Praise for

I have known Bobbie since ⎯⎯⎯⎯⎯⎯ ⎯⎯⎯⎯ of the Christian History Movement a half century ago. She is one of the foremost Christian educators in America. The title of the book gives the reader a glimpse of the treasured stories and truths that are in her volume. Mrs. Ames has a profound love for America that permeates her writing. She is a storyteller who knows how to take the reader into the events and lives of those who have created the American Miracle. This book is must reading for all those who want to restore our nation under God.

—MARSHALL FOSTER, *President & Founder, World History Institute*

A serious scholar and patriot whose love of America's Christian history is infectious, Bobbie Ames' book is an act of love—love for the Lord and for His Story. Her essays have graced the lives of many as she faithfully delivered her heart through her writing over decades. This collection sets the memorial stones in place as a trust for future generations who, if we have done our work, will ask, "What do these stones mean?" She tells the stories with a heartfelt faith honed through her years of founding Christian schools, teaching children, and investing the gifts God gave her in his people. There is no more meaningful way of renovating the age than learning and teaching America's Christian history.

—CAROLE ADAMS, *Founder & Board Member, StoneBridge School; President, Foundation for American Christian Education, Chesapeake, Virginia*

Nordskog Publishing is very strong on putting out materials that document well our nation's Judeo-Christian heritage. How great it is then to see this new book on celebrating America's Christian heritage, why it matters, and how it has been so threatened in our time. Also here in Bobbie Ames' new book is what we can do about it.

—JERRY NEWCOMBE, D.MIN., *Author and TV/Radio producer & host*

A life-long teacher, Bobbie Ames has lived her life immersed in our country's history, more than anybody I know. This book will enlighten its readers on our political life and more.

—TIM JAMES, *Alabama Businessman,*
Son of THE HONORABLE FOB JAMES, *Former Governor of Alabama*

Now that there have been two conservative originalist justices appointed to the U.S. Supreme Court, and it is anticipated that there will be more nominated in another term of a Republican President and Republican Senate majority, we joy in the expectancy that the U.S. Constitution will be restored, and that this nation will return to its founding principles. The writings of Bobbie Ames teach us what those founding beliefs and principles are in preparation for the sacred task ahead of us, the devoted citizens of this Constitutional Republic.

—THE HONORABLE TOM PARKER,
Chief Justice, Alabama Supreme Court

This beautiful book of essays lovingly written by Bobbie Ames is a treasure for all who love this great land. You will want to glean from these pages, and then share with family and others, the amazing truth of history, often obscured, of why this land is so blessed and how it can remain so. The eternal foundational truths held by our Founding Fathers are key and are exhibited throughout decades of Bobbie's writings and now in this collection of essays.

It is such an honor and joy to endorse this book, *Land That I Love*, given by my dear, long-time friend, Bobbie Ames, who faithfully writes of our true history for those who have a desire to know... *His Story*.

Blessed is the nation whose God is the LORD; and the people whom He hath chosen for His own inheritance. (Psalm 33:12)

—DOTTIE JAMES PARKER,
Wife of Tom Parker, Chief Justice, Alabama Supreme Court,
Editorial assistance to Bobbie on her monthly articles
for "The Education Station," published in The Alabama Gazette

Is there a second act for America? Does America get a second chance? If it could be so, Bobbie Ames's book, *Land That I Love*, has the moral, historical, and Biblical prescription for such a renewal. Many years ago, before her late husband died, he urged her to give herself fully to children and Christian schooling. He said, "If you do this, you cannot go wrong." Indeed, she has given herself to this wonderful Christian service for fifty years. Her book is a compilation of the wisdom and experience she passed to her Christian school children, a resource to be used for both Christian schools and homeschooling to "restore our Christian heritage."

—E. RAY MOORE, TH.M., *Chaplain (Lt. Col.) USAR Ret.,*
Director of Exodus Mandate

The Lord has blessed and enriched our lives through Mrs. Bobbie Ames. Our daughters (and through them, we) were taught the Biblical worldview using the Principle-Based Approach at Mrs. Bobbie's school, Emerald Mountain Christian School, from kindergarten through twelfth grade. They are both very talented, blessed, and successful. Mrs. Bobbie's influence on our lives has made for a very rich Christian life in service to our Lord and Savior. We wholeheartedly endorse Mrs. Bobbie's book and recommend it to all.

—RICH & SUSIE HOBSON
Rich serves as the Alabama Administrative Director of Courts
& Susie is a published author through Nordskog Publishing

Bobbie Ames, one of America's greatest Christian educators of the last fifty years, has written a critical book for every American, *Land That I Love*. Her book is more than just a collection of essays on civics; it is a comprehensive overview of how a Christian is to live out one's duty to country. Her book is more than concepts, but the truth and a vision of Christian nationalism that comes from her heart and is lived out in her life.

—THOMAS ERTL, *Zurich Publishing*

With joy I commend Bobbie Ames's book *Land That I Love* to the reader. I met Bobbie more than four decades ago as I was only beginning my adventure in the study of America's rich Christian heritage. Her love of the Pilgrims and their legacy caught my attention, since my calling to Plymouth was in its infancy. As you read this book, you will travel with Bobbie forward and backward through time as you mine the depths of Biblical and constitutional truths that are the pillars of our religious and civil liberty. These chapters are ready-made stories to read to your children, grandchildren, and great-grandchildren. Bobbie writes that the Pilgrims "brought the Reformation with them as their core values and intent." I agree, and over the years, when I might be discouraged as a Pastor, historian, and writer, I would get a call and hear the voice of a true patriot encouraging me. Bobbie writes, "Few today share the historic importance of our Pilgrim Fathers' impact on early America." This is unfortunately true, but I follow in the footsteps and path of pioneers like Bobbie Ames, and prayerfully, as we prepare here in Plymouth to commemorate the 400th anniversary of the arrival of those Pilgrims, we will all see a new generation appreciate what Bobbie longs to communicate, that America, because of her "Gilgal Stones" laid at her birth, will once again be the "land that I love"!

—DR. PAUL JEHLE, *President, Plymouth Rock Foundation, plymrock.org; Pastor, The New Testament Church of Plymouth, MA*

A Special Word from The Alabama Gazette

Mrs. Bobbie Ames has been our close friend at *The Alabama Gazette* for over a dozen years. Her monthly rumination in our publication on the spiritual history and spiritual course of our nation, which forms the basis of this book, serves as a beacon of wisdom, hope, and love in an era when many have been uninformed or misinformed as to the greatness of this country, its Founding Fathers, and the ongoing spiritual struggles that confront our Christian society today. Bobbie's erudite collection of prose will serve humanity, and more specifically, the Christian community, for generations to come. We at the *Gazette* are humbled and honored that Bobbie chose our publication to share some of her greatest treatises. Bobbie undoubtedly stands as one of the foremost Christian writers of this or any generation.

God Bless Bobbie and all who read *Land That I Love*. You will not be the same person when you finish it. May this book make a lasting change in our world, in our community, and in your heart.

—LORETTA GRANT, SAMUEL ADAMS, *Owners and Publishers,*
along with the staff of The Alabama Gazette

Secretary of the Continental Congress Charles Thomson designed the Great Seal of the United States featured on our cover. Thomson explained, "The colours of the pales are those used in the flag of the United States of America; White signifies purity and innocence, Red, hardiness & valour, and Blue, the colour of the Chief signifies vigilance, perseverance & justice. The Olive branch and arrows denote the power of peace & war which is exclusively vested in Congress. The Constellation denotes a new State taking its place and rank among other sovereign powers. The Escutcheon is born on the breast of an American Eagle without any other supporters [figures represented as holding up the shield] to denote that the United States of America ought to rely on their own Virtue."* The seal was adopted by the Continental Congress on June 20, 1782. See the seal in full color on the back cover.

Land That I Love

I Love

RESTORING OUR CHRISTIAN HERITAGE

BOBBIE AMES

Nordskog Publishing inc.

VENTURA, CALIFORNIA

Land That I Love:
Restoring Our Christian Heritage
by Bobbie Ames • © 2020 Bobbie Ames

ISBN: 978-1-946497-53-6
Library of Congress Control Number: 2020935589

Editing and Production:
Aaron Ford of digicomdesigns.com, Cover Design
Ronald W. Kirk, Theology and Lead Editor
Michelle Shelfer (benedication.biz), Managing Editor and Typesetting
Cheryl Geyer, Proofreader

* Charles Thomson quote on page vi is from "The Great Seal of the United States," U.S. Department of State Bureau of Public Affairs (July 2003).

Published by

Nordskog Publishing Inc.

Nordskog Publishing, Inc.
2716 Sailor Avenue, Ventura, California 93001
805-642-2070 • 805-276-5129
NordskogPublishing.com

Christian
Indie Publishing
Association

This book is dedicated to Verna Hall and Rosalie Slater, founders of The Foundation for American Christian Education. These ladies inspired me to put great emphasis on promoting true American history and to document the Judeo-Christian principles that are tightly interwoven with the providential historical events that make up the tapestry of our great nation's founding.

Verna Hall

Rosalie Slater

"WHERE THE SPIRIT OF THE LORD IS, THERE IS LIBERTY." II CORINTHIANS 3:17

The Foundation for
American Christian Education

TABLE OF CONTENTS

Foreword by Dr. Christina Fawcett Jeffrey

B obbie Ames, a friend since my grad-school days, is the most dedicated teacher I have ever known. Just the fact that she tracked me down on the campus of the University of Alabama, because she knew my mother, astounded me. Most people would not have gone to that trouble. As a result, I was conscripted into the Stop ERA movement, and then into Eagle Forum. But more important, I learned how to teach young children, as I visited her schools and listened to her talk about education. When Fob James became governor of Alabama, he appointed Bobbie to be chair of the Governor's Commission on the Alabama Year of the Child. This resulted in an excellent Report and improvements in the education and health-care programs for children in Alabama.

More recently, I have enjoyed helping Bobbie and her excellent editor, Dottie Parker, with a few of her columns in *The Alabama Gazette*.

I met Bobbie when she and her husband John were living in Marion, Alabama, where their first school, Perry Christian, was located (their second school was Dallas Christian School in Selma, Alabama). In those early years, when my husband and I were at the University of Alabama, we were involved in putting out an "underground newspaper," *VERITAS*. John Ames printed the paper for us.

After Selma, Bobbie and John moved to Montgomery, where a series of churches shared their education space with Bobbie's schools until she finally found the perfect place for a school, at Emerald Mountain, between Montgomery and Wetumpka, Alabama. There she was able to build a school and a library for the tens of thousands of precious volumes of books, most of which are not readily available in schools or libraries. I was happy to serve as the president of Friends of the Emerald Mountain School Library.

Bobbie's philosophy of education was identical with my parent's. Although I was one of eight children, and money was scarce on an Army officer's salary, my parents never failed to choose Christian education for us if it was available. Bobbie came from a strong Evangelical Presbyterian background, while my mother was a first generation American, a Scottish Catholic from Chicago. Yet they were friends and both members of Eagle Forum. In the old countries, our families would have been polarized—but not here in America! Here we know that we share the same Baptism, the same Savior, and the same strong support for Christian education.

My mother's father was sent from Chicago to try to reclaim International Harvester's nationalized (aka stolen) property from the Soviet Union following the Russian Revolution. He stayed in Russia for months and helped them stabilize their ruble, but he got not a single ruble to compensate International Harvester. Thanks to that experience, mother was born into a family well versed in the dangers of atheistic communism. Like Bobbie, mother understood the culture war that was being waged on the youth of America, that was my generation.

Mother wanted her children to engage the culture by becoming teachers and journalists. But only one of her eight children, a younger sister, became a journalist (mother was a prolific letter-to-the-editor writer and had studied journalism at Northwestern.) I was the only one of her children who wanted to be an educator. Bobbie's example strongly reinforced my mother's wish for me to become a teacher. Besides the students I've taught, my five children and grandchildren continue to benefit from this career choice.

In recent years, as Bobbie moved out of the classroom and into the editorial room, I learned even more about her philosophy of education and watched as she squeezed every word possible into her one-page articles. When I did not get to read her columns as she was working on them, I read them online. I still marvel at their content and the scope of her knowledge. Hers was a very popular column and for good reason—not only did she model the Christian approach to education, she taught her readers a great deal of real, American history.

I applaud Nordskog for publishing this book, containing as it does so many of the great articles from *The Alabama Gazette* Bobbie has written in recent years. The book will be a blessing to everyone who reads it.

Dr. Christina Fawcett Jeffrey (Mrs. Robert)
Spartanburg, SC
March, 2020

THERE EXISTS IN THE ECONOMY AND COURSE OF NATURE, AN INDISSOLUBLE UNION BETWEEN VIRTUE AND HAPPINESS, BETWEEN DUTY AND ADVANTAGE, BETWEEN THE GENUINE MAXIMS OF AN HONEST AND MAGNANIMOUS POLICY, AND THE SOLID REWARDS OF PUBLIC PROSPERITY AND FELICITY: SINCE WE OUGHT TO BE NO LESS PERSUADED THAT THE PROPITIOUS SMILES OF HEAVEN, CAN NEVER BE EXPECTED ON A NATION THAT DISREGARDS THE ETERNAL RULES OF ORDER AND RIGHT, WHICH HEAVEN ITSELF HAS ORDAINED: AND SINCE THE PRESERVATION OF THE SACRED FIRE OF LIBERTY, AND THE DESTINY OF THE REPUBLICAN MODEL OF GOVERNMENT, ARE JUSTLY CONSIDERED AS DEEPLY, PERHAPS AS FINALLY STAKED, ON THE EXPERIMENT ENTRUSTED TO THE HANDS OF THE AMERICAN PEOPLE.

GEORGE WASHINGTON,
First Inaugural Address, April 30, 1789
"First in war, first in peace, first in the hearts of his countrymen."
(from Henry Lee's Eulogy for Washington, December, 1799)

PUBLISHER'S WORD

We have no Government armed with Power capable of contend-
ing with human Passions unbridled by morality and Religion.
Avarice, Ambition and Revenge or Gallantry would break the
strongest Cords of our Constitution as a Whale goes through a
Net. Our Constitution was made only for a moral and religious
People. It is wholly inadequate to the government of any other.

—John Adams, to Massachusetts Militia, 11 October, 1798

I have known Bobbie Ames for several years. After I changed
vocations from publishing *Powerboat Magazine* to a focus on
publishing Christian and historical books, I became long-distance
friends with her as she taught her Principle Approach® Christian school in Alabama, Emerald Mountain Christian School and
Hoffman Education Center, founded years ago by Bobbie and
her husband. She served the Lord by teaching students to love
America (among other topics) for a half century of her life and
recently retired. Nordskog Publishing regularly sent her copies
of our *The Bell Ringer* e-newsletter by print, and she, in turn, sent

NPI reprints of her *Alabama Gazette* essays and articles, in which she wrote about the virtues and history of America.

One day, after reading one of her articles, I asked her if she would be interested in having us publish a book about her wisdom and writings, selectively on topics of Americana, historical and current events, and Biblical, constitutional principles that could stir up fellow patriots around the nation to learn and pursue the principles she learned and taught her students year after year. Graciously, she was excited and said yes.

Most Americans know we are in a battle for the survival of our nation and its precepts and virtues. Nearly half of Americans have been trained by secular government schools and colleges to live by unbiblical, unconstitutional, and erroneous doctrines, in contrast to the traditional all-American patriotic conservatives who believe we should follow the United States Constitution and Biblical truth. America achieved unprecedented prosperity and freedom by God's hand, but as we move away from Him, we lose God's blessings. To restore those blessings, we must see through the evil of secularism and once more adopt God's ways.

We are in the midst of a battle that is intense, and we want all Americans, whatever they have been taught in the past, to embrace the values, precepts, and courageous historical wisdom that has prevailed in this country since the Pilgrims landed at Plymouth Rock. Importantly, with the publication of this book, we honor this, the 400th anniversary of the year that (mostly) Christians landed on Plymouth Rock and entered a land preserved by God and reserved for the new Americans. The amazing Mayflower Compact was written on their ship prior to the Pilgrims' landing at Plymouth Rock. Thus we encourage all readers to join in, batten the hatches, and go for a ride of learning about the values and wisdom from above to God's beloved nation of America. Israel was God's first set-apart nation of "chosen people" (although they rejected God numerous times), and we can say the same about His second cherished nation, America, in our day and season.

Those who founded our nation looked with hopefulness to the shining example of God-given liberty that America could and would be for the world. In 1630, John Winthrop expressed the new Americans' eagerness to fulfill God's purposes in establishing this new nation when he spoke passionately of "a city upon a hill," from Matthew 5:14. Ronald Reagan and others over the decades echoed those words, affirming the exceptional character of America. We need to reinstill in our country's mindset this notion of American exceptionalism, returning to moral, ethical, and Biblical bedrock and love of liberty so that we can once again stand as that "city on a hill."

We have fallen badly, especially in the past century, in large part due to satanic attacks manifested in the government secular school system—a system that ought to be dismantled and replaced with free-enterprise educational entities. This much-needed overhaul of our education system is way overdue and very late in the game of our national life—a really serious circumstance as we attempt to pass on to the next generation the precious gift of our heavenly Father, Son (Jesus), and Holy Spirit.

Americans: it is imperative we be educated with the truth, and then become active and courageous students of God's Scripture, embracing our Redeemer, King Jesus, into our lives.

> Though the fig tree should not blossom
> And there be no fruit on the vines,
> Though the yield of the olive should fail
> And the fields produce no food,
> Though the flock should be cut off from the fold
> And there be no cattle in the stalls,
> Yet I will exult in the LORD,
> I will rejoice in the God of my salvation.
> The Lord GOD is my strength,
> And He has made my feet like hinds' feet,
> And makes me walk on my high places.
> (Habakkuk 3:17–19 NASB)

For the earth will be filled
With the knowledge of the glory of the LORD,
As the waters cover the sea.
(Habakkuk 2:14 NASB)

In my grammar (elementary) public school—in fifth grade—in Mrs. Birchwood's class in Los Angeles, I was cast as Patrick Henry in a small patriotic play. At that moment and at an early age, in her class I became a very young "patriotic American." While I did not recite the entire speech—only the last line—I became fascinated with all the Founding Fathers, especially the great orator from Virginia. As a remembrance for all Americans, here are the last two paragraphs of his speech that led to the passage of Henry's resolution to fight the British oppression with a well-regulated "militia" for the Virginia colony, pursuing the War of Independence:

Three millions of people, armed in the holy cause of liberty, and in such a country as that which we possess, are invincible by any force which our enemy can send against us.... The battle, sir, is not to the strong alone; it is to the vigilant, the active, the brave. Besides, sir, we have no election. If we were base enough to desire it, it is now too late to retire from the contest. There is no retreat but in submission and slavery! Our chains are forged! Their clanking may be heard on the plains of Boston! The war is inevitable—and let it come! I repeat it, sir, let it come!

It is in vain, sir, to extenuate the matter. Gentlemen may cry peace, peace—but there is no peace. The war is actually begun! The next gale that sweeps from the North will bring to our ears the clash of resounding arms! Our brethren are already in the field! Why stand we here idle? What is it that gentlemen wish? What would they have? *Is life so dear, or peace so sweet, as to be purchased at the price of chains and slavery? Forbid it, Almighty God! I know not what course others may take; but as for me, give me liberty or give me death!*[1]

---

1. Thomas B. Reed, ed., *Modern Eloquence*, vol. XIII (Philadelphia: John D. Morris & Company, 1903), 1178–81 (emphasis added). Available online at *The Avalon Project* at Yale Law School, avalon.law.yale.edu/18th_century/patrick.asp.

Patrick Henry appealed to the Creator of the universe, our Triune God, as he and almost all of the Founding Fathers were Christian gentlemen of great courage. Today we desperately need a revival from above and a reformation of our putrid society of the past few decades. We must ARISE, as the Bible mandates in many places. Americans need to get involved in the culture very actively with the Bible in one hand and a trowel or arms in the other, as when Israel rebuilt the temple and wall of Jerusalem under Ezra and Nehemiah.

> "As for Me, this is My covenant with them," says the LORD: "My Spirit which is upon you, and My words which I have put in your mouth shall not depart from your mouth, nor from the mouth of your offspring, nor from the mouth of your offspring's offspring," says the LORD, "from now and forever."
> "Arise, shine; for your light has come,
> And the glory of the LORD has risen upon you....
> Nations will come to your light,
> And kings to the brightness of your rising."
> (Isaiah 59:21; 60:1, 3 NASB)

Let's heed the words of our Founding Fathers:

All the miseries and evils which men suffer from vice, crime, ambition, injustice, oppression, slavery and war, proceed from their despising or neglecting the precepts contained in the Bible.[2] (Noah Webster)

Suppose a nation in some distant region should take the Bible for their only law book, and every member should regulate his conduct by the precepts there exhibited!... What a Utopia;

---

2. Noah Webster, "Advice to the Young," No. 53, *History of the United States* (New Haven: Durrie & Peck, 1832), 339.

what a Paradise would this region be.[3] ... The Bible is the best book in the world.[4] (John Adams)

Our all-gracious Creator, Preserver, and Ruler has been pleased to discover and enforce His laws, by a revelation given to us immediately and directly from Himself. This revelation is contained in the Holy Scriptures.[5] (James Wilson)

The Holy Scriptures ... can alone secure to society, order and peace, and to our courts of justice and constitutions of government, purity, stability, and usefulness.... Bibles are strong entrenchments. Where they abound, men cannot pursue wicked courses and at the same time enjoy quiet conscience.[6] (James McHenry)

The Bible contains more knowledge necessary to man in his present state than any other book in the world.[7] ... By renouncing the Bible, philosophers swing from their moorings upon all moral subjects.... It is the only correct map of the human heart that ever has been published.[8] (Benjamin Rush)

The Bible is the best of all books, for it is the Word of God and teaches us the way to be happy in this world and in the next.

---

3. John Adams, from diary entry of February 22, 1756, *The Selected Writings of John and John Quincy Adams*, ed. Adrienne Koch and William Harwood Peden (New York: Knopf, 1946), 5.

4. John Adams to Thomas Jefferson, December 25, 1813, *The Adams-Jefferson Letters*, ed. Lester J. Cappon (Chapel Hill and London: University of North Carolina Press, 1959), 412.

5. James Wilson, *The Works of James Wilson*, ed. James DeWitt Andrews, vol. I (Chicago: Callaghan & Company, 1896), 122.

6. James McHenry, *One Hundred and Ten Years of Bible Society Work in Maryland, 1810–1920*, ed. Bernard C. Steiner (Maryland Bible Society, 1921), 14. Found on wallbuilders.com.

7. Benjamin Rush, *Essays, Literary, Moral & Philosophical* (Philadelphia: Thomas & Samuel F. Bradford, 1798), 93.

8. Benjamin Rush, to John Adams, January 23, 1807, *Letters of Benjamin Rush*, ed. L. H. Butterfield, vol. II (Princeton, NJ: Princeton University, 1951), 936.

Continue therefore to read it and to regulate your life by its precepts.[9] (John Jay)

No book in the world deserves to be so unceasingly studied, and so profoundly meditated upon as the Bible.[10] ... The first, and almost the only book, deserving such universal recommendation, is the Bible.[11] (John Quincy Adams)

In the Second Great Awakening, the Rev. Charles Finney warned fellow Americans:

The Church must take right ground in regard to politics.... The time has come that Christians must vote for honest men, and take consistent ground in politics.... God cannot sustain this free and blessed country, which we love and pray for, unless the church will take right ground. Politics are a part of a religion in such a country as this, and Christians must do their duty to the country as a part of their duty to God. It seems sometimes as if the foundations of the nation were becoming rotten, and Christians seem to act as if they thought God did not see what they do in politics. But I tell you, He does see it, and He will bless or curse this nation, according to the course they take.[12]

> For the day of the LORD draws near on all the nations.
> As you have done, it will be done to you.
> Your dealings will return on your own head.
> (Obadiah 1:15 NASB)

As nations cannot be rewarded or punished in the next world, they must be in this. By an inevitable chain of causes and

---

9. John Jay, to Peter Augustus Jay, April 8, 1784, *John Jay: The Making of a Revolutionary, Unpublished Papers, 1745–1780*, ed. Richard B. Morris (New York: Harper and Row, 1975, 2:709.
10. John Quincy Adams, *Letters of John Quincy Adams, to His Son, on the Bible and Its Teachings* (Auburn, NY: Derby, Miller, & Co., 1848), 119.
11. John Quincy Adams, "The Value of the Bible," *A Compendium of American Literature*, ed. Charles D. Cleveland (Philadelphia: E. C. & J. Biddle, 1858), 310.
12. Charles Finney, *Lectures on Revivals of Religion* (New York: Leavitt, Lord & Co., 1835), 133–34.

effects, Providence punishes national sins, by national calamities.[13] (George Mason)

Whether this [American Revolution] will prove a blessing or a curse, will depend upon the use our people make of the blessings which a gracious God hath bestowed on us. If they are wise, they will be great and happy. If they are of a contrary character, they will be miserable. Righteousness alone can exalt them as a nation [Proverbs 14:34]. Reader! whoever thou art, remember this; and in thy sphere practise virtue thyself, and encourage it in others.[14] (Patrick Henry)

Our cherished Liberty Bell, still on display in Philadelphia, proclaims these words from Leviticus 25:10, reminding us of our Biblical mandate to love, cherish, and share God's gift of liberty:

Proclaim liberty throughout all the land
unto all the inhabitants thereof.

GERALD CHRISTIAN NORDSKOG
Mother's Day, May 10, 2020,
the 400th anniversary year of the landing
of the Mayflower at Plymouth Rock

---

13. George Mason, speaking at the Federal Convention, August 22, 1787, against the import of slaves to the United States of America.
14. Patrick Henry, *Patrick Henry: Life, Correspondence and Speeches*, ed. William Wirt Henry, vol. I (New York: Charles Scribner's Sons, 1891), 81–82.

AMERICA THE BEAUTIFUL

O beautiful for spacious skies,
For amber waves of grain,
For purple mountain majesties
Above the fruited plain!
America! America!
God shed His grace on thee
And crown thy good with brotherhood
From sea to shining sea!

O beautiful for pilgrim feet,
Whose stern, impassioned stress
A thoroughfare for freedom beat
Across the wilderness!
America! America!
God mend thine every flaw,
Confirm thy soul in self-control,
Thy liberty in law!

O beautiful for heroes proved
In liberating strife,
Who more than self their country loved
And mercy more than life!
America! America!
May God thy gold refine,
Till all success be nobleness,
And every gain divine!

O beautiful for patriot dream
That sees beyond the years
Thine alabaster cities gleam
Undimmed by human tears!
America! America!
God shed His grace on thee
And crown thy good with brotherhood
From sea to shining sea!

Prologue by Col. John Eidsmoe

Get ready for a voyage of discovery!

With Bobbie Ames as our pilot and guide, *Land That I Love* takes us on an expedition in which we explore America past and present. Not only do we see the mountains and shores from a distance; she repeatedly brings us ashore to study the land in minute detail.

We will go ashore in Massachusetts to visit the Pilgrims and their village of Plymouth. We will meet Governor William Bradford as he explains how these colonists first practiced communal living and found it a total failure, so they shifted to capitalism and then thrived. And through all their suffering and hardships, they were sustained by their firm Christian faith.

We will travel south to Virginia during the War for Independence. There we will meet Patrick Henry and hear him proclaim "Give me liberty or give me death!" Yes, we've heard that before, but our guide will explain the Biblical allusions throughout his speech.

We will meet George Washington, the father of our country and learn how his faith sustained him throughout an era of crisis, and how his character inspired his countrymen to sacrifice and fight for liberty.

We will study America's founding documents, the Declaration of Independence that established our nation and the Constitution that established our government. Through these documents we will understand the Founders' vision for a constitutional republic that would be a model for liberty-loving people throughout the world.

But our journey is not only to America's founding. Our guide also shows us how, step by step, the Founders' vision has been replaced by another. She shows us America's slide into Unitarianism, Darwinism, secularism, permissivism, postmodernism, and other alien ideas that are changing us into a very different nation, a country our Founders would not recognize.

And then she outlines a plan for restoring the American republic, a plan that is clear but a plan that is also hard—returning to the faith of our Founding Fathers, and limiting government to its proper constitutional limits.

What makes *Land That I Love* stand out above other books about America's heritage? The answer is the author, our pilot and guide, Bobbie Ames.

Bobbie has been my close friend for thirty years. As a teacher of American history and a founder of Christian schools, Bobbie has poured her life into this book. It is filled to the brim, not only with the massive knowledge and factual information she has acquired over the decades, but especially with the wisdom she has acquired over a lifetime.

This includes insights that have been largely forgotten, such as that of Father O'Gara, who devoted his life as a missionary to China and was imprisoned by the Chinese communists. Father O'Gara wrote that the Chinese communists used Darwinism, not just Marxism, as the cornerstone for their new political structure. He then noted that, after sending our soldiers abroad to fight against communism, we are nourishing in our breast at home the very viper whose head, with so much fanfare and sinister hypocrisy, we set out to crush in the far corners of the globe.

If you have vaguely sensed that something is wrong with the American dream, but you can't quite pinpoint the problem, read *Land That I Love*! Not only will you learn causes of America's malady and the solutions to making America great again; you will come to know this magnificent lady, Bobbie Ames. The wisdom of her lifetime is poured into this book.

THE TRANSFORMATION OF AMERICAN CULTURE:
1900–2014

February 2014

At the turn of the twentieth century, Americans believed in eternal life, in eternity. They believed that life continued beyond the grave. Perhaps not everyone believed in the depravity of man or in the necessity of redemption, but the culture reflected the moral law and Biblical principles for living one's life on earth. There was a universal hope of heaven. This was true from the earliest beginnings through the founding of America and beyond.

This was the world that I was born into in 1930. American education affirmed that we were *human*—body, mind, and spirit. Bible reading was a part of daily school life throughout elementary school. I first encountered the theory of evolution in a textbook in the grammar grades. My teacher, Mrs. Louise Beals, of Washington, North Carolina, assured us that this was a "theory being floated around by unreliable scientists who couldn't prove it." We were quite satisfied and dismissed the "strange theory" from our thoughts.

I never had a teacher in elementary school who did not have a deep faith and exemplary character. Little did I know that John Dewey had already boldly written in *The New Republic* (1922) and later reprinted in *Education Today* (1940), "We make a religion of our education, we profess faith in its possibilities, we point with pride to its advance." The religion that he defined had no place for the supernatural. The *Humanist Manifesto* identifies education as a "religious experience."[1]

By high school, evolution had gained a small following in the Southern States. By the time I reached my Methodist College in 1948, the "strange theory" of my childhood years was now taught as fact, as was the "old earth" millions-of-years theory that was so necessary to evolution's plausibility. While many of us were strong Christians, we were not equipped to debate or refute our professors. Our youth groups in church taught no apologetics at that time. Many of us did not believe the new theories, but many had their faith shaken.

What did the presentations of this pagan thought hide from us? I submit that evolution cut to the heart of our Hebrew-Christian faith, as it attacked *origins*. Are we created by God as His image bearers? Or did our existence result from a series of accidents and chance? Psalm 139:14 clearly states that we are "fearfully and wonderfully made."

Humanists see man differently. The humanist sees himself as a child of the cosmos, as one who puts his faith in *man* as the measure of all values, the measure of all things. One of the leading humanists in the early 1900s, E. Stanton Hodgin, wrote that public schools would take the place of the church in America, and that those schools would be based on the religion of humanism.[2] His writings so impressed Curtis W. Reese that he included them in his published collection of *Humanist Sermons*.[3]

Higher education circles in colleges and universities now challenged all of the teaching of my early years about the regenerated heart's role in living out one's life. To them, the heart is no more than a collection of muscles. Emotions are, then, simply reactions

---

1. *Humanist Manifesto I*, American Humanist Association, americanhumanist.org.
2. E. Stanton Hodgin, quoted in *School Education* vol. XXVII, Number 1 (January 1908): 49. "In a recent lecture on 'Standards of Education,' [Dr. E. Stanton Hodgin] said 'Religion is not going out of our public schools, but old dogmas are—that pure religion may come in.'"
3. Curtis W. Reese, *Humanist Sermons* (Chicago, London: The Open Court Publishing Co., 1927).

to chemical interactions. Yes, pagans have nothing to offer but distractions from the truth. The fundamental cornerstone of true education is to know who we are, who we really are—that God made us in His own image including the capacity to know Him and to know His Truth. Thus we can live all of life in relation to Him and to each other. Our view of origins and of eternity will determine how we invest our lives.

The modern culture reflects sin's hunger, which is never satisfied. The entertainment industry tracks the immense sales of video games and hardware. Sin's hunger drives children and adults to entertain themselves with increasingly violent and immoral sexual content. Information from a study by the National Institutes of Health, an arm of the U.S. Department of Health and Human Services, focused on "The Impact of Electronic Media Violence: Scientific Theory and Research."[4] The study showed that:

1. Children in the U.S. spend an average between three and four hours a day viewing television.
2. More than 60 percent of programs contain some violence, and about 40 percent contain heavy violence.
3. Children spend increasing amounts of time on video games, most of which contain violence. Video games are in 83 percent of homes with children.
4. Most of the games are violent. 94 percent are rated as violent by the game industry.
5. Video game use peaks during the middle childhood years, ages eight to ten.

As children experiment with these things in search of their own identity, the world offers nothing but distractions from God's Truth. Recognizing who we are and being schooled for our providential mission on this earth is the fundamental cornerstone of true education. That makes all the difference in our quality of life.

---

4. L. Rowell Huesmann, "The Impact of Electronic Media Violence: Scientific Theory and Research," National Institutes of Health, *Journal of Adolescent Health* vol. 41:6 (December 2007).

American education in the public schools has offered a substitute for the Bible's moral absolutes. Henry Nelson Wieman, a signatory for the *Humanist Manifesto II*, defines religion for the humanist mind: "Religion, then, as the word here is used, will mean a ruling commitment practiced by a community of individuals to what they believe creates, sustains, saves, transforms, human existence toward the greatest good."[5]

In the preface of the *Humanist Manifesto I*, Paul Kurtz wrote, "Humanism is a philosophical, religious, and moral point of view." He further declares that it "rejected orthodox and dogmatic positions." His idea of utopia is the new world community of humanism fulfilled.[6]

Just as Britain has abandoned Christianity, America is now in severe crisis as well. Recent research claims that the majority of Americans do not profess a personal faith in Christianity. How will the pulpits of our land respond to this urgent call? What will be the answer to abortion, euthanasia, drugs, crime, pornography, violence, and immorality, if not repentance? What will it take to rebuild family life, when the divorce rate has more than doubled since 1960?[7]

The spiritual fallout has taken its toll on academic achievement and general knowledge of history and literature and the world around us. Don Feder, in his book, *A Jewish Conservative Looks at Pagan America*,[8] quotes a National Endowment for the Humanities study: 68 percent of high school seniors don't know when the Civil War occurred. Two-thirds can't identify the Reformation, and 64 percent can't identify the author of *The Canterbury Tales*. Clearly our schools have failed their primary function to educate.

5. David A. Noebel, J. F. Baldwin, Kevin Bywater, *Clergy in the Classroom: The Religion of Secular Humanism* (Manitou Springs, CO: Summit Press, 1995), 77.
6. Paul Kurtz, *Humanist Manifestos I and II* (Amherst, NY: Prometheus Books, 1973), 7–10, also available online at americanhumanist.org.
7. W. Bradford Wilcox, "The Evolution of Divorce," *National Affairs* Number 41, Fall 2019, nationalaffairs.com.
8. Don Feder, *A Jewish Conservative Looks at Pagan America* (Lafayette, LA: Huntington House Publishers, 1993), 230.

The great stories of literature reflecting human greatness and its cause are becoming lost to this generation. The rise and fall of cultures throughout the centuries have powerful lessons to teach us. And underlying them all, the study will reveal if the nation has one God or many gods. Cultures reveal their religion.

The American Humanist Association has a religious tax exemption with the Internal Revenue Service. According to our friend Dr. David Noebel, an IRS agent verified this as a 501(c)(3) status and gave Dr. Noebel the actual federal ID number as proof.

In closing, let me say that there is no such thing as "value-neutral education." Many people do not want to take the time to be informed on the crisis in education, because they do not want to be involved; they do not want to be disturbed. The humanist worldview is not only real, it is the greatest threat to liberty, and it has gained many disciples in high places. Only through God's intervention can this republic be restored. Whose side are you on? Do you have on your armor? Are you ready for battle? The children and families of this nation need you. *Now.* Please, don't let them down.

CHAPTER 2

A Culture for Life or a Culture for Death: It Hangs in the Balance in America

April 2012

Wesley J. Smith, writing for *The Human Exceptionalist*, a newsletter of The Discovery Institute, asks, "Does every human life have equal moral value simply and merely because it is human?" He believes, as do many others, that the morality of the twenty-first century will depend on how we respond to this simple but profound question. He continues, "Answer yes, and we will have a chance of achieving universal human rights. Answer no, and it means we are merely another animal in the forest." Smith's passion is for those members of our population sometimes classified as "exceptional." There is no more important issue in the entire right-to-life battle than this issue of human exceptionalism. It is all inclusive in the basic issue of life, the first and foremost inalienable right, the gift of our Creator.[1]

In early March 2012, a jury awarded nearly three million dollars to a Portland-area couple in a "wrongful birth" lawsuit against a Portland, Oregon, hospital, Legacy Health. The couple sued because the hospital and staff missed diagnosing their daughter's Down's syndrome, thus depriving them of the opportunity to abort their baby. They insisted that they would have aborted the baby had they known of her disability.[2]

---

1. Wesley J. Smith, "The Human Exceptionalist," *Human Exceptionalism*, July 31, 2012, discovery.org.
2. Aimee Green, "Jury awards nearly $3 million to Portland-area couple in

The physicians did perform a prenatal test, taking tissue samples from Deborah Levy's womb, but assured the couple that they found a normal chromosome profile. The hospital attorneys called on experts who testified that the tests were properly done. The jury came to a different conclusion and "found" Legacy Health negligent on five counts. The jury, according to *The Oregonian* newspaper, "was emotionally moved by the Levys who were one of the rare couples who file a 'wrongful birth' lawsuit ... over a missed prenatal diagnosis." Experts commenting on the case noted that the couple "must be willing to say on the record that they would have aborted the pregnancy, and that they feel a burden—albeit financial—of raising the child."[3]

The case attracted national public debate, even the use of the contradictory term *wrongful birth*, as the majority of Americans view every life as a gift of the Creator—precious, miraculous, providential. As much as we would hope that this tragic lawsuit would be isolated and rare, the sad fact is that with the vast majority of babies diagnosed with Down's syndrome, physicians quietly abort the child in the mother's womb. Experts declare that mothers abort up to 90 percent of all babies diagnosed with this disability. Down's syndrome is a chromosomal abnormality of the twenty-first chromosome affecting development processes. It occurs more frequently in the pregnancies of older women.

A highly respected and long-standing organization in the right-to-life movement is the Minnesota Citizens Concerned for Life (MCCL). Their research reveals that a procedure approved by the FDA allows Stem Cells Inc. to inject the brain cells of aborted babies into the eyes of patients suffering from macular degeneration. The developing baby of twelve to twenty weeks would have fingers, toes, and a functioning brain.

'wrongful birth' lawsuit against Legacy Health," *The Oregonian/OregonLive*, March 9, 2012, oregonlive.com.

3. Dave Bohon, "Jury Awards Parents of Down's Daughter $3 Million for 'Wrongful Birth'," *The New American*, March 15, 2012, thenewamerican.com.

"Babies developing in the womb are being treated," noted MCCL's executive director, Scott Fischback, "simply as raw material for laboratory experimentation." He added that StemCells Inc. is not the only lab cashing in on aborted fetal tissue. Both MCCL and *World Magazine* have pointed to the problem, noting the University of Washington, Seattle's long involvement with research on fetal tissue. How few of us knew that the harvesting of aborted babies had been big business for decades, collecting the tissues from abortion centers across America, with the knowledge of our government, and especially, the National Institute of Health.[4]

In our postmodern culture, everything is "relative," to the secular mind. To that mind, "it may help society, it may cure diseases, or it may make a lot of lives better." And so, America continues down the slippery slope to destruction. A life can be destroyed, if found inconvenient.

Years ago, this writer was with Dr. Francis Schaeffer in Europe. I had the opportunity to ask him if there would be a measurement of some kind to know if America passed the point of no return from a Christian constitutional republic. He reminded me to look across world history. No nation could long stand which legalized abortion and homosexuality. It is something to ponder as America has legalized both.

Is there reason to hope? In February 2012, in the Alabama Supreme Court, we had a decision that affirms, in the strongest possible way, the defining of life in the womb. This case before the court originated in De Kalb County, brought by Amy H. against her physicians, charging that their "negligent and wanton acts" had wrongfully caused the death of her unborn son.

Previously, the court had held that a wrongful death action could not be maintained for the death of an unborn child who died before he was viable. The trial court held that the mother was not in a "zone of danger" and could not recover damages.

---

4. Dave Bohon, "Pro-Life Group Exposes FDA's Approval of Aborted Fetal Tissue in Research," *The New American*, March 27, 2012, thenewamerican.com.

Early in Amy H.'s pregnancy, she and her seven-year-old son had a rash, which she believed to be fifth disease, an infection caused by a parvovirus B19. She contacted her physician in mid-January, who drew blood during the appointment. Her doctor contacted her with the results of the blood test indicating she did have the parvovirus, and that she should have ultrasounds every two weeks. For reasons beyond her control, the medical people did not perform the ultrasounds in a timely fashion, and the second one came in late February. This second test revealed signs of anemia in the baby and signs of hydrops, which could lead to heart failure. In March, she noticed the decreased movement of her baby, and she developed flu symptoms. Another ultrasound revealed that the baby had died. They induced labor and the baby was stillborn. The doctors agreed that the baby had not reached viability.

The filed lawsuit alleged that the doctors had caused the death of her unborn son within the meaning of the Alabama Wrongful Death Act (Ala. Code [section symbol] 6-5-540 [1975]). Amy H. had amended the suit to claim "mental anguish and emotional distress." The defendants claimed, based on earlier decisions of the court: "The Supreme Court of Alabama has held that a plaintiff cannot maintain a wrongful death action for a fetus not viable to live outside of the womb." Finally, the Alabama Supreme Court upheld the lower court's ruling in part and reversed it in part. What concerns us here is the issue of personhood as it relates to the unborn child.

The Alabama Supreme Court in a majority opinion, authored by Justice Tom Parker, made clear that, for the purpose of the Wrongful Death Act, a "person" includes the unborn child at any stage of development. Nine other states permit legal recovery for the wrongful death of a previable unborn child either by statute or juridical construction. At least in this matter, it is comforting to know that Roe v. Wade does not control the issue of Wrongful Death Law in Alabama. We are aware that the courts use Roe to allow women freely to choose abortion, protected by her supposed "right to privacy."

The Alabama decision regarding personhood is a significant step toward protecting the lives of unborn children. Roe's damage is immeasurable, as it claims that babies in the womb are not persons within the meaning of the Fourteenth Amendment. Medical advancements make Roe's biased and unscholarly opinion unsupportable by serious thinking people. The theological consensus, across faith communities, has always been that human life begins at conception.

Hopefully, the U.S. Supreme Court will show the same wisdom as the Alabama Supreme Court and will, one day, overturn Roe v. Wade.

We pray that the Supreme Court will also realize that "the State's interest, if compelling after viability, is equally compelling before viability."

If I may, I would like to add a very personal note here. It comes with deep emotion. About twenty-six years ago, our granddaughter Ashley was born with a disability and with a short life expectancy. They diagnosed Trisomy 13, with the 13th chromosome abnormally formed. This disorder is very rare, and most of these babies live a matter of months or a few years. Ashley has defied all the odds, as she is healthy and very active every day. She has been a joy to the entire family and has the three most compassionate brothers you will ever meet. Her life has been a training ground for these brothers in Christian graces. She has been and continues to be an inspiration to other families who have family members with disabilities. Her parents are involved in numerous ministries in the River Region to assist others with such special needs as their daughter's. God's grace has served more than adequately for every challenge in Ashley's life. And, yes, challenges have come.

At this time, the evening of my life, I recall as vividly as yesterday walking the streets of communist China, cautioned by our tour guide not to express my Christian faith. Neither should I question their "one-child" family policy, or their choice of the sex of a child. I recall similar caution in communist Hungary during their darkest days, when we had to hand over our passport and wonder if we would get it back. My experience visiting the gas chambers of Germany went beyond anything I would want to put in print. Yes, I have been to those places where life was expendable and where a dictator declares man is the measure of all things. America was not founded on the corruption of humanity. We were given the rarest of all governments: the opportunity, under law, for each individual to freely live out the providential plan of the Creator, with the least restraint from external force. It requires that citizens embrace our Christian constitutional republic actively and passionately, or it is lost.

(Author's Note: This chapter does not contain a legal analysis of the case before the Alabama Supreme Court, but is used to praise the Court for the recognition that a new and unique human life is formed from the moment of conception. For more information, see Hamilton v. Scott, 97 So.3d 728 [Ala. 2012].)

What Is an American, This New Man in World History?

October 2014

Patrick Henry, speaking in the Continental Congress, 1774, declared; "The distinctions between Virginians, Pennsylvanians, New Yorkers, and New Englanders are no more. I am not a Virginian, but an American."

In a letter to Rufus King, Alexander Hamilton expressed these same convictions. "We are laboring hard to establish in this country principles more and more national and free from all foreign ingredients so that we may be neither Greeks nor Trojans, but truly Americans."

In his *Farewell Address*, George Washington addressed the same sentiment. "The name of American, which belongs to you, in your national capacity, must always exalt the just pride of Patriotism."

The American of 1776 and following was indeed a New Man. In courage, conviction, and sacrifice, he declared that the spiritual is supreme. That very First Principle of Americanism, declared in the Declaration of Independence, is that all men are *created* ... endowed by their *Creator*.

The First Principle: The Spiritual Is Supreme

Therein lies the First Principle: The spiritual is supreme. By spiritual we mean of the Holy Spirit of God. The Founding Fathers knew that the First Principle of America was religious in nature. Man is of divine origin and his spiritual nature is of supreme and eternal value to his Creator. His governmental philosophy rests on this First Principle. Never before in all of history has a governmental philosophy rested on the brotherhood of man under the Fatherhood of the Triune God. Only in a right relationship with God to man can man live in the right relationship with God and his fellow man.

As we look deep into the First Principle that the spiritual is supreme, we see the duty of every man to live under God's moral laws, to recognize the absolutes that bind upon all men at all times, under all circumstances. As we understand the remarkable heritage of civil and religious liberty in this light, we see that we will never enjoy these liberties without bearing the responsibilities that accompany them. We cannot separate the spiritual heritage from the responsibility of the accompanying stewardship. That stewardship sensibility should consider as paramount the protection of these God-given, unalienable rights that constitute the very heart of the Declaration of Independence.

In all the writing and journals of the founding period of America, our forefathers rejected all ideas, theories, and schools of thought that failed to affirm God as man's Creator and the sole source of his rights. Government exists to protect those rights.

Essential in the structure of our federal system was that the proposed federal government should have strictly limited powers. It also should have no jurisdiction or power in regard to religion. In the following years, the First Amendment would prohibit Congress from making any law "respecting an establishment of religion, or prohibiting the free exercise thereof." The Founding Fathers' conviction: Every man has supreme value because God created him. His Creator set his value. Therefore, the government must rest upon this truth: The spiritual is supreme. God's government supersedes man's government.

The Second Principle: Fear of Government over Man
The "Kentucky Resolutions," by Thomas Jefferson, makes this warning: "In questions of power, then, let no more be heard of

confidence in man, but bind him down from mischief by the chains of the Constitution."

Washington's *Farewell Address* speaks of the unity of government built on the very first Principle—that the spiritual is supreme. He declares:

> Interwoven as is the love of liberty with every ligament of your hearts.... The Unity of Government, which constitutes you one people, is also now dear to you. It is justly so; for it is a main Pillar in the Edifice of your real independence, the support of your tranquility at home, your peace abroad; of your safety; of your prosperity; of that very Liberty, which you so highly prize. But it is easy to foresee, that, from different causes and from different quarters, much pains will be taken, many artifices employed, to weaken in your minds the conviction of this truth; as this is the point in your political fortress against which the batteries of internal and external enemies will be most constantly and actively (though often covertly and insidiously) directed, it is of infinite moment, that you should properly estimate the immense value of your national Union to your collective and individual happiness.... The name of AMERICAN, which belongs to you, in your national capacity, must always exalt the just pride of Patriotism, more than any appellation derived from local discriminations. With slight shades of difference, you have the same Religion, Manners, Habits, and political Principles. You have in a common cause fought and triumphed together.

One of Washington's best-known admonitions is this one: "Of all the dispositions and habits, which lead to political prosperity, Religion and morality are indispensable supports. In vain would that man claim the tribute of Patriotism, who should labor to subvert these great Pillars of human happiness, these firmest props of the duties of Men and Citizens" (*Farewell Address*, September 17, 1796).

In a spiritual world of both godly and sinful men, fear of government makes an apt corollary, a valuable lesson of history. A mixture of good and evil lies in the heart of man. The resulting abuse of power, with injuries to individual and collective liberties, predominates in the history of every nation and culture. Would America be able to overcome the sin nature of man being prominent and dominant in the new government? What was the challenge to the American, this New Man?

J. Hector St. John de Crèvecoeur was a French immigrant who became a New York farmer. In 1782, he wrote essays compiled into his *Letters from an American Farmer*. In it, he describes the New Man in this light: "He is an American, who leaving behind him all his ancient prejudices and manners, receives new ones from the new mode of life he has embraced, the new government he obeys, and the new rank he holds.... The American is a new man, who acts upon his principles; he must therefore entertain new ideas, and form new opinions. From involuntary idleness, servile dependence, penury, and useless labour, he has passed to toils of a different nature, rewarded by ample subsistence. —This is an American."

Accordingly, until modernism set in, from the day of the Pilgrims and Puritans, Americans built from the ground up, an entirely new educational system. A system of Biblical principles formed the foundation for all knowledge. Dominant in early America, these principles now only fuel the curriculum of a few hundred Christian schools and home schools. Teachers in these Biblically grounded schools view, treat, and educate every child as uniquely created by God. They build on God's principle of individuality and covenant promise based on creation in God's image. These schools remain zealous for the safety of individual liberty. They treasure their God-given unalienable rights. The true American today, as before, continues to recognize government's overreach, with its secular religion in government schools, and opposes it in every lawful way.

We understand the wisdom of fearing government. We understand what Washington meant when he spoke of the "love of power and the proneness to abuse it." We see officials' human weakness and love of power, and we see the corresponding weaknesses in the people themselves.

Yet observation is not enough. We may be inspired when we think of unalienable rights, but do we always cleave to the moral basis from which they are derived?

Americans created government at all levels as a tool for preserving these rights, these liberties, and justice. They are the means of securing these rights for future generations. Instead, government now commonly violates and invades the historic checks and balances of national, state, and local representation, the boundaries of property rights, parental rights, and even our most private and personal decisions. All these cultural and civil currents have eroded American culture, erasing even the memory of our birthright in recent generations. This is the challenge of education today, of the Christian Church, and the family altar.

As a long-time teacher of American history, I was always so inspired by George Washington. In his *First Inaugural Address*, he addressed every generation—then and in the future. Referring to God-centered government, he admonished, "The preservation of the sacred fire of liberty, and the destiny of the republican model of government, are justly considered as deeply, perhaps as finally, staked on the experiment entrusted to the hands of the American people."

In order to protect the unalienable rights given by God, the Founding Fathers recognized the responsibility that accompanies every single liberty. There is no "just power" in the world that can morally violate these rights. To be the new man, the New American, each individual at the time of the new Constitution consented to his own limitations to some degree, in order to secure these unalienable rights.

Elbridge Gerry, writing in 1788, affirmed this in these words, "All writers on government agree ... that the origin of all power is in the people, and that they have an incontestable right to check the creatures of their own creation, vested with certain powers to guard the life, liberty, and property of the community."

Limited government was their passion. Alexander Hamilton wrote in the *Federalist*, no. 78,[1] "The executive ... holds the sword ... the legislature ... commands the purse ... the judiciary ... has no influence over either the sword or the purse.... Liberty can have nothing to fear from the judiciary alone, [as usurpers] but would have every thing to fear from its union with either of the other departments"—in usurping power.

The importance of a decentralized national government, limited in power, with the careful balance of the greater power in the states—and that limited as well—demonstrates the genius of the Founding Fathers, and their clear understanding that the spiritual is supreme. The Protestant Reformation brought the light of liberty to these shores. Dr. Joseph Warren, one of the greats of that generation, wrote in an oration on March 5, 1772, in Boston, "This eternal truth, that public happiness depends on a virtuous and unshaken attachment to a free constitution." And in his state's Massachusetts Bill of Rights, 1780, is this affirmation, "As the happiness of a people, and the good order and preservation of civil government, essentially depend upon piety, religion, and morality."

And since I am a history teacher, let me add Jefferson's words in closing, "[Through education of the young in public schools], the first elements of morality too may be instilled in their minds ... may teach them how to work out their own greatest happiness, by showing them that it does not depend on the condition of life in which chance has placed them, but is always the result of a good conscience, good health, occupation, and freedom in all good pursuits." (*Notes on the State of Virginia*, 1782).

---

1. Alexander Hamilton, John Jay, James Madison, *The Federalist Papers*. These were originally published in New York newspapers in support of the ratification of the United States Constitution. It is now available in numbers of mass market publications, such as published by Signet Classics and Dover Thrift. Online at congress.gov/resources/display/content/The+Federalist+Papers.

CHAPTER 4

America's Historic Education: The Christian Idea of Man and Government

May 2015

As men, we have God for our King, and are under the Law of Reason: as Christians, we have Jesus the Messiah for our King, and are under the law revealed by Him in the Gospel.

—John Locke, *The Reasonableness of Christianity*, 1695

The right to freedom being the gift of God Almighty.... The Rights of the Colonists as Christians ... may be best understood by reading and carefully studying the Institutes of the great Law Giver ... which are to be found clearly written and promulgated in the New Testament.

—Samuel Adams, "Rights of the Colonists," 1772

Ye shall know the truth, and the truth shall make you free.

—John 8:32

Thus was born a new civilization: the republican form of government. It was an exciting time in world history. The Protestant Reformation was in full force. It was a wonderful period of new discoveries in the universe. A liberating principle of individuality coupled with spiritual liberty brought true spiritual freedom for the individual. While this concept first permeated only the church of the day, it would soon advance to the State also.

What a contrast! This new idea opposed and contradicted the pagan world's view of man. In the old view of man, he had value only as he fitted into the structure of the political world around him. What were his contributions to the political system? While the elite ruling class might elevate some men, they ignored or abused the majority—the poor, the captives, the women. The struggle with these conflicting views continued for centuries. Even after Rome fell, the old view of man lived on. Man was only of value as he contributed to the State. Arbitrary power existed in the ecclesiastical as well as in the political realms.

With the Protestant Reformation came the brilliant thinkers who realized that the State exists for man, and not man for the State. Men like John Milton, John Locke, and America's Founding Fathers held to this eternal Truth.

America's history rests on two documents chiefly: The Declaration of Independence and The United States Constitution. The New Testament is the treasury of Truth from which these documents came to be. The idealistic goals of the Founders eventually established a new form of government designed to protect society with a political order built upon the Biblical mandate for man and government. This embraced the Christian individual, the family, and society. We often quote the Mayflower Compact's words. Their expressed colonial purpose was "for propagating and advancing the Gospel of the kingdom of Christ in those remote parts of the world."

What was it that they left behind in the pagan world of the past? The pagan view insisted that the major institutions of Church or State, whichever hierarchy ruled, must decide for man and culture as some kind of universal parent. Sovereignty resided in institution. The powerful must dictate to the individual man. They ignored the fact that the Creator created man in His very image, which meant inherent and eternal value, and the rightful liberty to pursue their God-given purpose.

Instead, centralization ruled as the norm. The flow of power and force always came from the top down in the pagan world. Power and force flowed through appointees, bureaucrats. Helpless, unregenerate man had no power to overcome it. This pagan idea of man and government prevailed for centuries, unchallenged. With the Protestant Reformation came the liberation of the individual man. Through the teaching of the Scriptures, Providence revealed him as free and independent, governed by the God who had created him, except when he practiced lawlessness. This Christian man saw himself as equal to any other individual under God's law, and under godly civil law as well. He increasingly understood that God provided this newfound liberty only under and within His law. The justice of God's law made liberty possible.

Liberty in civil society grew from the realization that the Protestant Church should be both local and self-governing, operating as a little republic. Likewise, the self-governing home and family must found the basis for society. The new realization of government based on eternal principles was liberating and challenging. With liberty living internally in the very soul of man, man's new government of grace by faith would flow from the inside out.

While the Old World awarded liberty to a few and never many, while enslaving the vast majority, the new Christian concept promoted voluntary union with diversity. Here union came by covenants of individuals, creeds, laws, and by elected representation. All the while this new way carefully guarded individual liberty of conscience under God's laws. "Conscience is the most Sacred of all Property."[1]

Where are we today in America? Is there evidence that we have lost the Christian idea of man and government as the basis of our political, social, and governmental structure? Is there evidence that the power of "We the People" has been usurped by a political force intent on promoting a one-world, centralized, totalitarian government? Are we losing the distinctive of our Christian idea of the individual created by God, for Gospel purpose, self-government,

---

1. R. J. Slater, and Verna M. Hall, *Teaching and Learning America's Christian History*, American Revolution Bicentennial ed. (San Francisco: Foundation for American Christian Education, 1975), 125–26.

and true liberty? And if so, how do we cast off the old pagan idea of top-down structures so predominant today?

The colonial records of the earliest colonists repeatedly express their convictions that their liberty is more precious than their very lives. For America to be the champion and example of Christian self-government once again, we must follow the same path of the Founders of this Christian constitutional republic.

For the individual with conviction, these steps would be a beginning toward restoration:

1. Search the Scriptures, believing that they are infallible.
2. Recover the language of liberty, found only in the 1828 Webster *Dictionary*.[2]
3. Study America's providential history and the truth of her glorious past.
4. Join with others—family, church, neighborhood, small groups, together on a mission to reclaim liberty, praying for revival and restoration for our beloved nation so blessed by God.

The long process of humanistic restructuring of American education has occupied nearly a century. First, they denied the infallibility of the Scriptures, teaching evolution as fact, rather than theory, and replacing accurate history with social studies. The use of terms such as *globalism* and *global age* gave us clues that change agents sought to implement atheistic models of government. The changes to civil government would primarily and obviously come through fundamental changes in education.

Progressive[3] educators began, decades ago, looking at Russia and even China as desirable models for implementing global objectives

---

2. Noah Webster, *American Dictionary of the English Language: Noah Webster 1828*, facsimile edition (Anaheim, CA: Foundation for American Christian Education, 2006). Webster's 1828 *Dictionary* is also available online at webstersdictionary1828.com/.

3. *Progressive* is a euphemism for progress toward socialism—centralized government control of any population, run by an elite that considers itself far superior to the people.

in education. Educators in the Reagan administration knew such disastrous ideas circulated, but unfortunately few became alarmed. The ideas have advanced through both Republican and Democrat administrations for decades, as the Federal Department of Education has expanded in power and determination. Education over decades has become totally secular now. The sex-education component of the national Common Core program, for example, is shockingly immoral but sold as health education. Moral absolutes are not to be found in government education.

Perhaps the greatest travesty of all is our national abandonment of the historic Christian family in American culture. Sons have no fathers. Mothers try to do the job, under great stress, of both parents. Parents surrender the education of their children to the State and its schools of indoctrination. As the home no longer functions under traditional Biblical influence as the primary influence in the nurture and character training of children, the accruing toll devastates the nation. The ancient Church concept of the body of Christ was the Church alive in the home. This is God's plan. The faithful Church was alive in Abraham's tent, and in David's palace. The Church: invisible and universal with outward local expressions in the lives of the saints is, was, and forever will be God's plan.

The Christian idea of man and government should be American Education 101. Yes, in the home, in the church, in every state, and at every national level thereby, prevailing once again in the public square. Could we together reclaim this heritage of Christian self-government with union? Thereby we may restore with God's help the Christian constitutional republic for our children, our grandchildren, for those of us who have experienced liberty, and for those who long for it. Then may its principles and practices extend to the uttermost parts of the earth.

CHAPTER 5

FOR RELIGIOUS LIBERTY TODAY, WE MUST RESTORE THE IMPACT OF OUR PILGRIM HERITAGE

November 2016

The England of the Pilgrim Fathers

By the latter sixteenth century, England had begun to experience societal changes transforming it from its former way of life to a modern one. The influence of the Renaissance awakened the English people to ask new questions about not only their culture, but about their civil governments as well.

Blessed and enlightened by John Wycliffe and other Reformers, the typical Englishman had access to the Scripture in his own language, and he was embracing the ideas of the Protestant Reformation. The speed of the printing press enabled dramatic ideas to be spread so widely and enthusiastically, that we might call it a spiritual revolution. This was accompanied by an economic revolution as well. The expansion of industry and commercialism was developing what we know as capitalism. It is evident that all of this would change the entire social structure of the land as well.

The nobility and the aristocrats saw their way of life threatened by these changes. The country gentlemen had considered their contribution as the backbone of society. Everything was changing.

Poverty had been a problem throughout their history, but now, it became more visible as farming decreased and industry increased. Many of the visibly poor congregated in cities. People assumed different attitudes about the poor. Some viewed them as "God's misfortunates." Some viewed poverty as a "holy state."

The Puritan work ethic began to spread widely. In this view we glorify the Lord by our work, and that it is a *calling* to pursue. Puritans taught about a Paternal Order. Servants must obey their master, but the master must care for their servants. They taught that every man has responsibility to care for the unfortunate ones.

The legacy of these ideas and movements dramatically affected the Pilgrims as they came west. They brought the Reformation with them as their core values and intent.

Few today share the historic importance of our Pilgrim Fathers' impact on early America. Public education has abandoned this glorious Christian history since I was in elementary school in 1936 and onward. Of course, many children and adults recognize the rendering of the falsely represented black-suited Pilgrim man, somber and often shown with a native Indian in the Massachusetts territory, but know little of his place in history.

The Truth about That First Thanksgiving

The Pilgrims received no bountiful harvest that first year in the New World. The Pilgrims celebrated a Thanksgiving before the Lord by faith, though they appeared in danger of starving. Enforced upon them by their financial backers, in the beginning they practiced communal agriculture, sharing everything equally. Not until they switched to private enterprise did they reap a plentiful harvest. They celebrated the first of this bounty with the Thanksgiving of 1623.

The Scrooby Congregation passengers on the Mayflower were distinctly Pilgrims as Bradford referred to them. Many were young adults, who made a covenant with each other and with the Lord to commit to worship and live in earnest, just as the Scriptures called for. They developed a compact for their church self-government.

Eventually, in order to fulfill their perceived calling, they traveled to America. It thrills me to recall that these Pilgrims took that church covenant and rewrote it as the Mayflower Compact in order to establish civil self-government. It is not an exaggeration to say that the Mayflower Compact is the forerunner to the U.S. Constitution. Because these Christian men and women had committed themselves to Christian self-government, directed by the Word of God, they accomplished three achievements that few people and few nations have ever seen or practiced:

1. They, as individuals, accepted the responsibility for governing themselves, and displaying a work ethic, likely excelled by none on the planet.

2. They interpreted their Biblical laws of nature to apply to society as a whole, leading to the constitutional law and the rule of law for all people, thus protecting their religious liberty.

3. They built an economic system that centered on personal responsibility. For example, the profit system was honest and provided opportunities for progress. A beautiful example of their sense of personal responsibility shines through twenty long years of their repaying their debt to the London merchants who financed their voyage. There was a great drive to develop tools for this economic system. The first water-powered gristmill was placed at the head of Plymouth Town Brook in 1636. Can you imagine the delight of the onlooking Indians as they watched this tool?

Forced by the merchants in the beginning to accept the arrangement of communal distribution, the Pilgrims patiently persevered and obtained rights to own land and to work to benefit their own families. If communism would ever have benefited a people, it would have worked for these Pilgrims, who loved each other and loved God above all else. It didn't work for them and cannot work for good for any people.

When the Mayflower ship returned to England, not one Pilgrim turned back. That little band of believers had introduced a new powerful force on the continent—that of individual religious liberty in practice.

All of these blessings of true liberty demand individual Christian character. There is no better example of this character than the Pilgrims of Plymouth Plantation.

Let's work diligently and pray sincerely for God to bring back in our nation individual liberty of conscience, Christian self-government, and a dedication to the U.S. Constitution and the rule of law. Let us pray for our America, a nation that stands uniquely as a Christian constitutional republic!

> The glories of Christianity are to be traced in the sufferings of confessors and martyrs of the sixteenth and seventeenth centuries; and it was under the influence of Christian principles, imbibed at this very period, that the Mayflower brought over the band of Pilgrims to Plymouth.... We should never forget that the prison, the scaffold, and the stake were stages in the march of civil and religious liberty which our forefathers had to travel, in order that we might obtain our present liberty....
>
> Before our children remove their religious connections ... before they leave the old paths of God's Word ... before they barter their birthright for a mess of pottage ... let us place in their hands the chronicle of the glorious days of the suffering churches, and let them know that they are the sons of the men "of whom the world was not worthy" and "whose sufferings for conscience sake" are here monumentally recorded.
>
> —John Overton Choules, August 12, 1843, preface to the 1844 reprint of Neal's *History of the Puritans* (1731), in *The Christian History of the Constitution*.

CHAPTER 6

A PORTRAIT OF PATRIOTISM

June 2014

This story of patriotism began in the life of a nine-year-old boy, standing on the deck of a sailing ship taking the Leutze family—the boy's parents, his sister, and young Emanuel—up the Delaware River to dock at the port of Philadelphia. Suddenly, the outline of the city, the largest in the New World, was visible, with its church steeples and tall buildings. Soon this boy's feet would touch the ground of the United States of America, his new home.

Emanuel Gottlieb Leutze was born March 24, 1816, in Gmünd, Württemberg, Germany. The village, thirty-one miles northeast of Stuttgaart, was famed as a center for silver craftsmanship. Emanuel's father Gottlieb was a skilled metal craftsman. He brought his wife, Catherine, daughter, Louisa, and son, Emanuel, to America to escape political oppression. Napoleon had completely humbled the Germany of the early nineteenth century, leaving her people frustrated. Poverty-ridden citizens despaired of life. Stories of faraway America, with its revolution of freedom for all peoples, offered hope.

Emanuel's mother, Catherine, also had two sons by a first husband who died young. Her son Jacob had immigrated to Pennsylvania in America, encouraging his mother and her family also to make such a venture. Emanuel's father Gottlieb had successfully built a comb manufacturing business. He thought he also could be successful in the New World. With his life savings, his manufacturing equipment and with state permission, they sailed in the summer of 1825, on the sloop *The William Henry*. The Leutzes would join other German-American colonists who settled mainly in the Pennsylvania and Virginia colonies. Those earlier immigrants had fought for the American side in the Revolution for Independence. German-American patriotism had stood in sharp contrast with the minds of many English colonists still torn between loyalties.

Emanuel had no doubt heard the stories of the Rev. Heinrich M. Muhlenberg, patriarch of the Lutheran Church in America, a great lover of freedom himself, and of his son John. John Muhlenberg was a colonel of the Eighth Virginia Regiment, personally commissioned by his intimate friend George Washington. In the colonel's Valedictory Address, in 1776, he called to his soldiers:

> The endangered fatherland, to which we owe wealth and blood, needs our arms—it calls its sons to drive off the oppressor. The Holy Scriptures says: There is a time for everything in this world. A time to talk, a time to be silent, and a time to preach and to pray. And also a time to fight and this time has come. Therefore whoever loves freedom in his new fatherland, he may follow me.

Young Emanuel absorbed all the stories of the Revolution. His love for the very sight of the Delaware River, so prominent in his life story, would last his lifetime. He lived near the river in Philadelphia, and traveled on it extensively throughout his life.

His father was well trained and successful as a silversmith. Yet when he contracted an incurable disease, his wife Catherine could hardly keep the comb manufacturing business going by herself. Emanuel must quit school to help the family survive. Though young, he sought odd jobs for small pay. With every precious spare hour, he would visit the collection at the Pennsylvania Academy of Fine Arts in Philadelphia. Established in 1805, it was the first highly noted art collection in the United States. Conceived in 1791, Charles Peale finally realized his dream of a great school of art to encourage and attract gifted young Americans. The academy's first major exhibition on the history of American Art displayed at

Independence Hall. The Peale Museum and the Franklin Institute were also close enough for this young boy to enjoy. Even then, he longed to study art and one day paint America's story on canvas.

With no money to finance formal study, Emanuel took his sketchbook to the museums, and for hours would study the oil portraits of the founders of our nation. His imagination absorbed the stories of Columbus, as he painted scenes from 1492. As he grew older, he drank in everything he could learn about George Washington, the father of his adopted country. He knew in his heart he was destined to be a painter and that he would paint scenes of the history of our country. He strove for excellence as an honor to those artists whom he studied in the museums—Benjamin West, Thomas Sully, John Trumbull, Henry Inman, and others. Dreaming was his escape from the sadness of his father's illness and the deep distress of the mother he adored. Yet amid his ambitions and pain, unselfishly and revealing his character, he found compassion to encourage his sister, Louisa, assuring her that he would always be there for her.

Trumbull's dramatized scenes from American history, "Burgoyne's Surrender at Saratoga," "Cornwallis; Surrender at Yorktown," "The Signing of the Declaration of Independence," and other historical paintings, brought Emanuel to envision the climax to his life's work would be to paint the scene for the most glorious of all the events of the Revolution. His painting must be massive and it must convey the courage and the danger in its subject, and point to what ultimately brought success to the Revolution. Even in his youth, he knew the challenge, the skills, and wisdom he must acquire to bring the dream about. He must study how to bring faces to life, how to draw details of clothing, and positions of the human frames, and much more. All the while he dreamed, he took odd jobs to help his mother and sister. To add to his personal burden, the Philadelphia Directory of 1831 lists, "Catherine Leutze, widow of Gottlieb Leutze, comb mfgr." His father died, and now Emanuel felt an even greater responsibility for the family.

Due to the expense and production limitations, few books were published in this era. Yet scarcely twenty-five years after his death, books about George Washington abounded. The most prominent story shared orally and in print was the story of George Washington crossing the Delaware River. But Emanuel Leutze lived in the very middle of many other historic events. Betsy Ross lived around the corner from the Leutze home. There she sewed the first American flag from a sketch George Washington gave to her. Just four squares away was the presidential residence of George Washington. Nearby Ben Franklin experimented with a front door key in one of his electricity experiments. Emanuel's neighborhood was filled with history. We can just imagine how he internalized these stories of independence and liberty and possibility for all.

As his artwork improved, he entered contests and won! He attended the Washington Birthday Ball at the White House at age twenty. He lived in Washington, D.C., for a time, where he quickly became known. Then he moved to Fredericksburg, Virginia. This was a time of tremendous growth for Emanuel through a chance meeting with a prominent citizen. This John Minor served as a mentor and secured commissions for him. Having a prominent aristocratic patron in John Minor greatly blessed Emanuel's efforts. Minor had given up his law practice and concentrated on Virginia history. He promoted the fables of Br'er Fox and Br'er Rabbit and had them published widely. During his time in Fredericksburg, Emanuel painted his first large canvas painting featuring Hagar and Ishmael in a scene illustrating hardship answered by overcoming power in the valiant. His charm, good looks, and obvious promise as an artist of the day placed his name on many tongues.

Even with growing success in America, Emanuel Luetze still felt the need of further personal development in the center of the art world in Europe. He chose to study in Düsseldorf, Germany, the city of his birth. During the daylight hours, he painted, and in the nighttime, he studied German and art history. He delighted the art critics in Düsseldorf, and before long the word *genius* attached to his name. His work was prominent in America, and now also came to be in Germany.

Emanuel received an invitation to exhibit his Columbus painting in the most prestigious art academy, where the most revered master teacher Karl F. Lessing offered him lessons. Lessing's own paintings "depicted grand historic characters whom he seeks to honor." This will also later be said of Luetze's painting of "Washington Crossing the Delaware." It too depicts strong men, the soldier-patriots, who opened the door for liberty for all. How proud Luetze would be that both his son and grandsons became admirals in the U.S. Navy, and that his descendants remain patriots to this day.

Years in Europe were successful in every way. He returned home with a dearly loved wife, four children, and fame. Emanuel realized his boyhood dream of painting George Washington crossing the Delaware River on a canvas twenty feet by twelve feet. The painting portrays the turning point in the War for Independence. Ann Hawkes Hutton, an authority and author on both Leutze and the painting, explains that the artist knew that his canvas "must bring to life that dramatic epoch in human affairs. It should portray that moment in Washington's career, when his thoughts, preparation, and experience converge into an action destined for victorious achievement. The face on the canvas must mirror his leadership and should reveal calm confidence to overbalance the fears and anxieties of the hard-pressed American troops. It must show nobility without aloofness and dignity without dullness."

Hutton cites the portrait as the climax of his career in his own mind. He had made endless sketches of Washington and separate sketches of every individual before he assembled all together in the painting. Washington is the central figure, of course. He wears yellow knee breeches, high boots, a dark coat lined with yellow, a gray military coat lined with red, and a black cocked hat. His sword hangs at his left side, and in his right hand he holds a spyglass. His expression dominates the painting in the same way that his personality dominates the crossing itself, a portent of the ultimate success of the American Revolution.

Most of the boats in the crossing were Durham boats ordinarily used to haul iron from the Durham furnace near Easton, Pennsylvania, down the Delaware to Philadelphia. Though the American flag had not yet been adopted in 1776, the artist rightly used it to symbolize the new nation. Actually, Washington no doubt flew a flag on the boat. We simply don't know which flag. Remember, Betsy Ross made the first American flag from the sketch Washington gave her.

Washington Crossing the Delaware, by Emanuel Leutze, 1851

In 1851, the United States Congress exhibited the famed canvas in the Capitol. Later, the Metropolitan Museum of Art acquired it. Leutze painted numerous smaller versions of Washington Crossing the Delaware, exhibited in numerous places. The Metropolitan Museum loaned the original to the Washington Park Crossing, a kind of homecoming for the painting. At one particular exhibit in New York, a speaker reminded those attending of the man and that historic hour:

It was at the gloomiest time of the long, the weary, and unequal strife with the gigantic power of England, that the passage of the Delaware took place. The darkest hour of that protracted night of peril had then overshadowed the noble spirits who held in their keeping the welfare of their country—the freedom of the world; but they quailed not, for he who was their leader stood firm, and, amid all their peril, hopefully before them; and resting, under God, on His unequalled wisdom and fortitude, they then saw that the deepest night does indeed foretell the coming day, for the dawn of their liberty—dim, rayless, almost chilling, but still dawn—soon struggled through the gloom ... with his eye fixed calmly on the desired shore, stands the Father of his Country.

In his *Farewell Address*, Washington still speaks to us today of that patriotism shared deeply by Emanuel Leutze, "The name of American which belongs to you, in your national capacity, must always exalt the pride of Patriotism."

Thank you to Ann Hawkes Hutton, *Portrait of Patriotism: Washington Crossing the Delaware* (Radnor, PA: Chilton Book Company, 1959), available online at archive.org/details/portraitofpatrio006992mbp.

CHAPTER 7

The Declaration of Independence, July 4, 1776

The Christian Idea of Man and Government in America's History

March 2017

Early in our country's history, the mother country England caused great distress among her children. Americans opposed the Declaratory Acts, the Stamp Act, and other measures as steps to absolute tyranny. Among the opponents were the Whigs, Patriots, and the Sons of Liberty. Others submitted willingly to the Crown. Both sides claimed to conform to English royalty and to the British Constitution.

In the writings of Buchanan, Locke, Milton, Sidney, and other historians, we find what we call the "Christian Idea of Man," embodying the very principles that formed the Declaration of Independence. This Christian Idea of Man became the basis of our very own theory of government. Those who signed the document were mostly Whigs—advocates of popular rights—prominent in their hometowns. In the beginning, Whigs did not have a large majority of support. Strong in conviction, their views invited fierce opposition. With their compelling arguments, these Whigs so grew in number they became a national party with tremendous influence.

The leading Tories, in opposition, still defended the principle of supremacy of existing authority, even if arbitrary against established English law. Many were indebted to the largess of the Crown for their positions, and so remained loyal, despite violations of law. They defended arbitrary power. Over time, the Whigs successfully created a mass network of committees of correspondence, the influential social media of the day. "Sons of Liberty," in opposition to the Stamp Act, marched to their banner, "Liberty, Property, and No Stamps."[1]

In Richard Frothingham's *The Rise of the Republic*, we read that the

> love of liberty under law was the reigning principle.... They nurtured the idea that devotion to the cause of justice was a higher obligation than fidelity to the old flag, when it was used to cover despotic power. They revolved [pondered] the saying of a great patriot, that freedom and security, under Providence, depended on themselves....
>
> [Then they turned to their own past history and to God's Word and reasoned, that] Englishmen in former ages had been justly renowned, and might turn the Great People to call on the name of the Lord, and to seek a redress of their grievances with the spear and lance at that glorious seat of justice, where Moses brought the Egyptians and Samson the Philistines.[2]

Through the Declaration of Independence and upon its principles, the patriots would establish a new American system with local government for the states and communities, and a national government for the union. Each would hold political sovereignty, each in its own sphere. In this, Americans freed themselves from foreign influences, rather acknowledging that their rights derive solely from the Creator—the unalienable rights of life, liberty, and the pursuit of happiness or property. We affirm that the rights of the new American system of government and culture came from the Christian Idea of Man.

---

1. Dennis Fradin, *Samuel Adams: The Father of American Independence* (New York: Clarion Books, 1998), 34.
2. Verna M. Hall, *The Christian History of the Constitution of the United States of America: Christian Self-Government* (San Francisco: Foundation for American Christian Education, 1966), 327.

Fifty-six patriots, true sons of liberty, signed the Declaration of Independence. Have you ever wondered who these men were and what happened to them after signing this document of our liberty?

A document distributed by the National Federation of Independent Business, of Washington, D.C., titled "The Price They Paid,"[3] says in part:

> What kind of men were they? Twenty-five were lawyers or jurists. Eleven were merchants. Nine were farmers or large plantation owners. These were men of means and education. Yet they signed the Declaration of Independence, knowing full well that the penalty could be death if they were captured.
>
> When these courageous men signed, they pledged their lives, their fortunes, and their sacred honor to the cause of freedom and independence.
>
> Richard Stockton returned to New Jersey in the fall of 1776 to find the state overrun by the enemy. He removed his wife to safety but was himself captured. His home, his fine library, his writings—all were destroyed. Stockton was so badly treated in prison that his health was ruined, and he died before the war's end.
>
> Carter Braxton was a wealthy planter and trader. One by one his ships were captured by the British navy. He loaned a large sum of money to the American cause; it was never paid back. He was forced to sell his plantations and mortgage his other properties to pay his debts.
>
> Thomas McKean was so hounded by the British that he had to move his family almost constantly. He served in the Continental Congress without pay, and kept his family in hiding.
>
> Vandals or soldiers or both looted the properties of [William] Ellery, [George] Clymer, [Lyman] Hall, [Thomas] Heyward, [Arthur] Middleton, [Benjamin] Harrison, [Francis] Hopkinson, and [Philip] Livingston.
>
> At the battle of Yorktown, Thomas Nelson Jr. noted that the British General Cornwallis had taken over the family home for

---

3. "The Price They Paid," National Federation of Independent Business (Washington, D.C.).

his headquarters. Nelson urged George Washington to open fire on his own home. This was done, and the home was destroyed. Nelson later died bankrupt.

Frances Lewis also had his home and properties destroyed. The enemy jailed his wife for two months, and that and other hardships from the war so affected her health that she died only two years later.

"Honest John" Hart was driven from his wife's bedside when she was near death. Their thirteen children fled for their lives. Hart's fields and his grist mill were laid waste. While eluding capture, he never knew where his bed would be the next night. He often slept in forests and caves. When he returned home, he found that his wife had died, and his children were gone.

Such are the stories and sacrifices typical of those who risked everything to sign the Declaration of Independence. These men were not wild-eyed, rabble-rousing ruffians. They were soft-spoken men of means and education. They had security, but they valued liberty more. Standing tall, straight, and unwavering, they pledged: "For the support of this declaration, with a firm reliance on the protection of the Divine Providence, we mutually pledge to each other, our lives, our fortunes, and our sacred honor."

Benjamin Rush (1745–1813) was one of the youngest signers of the Declaration in 1776. He was a distinguished physician and scientist who held the first chemistry professorship in America. In 1770, he published the first American chemistry textbook, *A Syllabus of a Course of Lectures on Chemistry*. He established the first free dispensary in America and published the first American work on mental disorders in 1813. He also helped form the first abolition society in America. He was appointed by President John Adams as the Treasurer of the U.S. Mint in 1797.

His passion for the Bible as the basic textbook in schools is understood in the context of his personal faith and passion for God's Word. Throughout his life, he advocated for the Bible as the source of knowledge.

Quoting from Benjamin Rush's writings and speakings:

1. Christianity is the only true and perfect religion; and that in proportion as mankind adopt its principles and obey its precepts they will be wise and happy.
2. That a better knowledge of this religion is to be acquired by reading the Bible than in any other way.
3. That the Bible contains more knowledge necessary to man in his present state than any other book in the world.
4. That knowledge is most durable, and religious instruction most useful, when imparted in early life.
5. That the Bible, when not read in school, is seldom read in any subsequent period of life

My arguments in favor of the Bible as a schoolbook are founded.

As a Scientist, Rush declared, "The memory is the first faculty which opens in the mind of children. Of how much consequence, then, must it be to impress it with the great truths of Christianity … so necessary for our happiness." Rush was very aware that many in the field of science were skeptics and this made him even more passionate about the necessity of the Bible as a school text book in America's schools. He spoke with passion, "We profess to be republicans and yet we neglect the only means of establishing and perpetuating our republican form of government; that is, the universal education of our youth in the principles of Christianity by means of the Bible; for this divine book, above all others, favors that equality among mankind, that respect for just laws, and all those sober and frugal virtues which constitutes the soul of republicanism."

Today, our challenge as Americans is to restore our heritage of this Christian Idea of Man and government, as mandated by the God of the Bible and the Hebrew-Christian religion. This writer has spent a lifetime in education that focuses on the Christian idea of man and government, through the Christian education of children.

George Washington,
the Father of Our Country, Part 1

The Building of His Character

April 2017

George Washington was born on February 22, 1732, to Augustine and Mary Ball Washington, in the family homestead of Bridges Creek, land not far from the Potomac River. George's father had been married before to Jane Butler, but only two of their three children survived, Lawrence and Augustine Jr. Their mother died in 1728, and August remarried in 1730 to Mary, the daughter of Colonel Ball. They had four sons, George, Samuel, John Augustine, and Charles, as well as two daughters, Elizabeth, called Betty, and Mildred, who died in infancy.

In the mid-1600s, the Washington family emigrated from England. Two brothers came together, John and Andrew Washington. They settled in the Virginia colony in 1657 and purchased land between the Potomac and Rappahannock Rivers. John became a leading figure in the colony's public service, prominent in the House of Burgesses, and as a successful plantation manager. He served as a colonel in the Virginia militia.

George grew up on a plantation of vast fields of tobacco, corn, and potatoes, rolling pastures, mountains, rivers, and an extended family of slaves owned by his father. These were often his companions and dear friends. There was harmony in the large Washington household. The father was serious, quiet, and in charge in the most ideal way. The mother enjoyed that security, but she had her hands full managing her domain, which was very large and commanding.

As a very young little boy, George learned to revere his family name. He daily recited from memory the Ten Commandments before his mother and father. They had a book, titled *The Young Man's Companion*, which taught manners. His father repeatedly emphasized that the Washington family does not lie, does not steal, does not cheat. All of George Washington's life is an example of that conduct, early learned at his parents' knees. His father expected obedience, honesty, patriotism, loyalty, and individual responsibility. His mother had the patience and resolve to see that George daily carried out these expectations of his father.

The Blacks on the farm felt a moral responsibility as well. Whether household servants or field workers, God was very real and personal to them. While we do not endorse slavery, it was very apparent from history that George Washington enjoyed close relationships and deep friendships with many of the slaves.

George's older brothers, Lawrence and Augustine, left home in their mid-teen years to go to England for their education. George expected to do the same, but plans changed dramatically when his father died unexpectedly when the young man was just twelve years old. His mother would not permit George to leave home for the schooling in England as his older brothers had done. While visiting the brothers in England at the Appleby Grammar School, George's father spent long hours with the headmaster there and brought back to Virginia numerous books of curricula. He was, of course, concerned for George's education, whether in England or at home.

George had early shown evidence of maturity but at his father's death, he assumed more responsibility, guided by his brother Lawrence. Back from England, Lawrence assumed headship of the family, while preparing George to lead in his own home in due season.

While he loved to roam the meadows and the fields, George had a great love for reading. One day he discovered a book from the Appleby Grammar School that had a long list of rules of conduct befitting a gentleman. He read and reread the book many times, copying every single rule in his own notebook. He would carry those rules in his heart and live them in his entire life. His notebook, with the rules carefully and neatly copied, exists today in the Washington Archives.

George's parents and older brothers were very involved and committed to his education, but no school of the quality of the Appleby Grammar School existed here in rural Virginia. The school that his brothers attended in England focused on character for manhood and promoted Christian faith and conduct. Though George expected to attend the Appleby School, nothing indicates any disappointment at staying home. For a time, George did attend a village school, guided by Hobby, the sexton of the parish, but he was not a well-educated teacher, so that George essentially studied under family tutelage at home. Still, the Appleby School had its influence through his brothers. Fortunately, Lawrence took a keen paternal interest in George after their father died, and George spent much time with him at Mt. Vernon.

Later, his mother decided to send George to live with his older brother Augustine, at Bridges Creek, where he studied at a fine village school led by Headmaster Mr. Williams. His manuscript notebooks still exist. George's execution in them is remarkably neat and accurate. Washington Irving and numerous other writers of the Washington biographies write of viewing his notebooks. Some of these same writers tell of viewing documents of his financial matters later in life, and that his keeping of accounts and financial transactions are near perfect.

Do we now see how young children benefit from such teaching in childhood? And through these young years, we see George as a self-disciplined young man in physical and also mental matters. He was passionate about exercise, running, leaping, wrestling, pitching quoits, and tossing bars.

As a teenager, he became interested in surveying, needed to measure the land and site boundaries. This interest made sense.

He loved mathematics and was enthralled with the land that his family owned. Moreover, George observed that land surveying was in great demand. He thus schooled himself through his teens to pursue this opportunity.

Lawrence's father-in-law, the Honorable William Fairfax, living at Belvoir, not far from Mt. Vernon, managed large landholdings for his cousin, Lord Fairfax. The Fairfax family actively assisted George to achieve success as a professional surveyor while yet a teenager, an accomplishment difficult to imagine out on the fringe of civilization.

Being asked to assist his sister Betty with her studies provided one of George's great learning experiences. Not only did it help him learn patience, which did not come naturally, it drew him ever closer to his sister. That closeness remained throughout their lives.

The friendship with the Fairfax family was a mutual blessing for them all. When Lord Fairfax came from England to view his vast lands, he delighted in forming a friendship with the young George Washington. George, not yet sixteen years of age, exhibited modesty with frankness. Because many of His Lordship's lands remained unsurveyed, George's passion for the land and surveying prompted favor and encouragement from this benefactor. They later entered together into contracts for the task. A few years later, George received the enviable appointment as public surveyor at age seventeen.

CHAPTER 9

GEORGE WASHINGTON, THE FATHER OF OUR COUNTRY, PART 2

His Character and Influence on Our Nation

May 2017

As a young boy, George engaged in his learning at home. At two different times, he attended a local village school, but most of his education came at home tutored by his father and older brothers, Lawrence and Augustine. Throughout his life, he praised his mother and acknowledged the great debt he owed her for the daily habits, particularly for her love of and faithfulness to Scripture. Mother and son quoted it daily together in the home. George also lived throughout his life by the "Rules of Civility" his father brought back from the Appleby School in England, which his older brothers attended. The book has continued in publication in America even to this day. I have a copy published in the 1980s as *110 Rules of Conduct*, which I treasure.

George had gone to visit cousins eighteen miles from home when his father became critically ill. He rushed home in time to see his father die the next day on April 12, 1743. Imagine the shock to them all, and the burden placed on Mary Washington. Fortunately, we have many records, some with amazing detail, of George's outstanding Christian mother. The early death of her husband proved her Christian character as firmly grounded. Her industriousness enabled her management of a huge burden of responsibilities, and that with few material resources yet with remarkable ability. Lawrence, in describing his stepmother, wrote "of her well-ordered household." He spoke of George's love of his mother, and of her trust in Divine Providence for her son. Those closest to Mary Washington knew that every day, without fail, she went to a secluded spot for her special time of prayer. We can imagine how much prayer went up for her youngest son, so often in danger, and always carrying staggering responsibilities.

One can imagine how difficult it was for George, after his father's death, to manage his schoolwork and farm labor. The serious study of agriculture had long interested him. His fascination with growing tobacco led to a great learning experience as he worked alongside the farm workers. The tiny little tobacco plants had to be transplanted in long field rows, and weeds had to be controlled. George must master the necessary skills to inspire the workers. So many journalists have pored over his notebooks, still in the Washington Archives, to learn in detail what he learned.

Upon August Washington's death, an inventory of his possessions established the details of his estate. Today we can review the entire list. The remarkable thing about the estate details is to see how very simply this family lived. There is no evidence of elegant, elaborate home furnishings. Everything spoke of sturdy adequacy but nothing of ornateness. Yet George received a great inheritance nonetheless. His life was full of energy, courage, wisdom, influence, and always ... assurance of eternal life. All of the research of the several centuries documents the fact that, throughout George's life, his parents gave their all to form a Christian character in their son. As we study his life, we see that he never, never, abused his power as Commander in Chief in the American Revolution or as President of the United States. Never did he bully his contemporaries or act less than the gentleman he was in fact. He never misused authority.

One of the first grown-up books George mentioned focused on living out the Christian faith. Written by the Rev. Thomas Comber, the book was entitled *Discourses*. On its first page, George would have read these words: "Prayer is the lifting up of the soul to converse with God and a means to obtain all of His blessings." He read of confessing one's sins, and assurance of forgiveness. It thoroughly explained such Scriptures as The Lord's Prayer and multitudes of Old and New Testament passages. The Anglican Church in that day reflected the great teaching of the Reformation.

Washington's First Great Achievement for His Nation

In the fall of 1753, French forces took command of the Ohio Valley. Governor Dinwiddie searched for someone to deliver a letter to the French commander, that this territory was British territory and that the French must withdraw. George, now twenty-one years old, volunteered to carry the letter. This was a thousand-mile wilderness journey undertaken during the winter months. His guide was Christopher Gist, known as "the most experienced frontiersman trader of the day." Both men left a written account of the journey, relating their contacts with Indians, including their efforts at Indian diplomacy. Gist wrote that the cold was so severe all of his fingers and some toes froze. At one time during the journey, the two men constructed a raft with but one small hatchet and no other tools. They wrote of being thrown off the raft at one point.

By virtue of this experience and his faithfulness, George would later serve as an aide to Virginia Lieutenant Governor Dinwiddie in another expedition against the French. The battle was chaotic and ended in defeat for George's forces. This would be the only defeat that George would experience throughout his life.

Greatly respected by now, the colony appointed George, at age twenty-three, to head the position of Commander in Chief of the Frontier Forces of Virginia. For three long years he fought against the French and Indian forces. Every day he must fight for food, for munitions, for uniforms, for transport, for military equipment, and for wages to pay his men. Through these experiences he learned the greatest lesson of all—discipline and self-government are the very soul of an army. In these three years, Providence would train him to lead the American Revolution.

Washington Irving's *Life of Washington* displays a steel engraving showing George Washington as a young man. A man who knew

Washington well wrote, after seeing the engraving, "It has been my privilege to see the best likenesses of the chief. The one of all others most resembling him is that prefixed to the first volume of Irving's *Life of Washington*." It well illustrates the character of America's great leader.

Perhaps His Greatest Achievement

For the eight long years of the American War for Independence, George carried its burden, inspired his soldiers, fought the British and displayed genius in leading his army to victory. Sometimes overlooked is the confidence of the folk back home in whom he had instilled total trust by his faith, by his leadership, and by his vision for our new nation.

The world watched. No revolution was like this Revolution. Ours should be called The War for Independence, for that is what it was. The only objective was freedom for the new nation as against the unlawful tyranny of England. George trained his leaders carefully, and they, in turn, trained the troops for the entire army. Discipline and courage prevailed. Military experts claim that George Washington accomplished more with fewer resources than any military leader in world history. He determined to have a union of thirteen colonies, where each one would retain both their liberty and rule of law.

The tragedies and suffering at Valley Forge in the winter of 1777 and 1778 press our imaginations beyond ability to comprehend. Supplies did not come, and pay lagged four to five months behind. Winter set in. Soldiers had no barracks, huts, or any real shelter. Tents hardly served. Food and clothing were far from adequate. Even given the general sturdy Christian character of the colonial patriots, only Washington's leadership can fully explain the fact that several thousand soldiers remained to endure such pain. He walked among the troops during the night hours. They recorded in their journals that on many occasions they saw tears on the general's face. The Valley Forge story gives us a glimmer of the price that many paid for our liberty. Looking back over that time period, Washington later wrote: "Naked and starving as they are, we cannot enough admire the incomparable patience and fidelity of the soldiers."[1]

U.S. Senator Albert J. Beveridge made a thorough study of Washington's life, career, and achievements. He concluded from his study, "Washington was the soul of the American cause. Washington was the government. Washington was the Revolution."[2]

The Senator was correct in his assessment. George Washington was the only American leader we could name who held the complete trust of the American people. They had entire trust in his leadership, and, in turn, he instilled in them a trust in the union then forged for their liberty. Under different leadership, we may never have had the Constitution that we have today. Miraculously, it seems, the people of the American colonies both retained their liberty and rule of law as newly formed states, while also forming a new union. Thanks to Washington's leadership, the Constitution became a reality. He instilled assurance and confidence that this was God's providence for the new nation. Thirty of the fifty-five delegates to the Constitutional Convention had been officers under his command during the Revolution. Think about that.

Within the new government, factions warred against one another. Washington had the patience and wisdom to cut through the chaos, reaching out to the ordinary citizens for support. Gouverneur Morris, in a speech on George Washington's passing, cited Washington as saying, "Let us raise a standard to which the wise and the honest can repair. The event is in the hand of God."[3] John

1. William J. Bennett, ed., *Our Sacred Honor: Words of Advice from the Founders in Stories, Letters, Poems, and Speeches* (New York: Simon & Schuster, 1997), 179.

2. Albert J. Beveridge, *Life of John Marshall*, vol. 1 (Washington, D.C.: Beard Books, 2000), 121.

3. Gouverneur Morris, "An Oration upon the Death of General Washington," in Max Farrand, ed., *Records of the Federal Convention of 1787*, vol. 3 (New Haven: Yale University Press, 1911), 381–382, available online at *Online Library of Liberty*, oll.libertyfund.org.

Fiske wrote of his influence throughout the convention, noting "Washington's glorious spirit."[4]

It is likely that Washington would have liked to retire to his farm after the war was over. However, Providence had prepared him to take the presidency. He was the only man in whom every state could place their trust. By this time, he had the respect of many foreign nations. His sincerity and modesty were evident at his inauguration. In his first official act, he promised "my fervent supplications to that Almighty Being who rules over the Universe, who presides in the Councils of Nations, and whose providential aids can supply every human defect."[5]

Looking over his two terms as president, he prayed for our nation:

That Heaven may continue to [grant] you the choicest tokens of [His] beneficence; that your union and brotherly affection be perpetual; that the free Constitution, which is the work of your hands, may be sacredly maintained; that its administration in every department may be stamped with wisdom and virtue; that, in fine, the happiness of the people of these States, under the auspices of liberty, may be made complete.[6]

I quote here one of the two scholars who founded the Foundation for American Christian Education in the 1960s in San Francisco, California. They compiled more primary research on Washington that any current foundation in the nation. Their book referenced below is a treasure. Quoting Verna Hall on Washington's character:

If one is not himself knowledgeable of the admonitions in the Bible, the fruits of the Spirit, the fruits of the flesh, he cannot

4. John Fiske, *The Historical Writings of John Fiske*, vol. XII (Boston: Houghton Mifflin, 1882), 276.

5. George Washington, "Washington's Inaugural Address of 1789," *National Archives*, Founders Online, archives.gov/exhibits/american_originals/inaugtxt.html.

6. George Washington, "Farewell Address, 19 September, 1796," *National Archives*, Founders Online, founders.archives.gov/documents/Washington/99-01-02-00963.

fully comprehend the life of George Washington. Additionally, even a Christian must not judge Washington from a doctrinal or sectarian prejudice, otherwise, the full wonder of this Bible-Christian life cannot be recognized.

George Washington is unique, but not unique for his time. He is the natural product of a Bible-believing people. If one would really know George Washington, he must be a Bible-believing scholar such as he. (Verna M. Hall, Foundation for American Christian Education)[7]

Virginia gave us this imperial man;… this unblemished gentleman: What shall we give her back but love and praise? (James Russell Lowell)[8]

Let vice and immorality of every kind be discouraged as much as possible in your regiment; and see, as a Chaplain is allowed to it, that the men regularly attend divine Worship. Gaming of every kind is expressly forbid as the foundation of evil, and the ruin of many a brave, and good officer. Games of exercise, for amusement, may be not only allowed of, but encouraged. (George Washington, 1777)[9]

The Marquis de Lafayette arrived from France in 1777 and developed a father-son relationship with George Washington. He fought in many battles and was wounded at Brandywine. His love for Washington led him to name his own son George Washington Lafayette.

So that we do not imply otherwise, we note in expounding on the life of this great man that we magnify God for His glory, and on His Providence, not on any man who owes everything to Him.

---

7. Verna M. Hall, *George Washington: The Character and Influence of One Man* (San Francisco: Foundation for American Christian Education, 2000), 152–53.
8. James Russell Lowell, *Poems of James Russell Lowell* (London: Oxford University Press, 1917), 527.
9. Jared Sparks, *The Writings of George Washington*, vol. IV (Cambridge: Folsom, Wells, & Thurston, 1834), 436–37n.

CHAPTER 10

THE EMERGENCE OF LIBERTY

September 2012

Montesquieu expressed what should be obvious to all, "God is related to the universe as Creator and Preserver; the laws by which He created all things, are those by which He preserves them. He acts according to these rules, because He knows them; He knows them, because He made them; and He made them because they are relative to His wisdom and power" (*The Spirit of the Laws*).[1]

The Biblical Law of Liberty represents the very core of our Christian heritage, serving as the foundation of Western civilization and the source of every advancement in the culture. Men do not create, produce individual excellence, or otherwise contribute very much in a state of slavery. Sinful men love to enslave others. Therefore, the history of liberty is one of strife. Liberty always came at a price, the price of the blood of martyrs paid over centuries. To each martyr, God's Word held fundamental meaning, liberating the soul even in the face of death. Remembering the strife, the cost of liberty helps to protect it.

Memory is so important. Without memory, we repeat the fallacies of the past. We must revisit our memories of the steps on the path to liberty. For example, remember how an army of God set up camp on the green meadow at Runnymede the fifteenth day of June, 1215. Their banners flew as barons and lords bravely stood

---

1. Baron Montesquieu, *The Spirit of Laws*, vol. 1 (London: S. Crowder, C. Ware, & T. Payne, 1773), 2.

their ground upon their noble horses. Would the day end in a civil war, or would Englishmen have the liberties rightfully theirs?

King John, brother of Richard Coeur de Lion, lurked about in Windsor Castle, overlooking the meadow, the while barons gathered. A wicked man, John had acted quickly at Richard's death to seize his money and his throne. No one in the English kingdom of those days knew any liberty except those closest to the wicked king. Meeting the barons, at sword point King John realized that he must accept free elections and their demands. Thus, King John set the great seal on the Magna Carta—the Greater Charter. The church should be free and have its own elections. No freeman should suffer criminal punishment without a lawful judgment of his peers at trial. The people may move about freely at will. No one would be denied justice. The Magna Carta provided for fairness in the marketplace and made other provisions in the interest of liberty and justice. Tyranny of the monarchy should end.

The Great Charter became a battle cry for freedom. Soon, a Great Council of barons, archbishops, bishops, and earls formed to decentralize government power and make it more representative. Thus, Parliament established the beginning of representative government, however imperfect. The Magna Carta did not solve all injustices, but the fundamentals of unalienable rights affirmed in that document paved the way for liberty in every land across the sea where Englishmen have settled. I saw the crumpled parchment displayed in the British Museum. It is but a piece of sheepskin, but the Magna Carta powerfully symbolizes the liberties that we have come to enjoy. Every baron and every lord came ready for civil war that June day in the lush green meadow. I have taken students to walk in its grasses. We all could imagine being there that fateful day. No blood spilled that day, though it would spill on many other days to come. The founding patriots of our own United States spilled much blood in the fight for liberty and its necessary sacrifices.

Henry III made amendments to strengthen the Great Charter in 1225. Many who fought oppression in England and America have since studied and quoted its provisions in the various battles for liberty and justice. We cannot overstate its historical significance in the heritage of liberty.

A century passed upon the Magna Charta. The passion for liberty still burned in the hearts of Englishmen, though liberty had not yet come to the serfs, called *villains* (people serving aristocratic lords, farm servants), who must pay taxes to the king, the barons, and priests. They could not read and had no schools and no advocates. Monks and friars were everywhere, as their church held half the land in England and more wealth than the king. Superstition abounded due to the ignorance of the masses. The Bibles belonged to the church but remained chained to the pulpits in the churches and cathedrals (before the days of the printing press). They were written by hand by the scribes, and they took many years to complete. Yet the clergy refused to teach the people its content, which would make them strong and free in Christ.

England's greatest scholar John Wycliffe preached against the immoral practices of the monks and friars. He preached repentance (fundamental change toward God) to all men, that they might live righteous and blessed lives. He preached limited rightful authority of the king and of the priests, each within their own spheres. Wycliffe preached individual liberty of conscience and opinion. This teaching threatened the arbitrary authority of both church and state and so their officials pushed back. Ruling officials called Wycliffe to appear before the Bishops Court. Then, summoned to appear before the pope in Rome, Wycliffe refused. Instead, he remained in England, where he translated the Bible from the Latin Vulgate version to the English language of his own dialect. Until this time, aside from the fact that few Bibles existed—and those were chained down, they remained available only in Latin and Hebrew. Only highly accomplished scholars could read them. Dr. Wycliffe believed that every person had the right to read the Scriptures, despite the decree of the Pope that only the clergy could do so. As there was no universal English language at the time, providentially Wycliffe used his own dialect because it was the most expressive and vigorous. Clearly, Wycliffe believed God intended the Bible for the people and not only for an elite ruling class. The people listened with great enthusiasm to public Scripture reading. They began to think new thoughts, leading to more dreams of individual liberty, as the Word penetrated their understanding.

One of Dr. Wycliffe's friends, Geoffrey Chaucer, a poet, helped the cause of liberty through his writing of *The Canterbury Tales*. Together, these two men laid the foundation for the strongest, most aggressive language of expression in the history of the world—our very own English language, the language of liberty. Holding up bad religious practices to ridicule in his writing, he also used a valuable Norman vocabulary, enriching his writing and expanding literacy. Authorities forced Chaucer to flee England twice, but he was able to return and die a peaceful death in 1400. He made a contribution to human freedom in exposing evil.

In 1385, Dr. Wycliffe died and was buried. A steady stream of pilgrims came to the gravesite. Forty-one years later, mainstream monks and friars had all they could take of these pilgrimages. The Council of Constance ordered Wycliffe's bones dug up and burned. The ashes were thrown into the sea. Did they succeed in being rid of John Wycliffe? No! His followers, called Lollards, carried the language of liberty over all of England, all of Bohemia, and elsewhere.

A Bohemian priest, John Hus, read the Wycliffe Bible and converted to Christ. Working to spread the Gospel and achieve a translation of the Bible into Bohemian, Hus sought protection from the king and received it for some time. Protection did not prevail, and Hus burned at the stake. Yet, following his martyrdom, once more the message of Christ prevailed, penetrating Bohemia.

Moving ahead, sixty years passed since Wycliffe's ashes went into the sea. Responding to the Wycliffe Bible, two Reformers providentially advanced the Gospel as never before: Lawrence Coster and John Guttenberg. Coster and his family lived in Holland, where he crafted his revolutionary invention. Up until this time, all books were printed by hand with a pen on parchment—animal skin. An idea came to Coster as he carved his child's name on a piece of tree bark. He thought, "I might carve letters on a wood block, ink them over, arrange the letter so, and stamp any word in the language." His experiment worked well. He invented movable type. He hired a young apprentice, John Guttenberg. Movable type revolutionized the world of printing. It made the Bible affordable. It gave every man access to knowledge. Wow! When Coster died, Guttenberg took the Coster secret with him up the Rhine, and settled in Strasburg working as a typesetter.

He realized that the wooden blocks wore out, and he longed to make them metal to withstand the pressure of the printing press. He must make a metal mold. A goldsmith assisted him. Success! Guttenberg published his book in 1450, with the new metal movable type. It was the Bible, of course. Now, the Bibles were more affordable with the Guttenberg Press. Wycliffe's legacy lives on in mechanically printed Bibles, spreading the language of Gospel liberty.

The story of Christian liberty continued into the next century. It was one of great upheaval and transition due to the Protestant Reformation. John Calvin's thought and influence went deeper and impacted every major societal issue touching on religious and civil liberty. The teaching of Calvin influenced his own native French Huguenot successors, the Scottish reformers, English and New England Puritans, and American colonial founders. Calvin was born in Noyon, France, in 1509 and died in 1564.

We recommend the writing of Dr. Douglas Kelly, a brilliant theologian and seminary professor and an authority on Calvin's impact on our heritage. Dr. Kelly rightly claims that Calvin's influence "helped hold together a skeletal system of political, economic, and religious life in the western nation states for the last four hundred years." Kelly writes of Calvin's lifelong interest in political matters and government. He studied law, which equipped him to write the first edition of his *Institutes of the Christian Religion* as a political treatise. In dedicating it to the King of France,

Calvin focused his last chapter on "Freedom, and Ecclesiastical and Civil Power." He dedicated numerous works to rulers in Europe in hopes of support for the Reformation. In writing of the benefits of Calvin's superior legal and Renaissance education, Dr. Kelly states, "Combining both theological and philosophical and legal scholarship goes far toward explaining the lifelong and fruitful marriage in the thought and activity between the theological and legal concerns."[2]

Space does not allow us to dwell on the years in Geneva when Calvin led the Reformed Church. However, Calvin continually preached on proper forms of civil government and limitations on civil authority.

John Knox and other reformers took refuge in Geneva, where Knox became the pastor of an English-speaking church for refugees. Following the death of Mary Tudor, Knox returned to his native Scotland, and passionately taught the theology that we know as the Covenant Concept. The Covenant binds the people and the government under the Law of God as revealed in the Scriptures. Knox and the reformers labored long to secure limited powers and church-state balance.

The Covenanting movement prevailed in 1638 with the passage of The National Covenant, protecting the lordship of Christ over their church and worship, and proclaiming Christ's lordship over the nation of Scotland. The Long Parliament summoned the Westminster Assembly, which gave us the *Westminster Confession of Faith*. One of the commissioners was Samuel Rutherford, author of *Lex Rex*, or *Law is King*. John Locke studied at the school at Westminster Abbey when the Westminster Assembly took place. *Lex Rex* came out while Locke studied there. Locke drew heavily on the Calvin Covenant concepts, and his writing was embraced by our prominent Founding Fathers in the formation of our Christian constitutional republic.

---

2. Douglas Kelly, *The Emergence of Liberty in the Modern World: The Influence of Calvin on Five Governments from the 16th through 18th Centuries* (Phillipsburg, NJ: Presbyterian and Reformed Publishing, 1992).

In the next chapter, we will look at the emergence of liberty throughout the movements of the French Huguenots, the Scots, the English Puritans, and the American colonies. Further, we will expose the death threats to liberty in America today.

CHAPTER 11

THE EMERGENCE OF LIBERTY
AS CHRISTIANITY MOVES WESTWARD

October 1, 2012

In Dr. Douglas Kelly's book *The Emergence of Liberty*, Kelly
writes:

> John Calvin saw theology as a *scientia practica*, and so from
> the beginning to end he integrally related doctrinal concerns
> with legal and political questions.... He believed in a relatively
> independent church supported by a Christian civil magistrate.
> In other words, Calvin held the ancient "two-powers" view
> that both church and state are ordained by God with neither
> subordinate to the other and neither entitled to control the
> other. Both have coordinate authority, under God's ultimate
> authority, which is expressed in His infallible Word. Calvin
> held a much more positive view of the guidance of God's law
> for Christian life and polity than did Martin Luther, the elder
> statesman of the Reformation.[1]

Speaking of Calvin's view of the limited power of all human
authorities and institutions of the law, Dr. Kelly writes,

> They are all equally under the higher law of God's transcendent
> law, including natural law engraved on the consciences of all
> men, and most importantly, the revealed law of Scripture. This
> means that under extreme circumstances the people have a right

---

1. Kelly, *The Emergence of Liberty in the Modern World*.

to resist tyranny in the name of that higher covenant law, in so far as they are led by duly constituted lesser magistrates.[2]

Several decades after Luther nailed his paper on the church door at Wittenberg, priest James Lefevre translated the Bible in France. The French who could read now learned the message of repentance and salvation and righteous living, and they experienced a life change. The mob ridiculed them, calling them *hugunons*, meaning people who sing psalms in the streets. The established church followed with formal persecution, and in the town of Meaux, they burned its inhabitants. They maimed others. Then they forbade further printing of the Bible.

John Calvin held a dynamic influence in his native land for more than two hundred years. His teaching on religious and political liberties had an even greater impact on the nations of Scotland, the Netherlands, England, and certainly the American colonies. Lasting tenets of his teaching stressed the political sovereignty of the people, granting them inherent rights to resist the abuse of their God-given rights. Always a minority, the French Huguenots appeared never more than 20–25 percent of the population. While the French government based in Roman Catholic authoritarianism viewed them as a danger, the Protestants did have some support among the nobility and some intellectuals. Reformed leaders did not all agree on revolutionary action. Calvin and Theodore Beza warned against it. John Knox favored resistance to oppressive tyranny.

The first massacre of French Protestants took place in a worship service at Vassy in March of 1562. The Huguenot response? The Reformed church's *Confession of Faith* and *Book of Discipline* articulated the authority of Scripture, the Word transcendent over all human documents. The doctrine of God's providence gave comfort, knowing that God is in control and working all things for the good of the elect (Romans 8:28).

---

2. Kelly, *The Emergence of Liberty in the Modern World*, 139–40.

Catherine de Medici, the Queen Regent and mother of the young and weak king, Charles IX, took up arms against the Protestants, approving the massacre of many tens of thousands in Paris and elsewhere on St. Bartholomew Eve, August 1572. Civil war resulted. Ultimately, many Huguenots made an exodus to England, Scotland, or elsewhere. Published and circulated Huguenot tracts traced French history to ancient and feudal times, times of common law and principles of constitutional tradition. For example, a king's subjects could remove him from his throne for violation of his rule.

Lutherans in their Magdeburg Confession asserted the duty of a people to depose a ruler who abused his duty to religion. The Huguenots may have made their most important contribution to liberty when they expanded their emphasis from primarily religious and church covenantal purposes to also include civil constitutional and political theory. This matured their thinking toward representative government and a Parliament representing the people. Later, the Scottish Presbyterians would adopt the concept of *separation of powers*. Certainly, the French Huguenots influenced both English and Scottish Protestants with their strong views of limited powers, sovereignty of the people, and the right to resist tyranny.

Dr. Kelly claims that Knox's Scotland exemplified Calvinism more fully than any other country on a national scale. He writes, "Calvin's teaching on God, authority, law, and church and state developed further in Scotland than in France or England.[3] The minority of Huguenots in France limited their influence. In England, the complex of competing theories of church-state relations hindered them. A crucial concept in Reformed Scotland claimed that the church as a body is equal in legal standing as the civil state. Another claimed the covenantal idea of the direct right of the people to hold the magistrates accountable to them for the functions of their offices."

---

3. Kelly, *The Emergence of Liberty in the Modern World*.

Knox's sojourn in Geneva, where he served as pastor to an English-speaking church, brought him to Calvin. Knox described Calvin's Academy as "the most perfect school of Christ since the days of the apostles."[4] Understanding Calvin's influence on Knox, Scotland's Reformation, and on Presbyterian and Reformed bodies today is vital. Christians, as true believers, live in covenant relationship with the God of Creation, through Christ alone, by faith alone. Knox drew heavily from Old Testament sources to support his views on covenant and to support his views justifying the right to rebel against ungodly rulers. Scotland's struggles continued, but the two-spheres-of-authority concept prevailed: Christ is over the Church, and though the state may have a king, he is under the authority of God through the representation of the body of Christ, His church.

At the heart of the English Puritan movement lay the Word of God, with its authority in the peoples' lives and culture. They believed in what they called a *regulative principle* that governed all of life, work, church worship, home, and state. Everything must be in harmony with the teaching of God's Word. The Westminster Assembly gave direction to Scotland and England, and later, to America—a model toward achieving personal and national liberty in a balance with state authority. Not all Protestants agreed. The Arminians, for example, favored a man-centered theology. Arminians could accommodate monarchical absolutism.

The English Puritans of New England, and the Scotch-Irish of the Middle Colonies, took their Calvinist theology with them to America. Their colonial charters permitted them to draw up their civil compacts in harmony with their church charters. Carving a Christian constitutional republic over time made them far ahead of any people in the world in terms of liberty. Calling the American Revolution a *Presbyterian Rebellion* didn't miss the mark very far. The Baptists held council to produce their wonderful *Confession of 1689*, proving them alive and well. The election-day sermons

---

4. Roger E. Olson, *The Westminster Handbook to Evangelical Theology* (Louisville: Wesminster John Knox Press, 2004), 17.

of the Congregational pulpits continued to ring out strong. The Declaration of Independence portrayed King George III, a tyrant, "unfit to be the ruler of a free people."

My favorite American history is the Pilgrim story. A church congregation relocated to a wilderness, as they lifted the sails on The Mayflower in 1620. Their example of individual devotion to religious liberty has inspired me for more than half a century. These brave Pilgrims and the Puritans, who followed ten years later and learned from the Pilgrims, continued to influence the colonies for a century more. America fulfilled the dreams of the Huguenots and all those who will not compromise God's Word. America has been faithful to the promise of Christian liberty.

What Happened?

The Congressional Record, October 1, 1965, published a lead article—actually a reprinted sermon written by a pastor from Arizona, Dr. Charles Polling. Dr. Polling titled the sermon, "How a Republic Died."[5] How I wish that every congressman in the Congress had read the sermon then and taken it to heart. It is prophetic, if I may use that word. I urge you to get a copy from your congressman and distribute it to your circle of influence and to your church for the purpose of prayer. Quoting some of it:

> There are certain world crises that all thoughtful Americans must recognize. We cannot go on bearing the expense of unbridled government spending without eventually crashing head-on with a cataclysmic day of reckoning. We cannot continue to ignore the charter of our freedom, The Constitution, which has made us the strongest, richest, and greatest Nation this world has ever known, and survive. Even while I speak, we face national bankruptcy and the slavery of socialism, the chains of dictatorship, and a police state. We have toyed dangerously with statism and a planned socialist economy. Government

---

5. Charles Polling, "How a Republic Died," *The Congressional Record*, originally presented in Eighty-Ninth Congress, First Session, January 4, 1965 to October 23, 1965.

is no longer our servant; it is our master. To a greater degree than we realize, the Congress is no longer the legislative arm of America. Under the provision of the Spence Act, the President has power over the entire life of the Nation, empowered to do as he personally pleases. And one leader, one demagogue, with delusions of infallibility, can lead a proud and mighty nation down the dark road to oblivion. A hasty glance at history supports this statement. Today we have the judiciary and the executive branches of government in violation of the Constitution, usurping and assuming the functions and authority granted only to the legislative arm of our government. Now all that is transpiring in our society and government today is vitally related to the church and the kingdom enterprise. The record of history reveals that as the Church goes, so goes the Nation.

Dr. Polling makes the call for Christians to become involved in government affairs. We must challenge one another to pray without ceasing for our nation.

CHAPTER 12

They Preached Liberty

July 2016

Years ago, D. James Kennedy sent me a book by this title he had published through Coral Ridge Ministries. He made a passionate search of sermons preached throughout New England by virtually all the ministers of the period, from the 1700s through the period of the American Revolution and beyond. Early American pulpits preached these election sermons and artillery sermons. Then they commonly printed and widely distributed these sermons among American citizens. This one fact should give cause to read them carefully and discover that civil liberty was of utmost importance to those ministers. Facing constant dictatorial peril from the mother country, *liberty*—with its necessary companion *justice*—impassioned colonial citizens.

In early America, an opportunistic and greedy English government kept liberty under fire as it is today. History has rightly called the New England Puritan clergy "watchmen on the wall." These clergymen were the most highly educated in the entire community. Most of them had graduated from Harvard and Yale when these institutions still stood solidly and soundly in historic Biblical theological orthodoxy on the tradition of the Reformation. These were remarkable men, skilled not only in Old Testament and Reformation Theology, but in other fields of knowledge, in a broad liberal education. The colonial pastors learned the sciences, industrial arts, history, literature, and civil government. Dr. Kennedy particularly highlighted the fact that these pastors established the American Academy of Arts and Sciences in 1780.

These pastors' sermons clearly communicated their passion for ordering civil government in a godly fashion. They deemed Biblical faith applied to political subjects and admonitions most worthy subjects for sermons. Political order protects a peoples' ability to serve God as a people ought. Without godly order, "if the foundations be destroyed, what can the righteous do?" (Psalm 11:3). Thus, they delivered these sermons to motivate and instruct the citizens in principles and active best-stewardship practices, to maintain and protect the Christian liberty of our young nation.

Yes, of course, many Tories strongly objected to the Puritan views. Yet the ministers responded Biblically: "Where the Spirit of the Lord is, there is liberty" (Second Corinthians 3:17), and "Ye shall know the truth, and the truth shall make you free" (John 8:32).

Holding Biblical history sacred, the colonial pastors often referred to the ancient Hebrews. They related America's condition to that of the Hebrew children leaving their land of bondage and inheriting the Promised Land, on the ground of receiving and obeying Moses' Law by faith. They must do so! Jesus said, "If ye love Me, keep My commandments" (John 14:15).

Through intense study of the ancient Hebrews, they understood that every nation had fallen into established idolatry by the time God raised Moses up as a deliverer of His people. Moral and social evils beyond description and imagination reigned in those cultures. With every nation suffering grasping tyranny, no people enjoyed anything like a constitution to protect liberty and self-government, as we have known in America. The children of Abraham, the Israelites, had even ceased to worship the One True God.

That One True God used Moses to establish the means of a political-religious constitution to insure liberty, a fundamental purpose of Providence. He would use the true faith and religion to establish government, and then use the resulting righteous government, justice, to protect the true religion. The Jewish lawgiver gave us the means to secure liberty, which can be achieved in no other way. We learn from Moses that the worship of the One True God in Christ by faith must be the *first* principle of civil polity. Obviously, our adversary Satan purposes to destroy that idea in our pubic square.

The revolutionary pastors distinguished between natural rights and civil rights. Men possess *natural,* or inherent, God-given rights. But men enforce civil rights through godly laws. Righteous civil government of men by compact or constitution must guard the natural rights of every man. God made a compact with Noah, Moses, and Joshua. We citizens who elect imperfect men to office have a duty to limit their power and monitor their performance in office.

The greatest insight to gain from these early sermons is the fact that liberty is grounded solely in Scripture's way. Franklin P. Cole, author of the book, *They Preached Liberty*, wrote of the Puritan ministers: "They wished to conserve the best from the past, including Magna Charta, and their own colonial charters. In their opinion, the real radicals were those in the British government who were departing from the laws and traditions of old. The clergy opposed what Samuel Langdon, D.D., President of Harvard College, called the many artifices to stretch the prerogatives of the crown beyond all constitutional bounds."[1]

Can you understand that in opposing and resisting tyranny, the patriots defended the ancient liberties? These ministers defended political and civil liberty, but they also stressed the *religious liberty* only possible through education into these ancient truths. They faithfully pointed out the obligations and the *cost* of liberty. Our forefathers fought an apparently impossible war to obtain it. My generation fought a war to preserve it (WWII).

Before the beginning of the American Revolution, the New England clergy pled the cause of the African slaves, victims of man

---

1. Franklin P. Cole, *They Preached Liberty: An Anthology of Timely Quotations from New England Ministers of the American Revolution on the Subject of Liberty, Its Source, Nature, Obligations, Types, and Blessings* (Indianapolis: Liberty Press, 1976). Succeeding quotations in this chapter come from this book.

stealing (Exodus 21:16). In the original draft of the Declaration of Independence, Jefferson denounced the British government for the slave trade, but the colonies of South Carolina and Georgia succeeded in striking this from the Declaration.

Meet Jonathan Mayhew (1729–1766)

Robert Treat Paine, a signer of the Declaration of Independence and later Attorney General of the United States, declared New England minister Jonathan Mayhew "The Father of Civil and Religious Liberty in Massachusetts and America." Others, including James Otis, John Adams, and Samuel Adams, all his intimate friends, recognized Mayhew for his convictions, persuasive writings, and influence. Patriot statesmen of his day widely read his works.

Twenty-six years before the Declaration was penned, Mayhew proclaimed, "Nothing can well be imagined more directly contrary to common sense than to suppose that millions of people should be subjected to the arbitrary, precarious pleasure of one single man,—who has naturally no superiority over them in point of authority,—so that their estates, and everything that is valuable in life, and even their lives also, shall be absolutely at his disposal, if he happens to be wanton and capricious enough to demand them."

In 1754, Mayhew's Election Sermon included this challenge:

God forbid that any son of New England should prove such a profane Esau as to sell his birthright! Our ancestors, though not perfect and infallible in all respects, were a religious, brave, and virtuous set of men, whose love of liberty, civil and religious, brought them from their native land into the American deserts. By their generous care it is, under the smiles of a gracious Providence, that we now have a goodly heritage.

In 1750, warning against unlimited submission, Mayhew declared:

Tyranny brings ignorance and brutality with it. It degrades men from their higher rank into the class of brutes. It dampens their spirits, it suppresses arts; it extinguishes every spark of noble ardor and generosity in the breasts of those enslaved by it; it makes naturally strong and great minds feeble and little, and triumphs over the ruins of virtue and humanity.

In no other country in world history has there been a government like ours. In early America, for a season, civil and religious liberty combined in harmony. In Charles Turner's Election Sermon of 1773, he warns the patriots, "Religious liberty is so blended with civil that if one fails, it is not to be expected that the other will continue."

In Ebenezer Bridge's Election Sermon of 1767, he declares, "As to religion and religious privileges, what people in the whole world are so highly favored as our nation? We have the Gospel, the freest use and the fullest enjoyment of it."

The fundamental principles of the ancient Hebrew and the American constitutions are prominently republican. True republican government is a system of godly, truly relational representation on a common faith. In such a republic, confidence rests in the people faithfully to administer great power justly. The republican governmental model assumes a people of the Biblical faith, for the Holy Spirit of God governs through them. The republic imposes a great need for people of faith to read, research, and embrace our Biblical Christian history. It is a matter of sustained and generational character if liberty can long last in our or any nation.

Minister Jonathan Mayhew declared in 1754, "Rulers derive their power from God, and are ordained to be his ministers for good." Many New England election sermons, directing their admonitions to those elected to office, emphasized this charge over decades.

An evil force in our nation works tirelessly to undermine the true Source of our own liberty in America—the law of Moses. We implore your careful reading here to inspire continued deep study in the Biblical principles of Christian liberty, recognition of the responsibility to represent God in society, and responsible action for the stewardship of the public square to preserve both religious and civil liberty. Prayer is essential, but so also a well-informed, wise, and active constituency. I pray for the ministers of America's churches to "Proclaim Liberty Throughout the Land" once again.

> God never gives men up to be slaves till they lose their national virtue, and *abandon themselves* to slavery. (Rev. Richard Salter, emphasis added, Mansfield, Connecticut, *Election Sermons*, 1768)

> But be ye doers of the word, and not hearers only, deceiving your own selves. (James 1:22)

> And all thy children shall be taught of the LORD; and great shall be the peace of thy children. (Isaiah 54:13)

CHAPTER 13

The Origin of Old Glory, Our American Flag

January 2016 & February 2017 combined

The story of the Stars and Stripes is the story of our nation. It is the story of freedom, liberty, and equal justice under law. Our development of the American flag has paralleled the evolution of our ideas and of our free institutions. The flag is our symbol—an emblem for our ideas, our faith, and our laws.

In our early days as thirteen British colonies, the banners borne by the Revolutionary forces varied widely.

The local flags and colonial devices, displayed in many places on land and sea during the first months of the American War for Independence, carried the various grievances the colonists held against the mother country.

The Massachusetts Spy, a Boston newspaper, published the first public reference to a national flag on March 10, 1774. They ran this poem as a tribute to the flag:

> A ray of bright glory now beams from afar,
> Blest dawn of an empire to rise;
> The American Ensign now sparkles a star,
> Which shall shortly flame wide through the skies.

In Taunton, Massachusetts, a flag unfurled in 1774, which carried the traditional British crosses of Saint Andrew and Saint George in the canton, with the words "Liberty and Union" printed on it.

In the summer of 1775, George Washington accepted his appointment as Commander in Chief of the Continental Forces for the defense of American Liberty. At that time, the Continental Congress continued to correspond with King George, urging their grievances. Reflecting a dual love of England and the desire for liberty and justice in the colonies, by autumn of 1775, citizens ready to revolt chose a flag simultaneously reflecting their sense of unity with the mother country and their claim to justice and liberty.

The famous Rattlesnake Flag, carried by the Minutemen in 1775, showed thirteen red and white stripes with a rattlesnake emblazoned across it with the warning, "Don't Tread on Me."

In 1775, the banner that flew over Fort Moultrie displayed a crescent on a blue field with the word "Liberty" printed in white. When enemy muskets shot this flag down, a brave sergeant named Jasper nailed it back to the staff at the risk of his life.

The Pine Tree Flag, which flew over the troops at Bunker Hill in 1775, displayed the pine tree symbol of the Massachusetts Bay Colony. It was a white flag with stripes of blue at the top and bottom. It displayed a green pine tree with the words "Liberty Tree—An Appeal to God."

John Paul Jones raised the first flag representing the colonies at sea from the deck of the *Alfred* on December 3, 1775. One month later, George Washington displayed the same design and named it the Grand Old Flag, on January 2, 1776. Also called the Continental Colors, it had thirteen alternate red and white stripes and a blue field with the crosses of Saint Andrew and Saint George on it.

After July 4, 1776, the people of the colonies felt the need for a new flag—a truly national flag, an emblem of internal unity and independence as a nation. The Continental Congress acted with this resolution: "Resolved, that the flag of the thirteen united states be thirteen stripes, alternate red and white; that the union be thirteen stars, white on a blue field, representing a new constellation." The significance of the colors was defined thus: *white* signified Purity and Innocence; *red*, hardiness and valor; *blue*, vigilance, perseverance, and justice. Francis Hopkinson, signer

Betsy Ross Sewing Flag,
after G. Liebscher, c. 1908
(Library of Congress)

of the Declaration of Independence and a member of the Continental Congress, is credited with having designed the American Flag.

Historians of the period credit Betsy Ross, the flag maker in Philadelphia, with having made the first flag and having suggested that the stars be five pointed. Betsy Ross's home in Philadelphia at 239 Arch Street is a national shrine, and her flag flies on a staff from her third-floor window. Her grandson William J. Canby wrote in 1857 that he vividly recalled as a boy of eleven hearing the story from his then-eighty-four-year-old grandmother Betsy Ross.[1]

It is not tradition, it is report from the lips of the principal participator in the transaction, directly told not to one or two, but a dozen or more living witnesses, of whom I myself am one, though but a little boy when I heard it.... Colonel Ross, with Robert Morris and General Washington, called upon Mrs. Ross, and told her they were a committee of Congress, and wanted her to make the flag from the drawing, a rough one, which, upon her suggestions, was redrawn by General Washington in pencil in her back parlor. This was prior to the Declaration of Independence. I fix the date to be during Washington's visit to Congress from New York in June 1776, when he came to confer upon the affairs of the army, the flag being, no doubt, one of these affairs.

---

1. George Henry Preble, *History of the Flag of the United States of America* (Boston and New York: Houghton, Mifflin & Company, 1894), 266–67.

There is in the archives of the Navy an order "for making ship colours" for fourteen pounds, twelve shillings and two pence, to Mrs. Elizabeth Ross of Philadelphia.[2]

The Marine Committee adopted on June 14, 1777 the theme of the red and white striped Union Flag of Holland to the flag of the thirteen United States of America. Ezra Stiles, President of Yale University, recorded in his diary the resolution passed by Congress in 1777: "The Congress have substituted a new constella of thirteen stars (instead of the English Union) in the Continental Colors."[3]

On May 1, 1795, our flag received a revision to fifteen stars and fifteen stripes with the inclusion of Vermont (1791) and Kentucky (1792) into the Union. This was the flag seen "so gallantly streaming" over Fort McHenry when Francis Scott Key wrote "The Star Spangled Banner." The fifteen-stars-and-stripes flag flew for twenty-three years from 1795 to 1818. Five presidents served under this flag; George Washington (1789–1797), John Adams (1797–1801), Thomas Jefferson (1801–1809), James Madison (1809–1817), and James Monroe (1817–1825).

During the night of September 13, 1814, the British fleet bombarded Fort McHenry in the harbor at Baltimore, Maryland. Francis Scott Key, a thirty-four-year-old lawyer-poet, watched the attack from the deck of the British prisoner exchange ship. He had gone to seek the release of a friend, but the British refused permission to the party to go ashore until after a planned attack. On the following morning, Key turned his telescope to the fort to see the American flag still waving. The sight so inspired him that he pulled a letter from his pocket and began to compose his famous poem on it. Key returned to Baltimore and later that day took a room at a Baltimore tavern, where he completed the poem. Eventually, the United States adopted this poem as the National

---

2. Preble, *History of the Flag*, 270.
3. Hon. Claiborne Pell of Rhode Island, "The Untold Story Behind Our Country's Flag: Extension of Remarks," Monday, February 19, 1962, from *Congressional Record—Appendix*, A-1150.

Anthem of the United States—"The Star-Spangled Banner." Years later, Key told a hometown audience in Frederick, Maryland:[4]

> I saw the flag of my country waving over a city—the strength and pride of my native state—a city devoted to plunder and desolation by its assailants. I witnessed the preparation for its assaults. I saw the array of its enemies as they advanced to the attack. I heard the sound of battle; the noise of the conflict fell upon my listening ear, and told me that "the brave and the free" had met the invaders.

On April 4, 1818, Congress enacted the following law, which is still in effect:

> An Act to Establish the Flag of the United States. Sec. 1. Be it enacted. Etc., That from and after the fourth day of July next, the flag of the United States be thirteen horizontal stripes, alternate red and white; that the union have twenty stars, white in a blue field. Sect. 2. And be it further enacted, That on the admission of every new State into the Union, one star be added to the union of the flag; and that such addition shall take effect on the fourth of July next succeeding such admission.[5]

The First Flag Flown in Battle, Fort Stanwix, New York, August 3, 1777.

The city of Rome, New York, now occupies the spot where Fort Stanwix was situated. On August 2, 1777, British and Indians attacked the fort, which was defended by Colonel Peter Gansevoort with six hundred men. Lt. Col. Mellon arrived at the fort that afternoon with ammunition and supplies. He also brought newspapers carrying the accounts of the newly enacted flag resolution.

Soldiers gave up their white shirts. One of the wives at the fort donated her red flannel petticoat, and Captain Abraham Swartwout

---

4. Marc Leepson, *What So Proudly We Hailed: Francis Scott Key, A Life* (New York: St. Martin's, 2014), 161.
5. Bureau of Equipment, Department of the Navy, *Flags of Maritime Nations* (Washington, 1899), 6.

donated his coat made of blue cloth to provide the blue field for the Union.

In the battle for Guilford Courthouse, March 15, 1781, the North Carolina militia of the American Army in the Revolutionary War first carried the Stars and Stripes with its thirteen eight-pointed stars.

A bronze historical marker close to the Detroit River identifies the spot where the first American flag flew along the Great Lakes on July 25, 1791.

When George Washington transferred his army from Boston to New York, he carried the Grand Flag with him and raised it over his headquarters.

On April 24, 1778, John Paul Jones wrote, "Following the first naval victory, I hoisted the 'American Stars'."

When Congress established the army in 1789, its raised colors consisted of a blue field embroidered with an eagle. During the War of 1812, the flag contained an eagle bearing a striped shield in its breast. As each state gained admission into the Union, Congress rearranged the stars around the eagle's head to include the new one.

In 1834, the artillery and the 184th infantry carried the colors.

Each state flag conveys her individuality. Alabama's flag consists of a diagonal cross, and the square shape of the flag recalls the Battle Flag of the Confederacy, organized in Montgomery in February of 1861. Alabama entered the Union in December 1819 as the twenty-second state.

Our national Flag Day celebrates the birthday of our Flag, June 14, 1777. By the 1890s, Flag Day became a popular event. In 1916, President Woodrow Wilson issued a proclamation calling for a nationwide observance of Flag Day. Although still not an official national holiday, Congress eventually established Flag Day as a permanent observance. President Harry Truman signed it into law in 1949.

Food for Thought

Numbers 2:1–2 (NASB)

Now the LORD spoke to Moses and to Aaron, saying, "The sons of Israel shall camp, each by his own standard, with the banners of their fathers' households; they shall camp around the tent of meeting at a distance.

Isaiah 5:26 (NASB)

He will also lift up a standard to the distant nation, And will whistle for it from the ends of the earth; And behold, it will come with speed swiftly.

Isaiah 11:10

In that day there shall be a root of Jesse, which shall stand for an ensign of the people; to it shall the Gentiles seek: and His rest shall be glorious.

Isaiah 11:12

He shall set up an ensign for the nations, and shall assemble the outcasts of Israel, and gather together the dispersed of Judah from the four corners of the earth.

Isaiah 18:3 (NASB)

All you inhabitants of the world and dwellers on earth, as soon as a standard is raised on the mountains, you will see it, and as soon as the trumpet is blown, you will hear it.

Isaiah 30:17 (NKJV)

One thousand shall flee at the threat of one, at the threat of five you shall flee, till you are left as a pole on top of a mountain and as a banner on a hill.

Isaiah 31:9 (NASB)

His rock will pass away because of panic, and his princes will be terrified at the standard.

Zechariah 9:16 (NKJV)

The LORD their God will save them in that day, as the flock of His people. For they shall be like the jewels of a crown, lifted like a banner over His land.

Psalm 74:4

Thine enemies roar in the midst of thy congregations; they set up their ensigns for signs.

CHAPTER 14

PATRICK HENRY...
"GIVE ME LIBERTY OR GIVE ME DEATH"

September 2018

The name Patrick Henry comes to mind when we think of the American Revolutionary period. Every American over fifty has heard of his memorable words, "Is life so dear, or peace so sweet, as to be purchased at the price of chains and slavery?" Government schools in recent generations have deprived their pupils of our true history, and with the resulting ignorance, we have lost much of the liberty for which Patrick Henry gave his life.

We harbor no doubt that Patrick Henry distinguished himself as the greatest orator of the colonial South. Born in Studley, Virginia, in 1736, Henry married at age eighteen. He tried several occupations before deciding on law and practicing at Hanover. He was one of the earliest public leaders to recognize the inevitability and necessity of armed resistance to Great Britain. He served as governor of his state for three terms but turned down several offers made by George Washington of public office.

One short biographical sketch reads:

Here he seized the occasion to introduce the first resolution relative to the British imposition of stamp duties and thus initiated the American Revolution. He was one of the first to see the inevitable necessity of armed resistance to Great Britain, and to advocate war preparations. He was successively governor of his state for three years, and member of the House of Burgesses.... He declined the offer of Washington to appointments as Secretary of State and of Chief Justice of the United States, but would have acceded to Washington's appeal to reenter the state legislature had not death, which came to him June 6, 1799, put an end to his activities.[1]

Speaking to the convention of delegates at the First Continental Congress at Philadelphia in 1775, he realized that destiny hung in the balance of the moment.

St. John's Church, Richmond, Virginia, March 23, 1775

MR. PRESIDENT: No man thinks more highly than I do of the patriotism, as well as abilities, of the very worthy gentlemen who have just addressed the House. But different men often see the same subject in different lights; and, therefore, I hope that it will not be thought disrespectful to those gentlemen, if, entertaining as I do, opinions of a character very opposite to theirs, I shall speak forth my sentiments freely and without reserve. This is no time for ceremony. The question before the House is one of awful moment to this country. For my own part I consider it as nothing less than a question of freedom or slavery; and in proportion to the magnitude of the subject ought to be the freedom of the debate. It is only in this way that we can hope to arrive at truth, and fulfil the great responsibility which we hold to God and our country. Should I keep back my opinions at such a time, through fear of giving offense, I should consider myself as guilty of treason toward my country, and of an act of disloyalty toward the majesty of heaven, which I revere above all earthly kings.

Mr. President, it is natural to man to indulge in the illusions of hope. We are apt to shut our eyes against a painful truth, and listen to the song of that siren, till she transforms us into beasts. Is this the part of wise men, engaged in a great and arduous struggle for liberty? Are we disposed to be of the number of those who, having eyes, see not, and having ears, hear not, the things which so nearly concern their temporal salvation? For

---

1. Thomas B. Reed, ed., *Modern Eloquence*, vol. XIII (Philadelphia: John D. Morris & Company, 1903), 1178.

my part, whatever anguish of spirit it may cost, I am willing to know the whole truth; to know the worst and to provide for it.

I have but one lamp by which my feet are guided; and that is the lamp of experience. I know of no way of judging of the future but by the past. And judging by the past, I wish to know what there has been in the conduct of the British ministry for the last ten years to justify those hopes with which gentlemen have been pleased to solace themselves and the House? Is it that insidious smile with which our petition has been lately received? Trust it not, sir; it will prove a snare to your feet. Suffer not yourselves to be betrayed with a kiss. Ask yourselves how this gracious reception of our petition comports with these war-like preparations which cover our waters and darken our land. Are fleets and armies necessary to a work of love and reconciliation? Have we shown ourselves so unwilling to be reconciled, that force must be called in to win back our love? Let us not deceive ourselves, sir. These are the implements of war and subjugation; the last arguments to which kings resort. I ask gentlemen, sir, what means this martial array, if its purpose be not to force us to submission? Can gentlemen assign any other possible motives for it? Has Great Britain any enemy, in this quarter of the world, to call for all this accumulation of navies and armies?

No, sir, she has none. They are meant for us; they can be meant for no other. They are sent over to bind and rivet upon us those chains which the British ministry have been so long forging. And what have we to oppose to them? Shall we try argument? Sir, we have been trying that for the last ten years. Have we anything new to offer upon the subject? Nothing.

We have held the subject up in every light of which it is capable; but it has been all in vain. Shall we resort to entreaty and humble supplication? What terms shall we find which have not been already exhausted? Let us not, I beseech you, sir, deceive ourselves longer. Sir, we have done everything that could be done to avert the storm which is now coming on. We have petitioned; we have remonstrated; we have suppli-cated; we have prostrated ourselves before the throne, and have implored its interposition to arrest the tyrannical hands of the ministry and parliament. Our petitions have been slighted; our remonstrances have produced additional violence and insult; our supplications have been disregarded; and we have been spurned, with contempt, from the foot of the throne. In vain, after these things, may we indulge the fond hope of peace and reconciliation. There is no longer any room for hope. If we wish to be free—if we mean to preserve inviolate those inestimable privileges for which we have been so long contending—if we mean not basely to abandon the noble struggle in which we have been so long engaged, and which we have pledged ourselves never to abandon until the glorious object of our contest shall be obtained, we must fight! I repeat it, sir, we must fight! An appeal to arms and to the God of Hosts is all that is left us!

They tell us, sir, that we are weak; unable to cope with so formidable an adversary. But when shall we be stronger? Will it be the next week, or the next year? Will it be when we are totally disarmed, and when a British guard shall be stationed in every house? Shall we gather strength by irresolution and inaction? Shall we acquire the means of effectual resistance by lying supinely on our backs, and hugging the delusive phantom of hope, until our enemies shall have bound us hand and foot?

Sir, we are not weak, if we make a proper use of the means which the God of nature hath placed in our power. Three [or The] millions of people, armed in the holy cause of liberty, and in such a country as that which we possess, are invincible by any force which our enemy can send against us. Besides, sir, we shall not fight our battles alone. There is a just God who presides over the destinies of nations; and who will raise up friends to fight our battles for us. The battle, sir, is not to the strong alone; it is to the vigilant, the active, the brave. Besides, sir, we have no election. If we were base enough to desire it, it is now too late to retire from the contest. There is no retreat but in submission and slavery! Our chains are forged! Their clanking may be heard on the plains of Boston! The war is inevitable—and let it come! I repeat it, sir, let it come!

It is in vain, sir, to extenuate the matter. Gentlemen may cry peace, peace—but there is no peace. The war is actually begun!

The next gale that sweeps from the North will bring to our ears the clash of resounding arms! Our brethren are already in the field! Why stand we here idle? What is it that gentlemen wish? What would they have? Is life so dear, or peace so sweet, as to be purchased at the price of chains and slavery? Forbid it, Almighty God! I know not what course others may take; but as for me, give me liberty or give me death![2]

Give Me Liberty, or Give Me Death!, Currier & Ives, 1876

---

2. Reed, *Modern Eloquence*, 1178–81. Available online at *The Avalon Project* at Yale Law School, avalon.law.yale.edu/18th_century/patrick.asp.

CHAPTER 15

THE STORY OF A PARCHMENT: THE DECLARATION OF INDEPENDENCE

July 1, 2012

W e here quote David C. Means, Assistant Librarian of the Library of Congress, in the publication, *The Story of a Document* (Washington, 1950).

> The story of the Declaration is a part of the story of a national legacy, but to understand it, it is necessary to understand as well its makers, the world they lived in, the conditions which produced them, the confidence which encouraged them, the indignities which humiliated them, the obstacles which confronted them, the ingenuity which helped them, the faith which sustained them, the victory which came to them. It is, in other words, a part, a very signal part of a civilization and a period, from which, unlike his Britannic Majesty, it makes no claim to separation. On the contrary, unsurpassed as it is, it takes its rightful place in the literature of democracy. For its primacy is a primacy which derives from the experience which evoked it. It is imperishable because that experience is remembered.[1]

Representatives signed the Declaration August 2, 1776, filing it with the office of the Secretary of the Continental Congress at Philadelphia. They rolled up the parchment to rest there undisturbed except when it came out for signature or to be signed by other delegates. When Congress, in order to avoid the British, reconvened in Baltimore, they transported the document in a light

---

1. David C. Means, *The Story of a Document* (Washington, D.C., 1950).

wagon where it remained until they could safely return it to Philadelphia. Over time the Declaration found temporary lodging in a number of locations—the courthouse at York, Pennsylvania, Annapolis, Maryland, Trenton, New Jersey, and New York's City Hall. When the First Congress convened under the U.S. Constitution, the Declaration they gave into the custody of the Secretary of State returning to Philadelphia. President John Adams directed its move to the Federal City in the District of Columbia in 1800. In the summer of 1814, the threat of unfriendly British caused Secretary of State James Monroe to order its evacuation. It was stored in the home of a Reverend. Mr. Littlejohn at Leesburg, Virginia, for several weeks. Then it was safely returned to the District of Columbia.

In 1823, the government announced that a prominent engraver, Mr. William J. Stone, had for three years worked on and had then completed a facsimile of the Original Declaration of Independence. Now stored in archives, the government declared that this new version, "is executed with the greatest exactness and fidelity; and that the Department of State has become the purchaser of the plate."[2] This enabled American citizens to obtain personal copies of this, America's birth certificate, while also protecting the original from unnecessary exposure. Since that time, what school child of almost any generation, except perhaps the present, would not recognize this parchment?

Daniel Webster, Secretary of State in 1841, ordered various articles, including the Declaration, transferred to the National Gallery. Unfortunately, the Declaration, along with Washington's Commission as Commander in Chief, hung on the wall for viewing, and both were exposed to "the chill of winter and the heat of summer."[3]

The Declaration went back to Philadelphia for the one-hundredth anniversary, celebrated with a national exhibition. A grandson of Richard Henry Lee spoke on the occasion. The Philadelphia

---

2. H. Niles, ed., *Niles' Weekly Register* (June 14, 1823): 237.
3. "Annual Report of the Librarian of Congress" (June 30, 1949): 37.

Press described the document as "age dimmed."[4] At this time, in August 1876, Congress adopted a Joint Resolution that a commission, consisting of the Secretary of the Interior, the Secretary of the Smithsonian Institution, and the Librarian of Congress, be empowered to find the means to restore the writing of the original manuscript and the signatures.

Throughout the years, the care and preservation of the historical documents of our history have been a primary concern for the Chief of Manuscript Division of the Library of Congress. In 1903, the government transferred papers of George Washington, James Madison, Thomas Jefferson, Alexander Hamilton, and Benjamin Franklin from the Department of State to the Library of Congress. They focus our legacy, a legacy unlike any other nation has ever enjoyed, a legacy of Christian self-government.

In the building housing these Archives, the Declaration has a permanent home in display, known as the Shrine, something far grander than an exhibit. Designed by Francis Bacon (brother of Henry Bacon, architect of the Lincoln Memorial), the Shrine resides on the second floor of the Great Hall of the Thomas Jefferson Building. Into New York black marble is inscribed, "The Declaration of Independence and the Constitution of the United States." Surrounding the entire shrine is a solid white balustrade of Italian marble, suggesting the chancel rail before an altar, which from the outside would provide a clear view of the charters.

After the attack on Pearl Harbor, the government removed the national documents and safely deposited them at Fort Knox, until all danger had passed. Hundreds of thousands of citizens now gaze at the Declaration of Independence parchment annually.

Some have understanding of their significance, but many do not. Jefferson wrote about the greatest gift of all, liberty. Our Holy Triune God created us so that we are all born with certain unalienable rights, and that among these are the right to life, liberty, and the pursuit of happiness. This right of liberty—what is right in

---

4. "Annual Report of the Librarian of Congress": 38.

the nature of God's moral universe—will result in all manner of inequalities as we live our individual lives. When the Declaration states we are created equal, it means in inherent value as the image of God and therefore in the rights of equal justice. Yet the ones who work the hardest by faith usually get ahead, God blessing as He wills. Frugal ones seek with prudence to avoid perpetual indebtedness. The One Who gave us rights blesses those individuals who practice obedient, faithful, and good stewardship of them.

Patrick Henry pronounced thoughtful warnings: "Guard with jealous attention the public liberty. Suspect everyone who approaches that jewel. Unfortunately, nothing will preserve it, but downright force."[5]

In Jefferson's last letter to James Madison, fifty years after they met, he wrote, "It has also been a great solace to me, to believe that you are engaged in vindicating to posterity the course we have pursued for preserving to them, in all their purity, the blessings of self-government, which we had assisted too in acquiring for them [the people]."[6]

Madison responded, "You cannot look back to the long period of our private friendship and political harmony, with more affecting recollections than I do.... And I indulge a confidence that sufficient evidence will find its way to another generation, to ensure, after we are gone, whatever of justice may be withheld whilst we are here."[7]

The Founders did not write the Declaration of Independence as a legal document, praise the Lord! Jefferson was not a lawyer, nor Washington or Franklin. Rather, the educated heart of Thomas Jefferson upon our Christian heritage poured out the Declaration as an impassioned declaration of manifest truth. In his *First*

---

5. David Wootton, ed., *The Essential Federalist and Anti-Federalist Papers* (Indianapolis: Hackett Publishing, 2003), 26.

6. Paul Leicester Ford, ed., *The Writings of Thomas Jefferson*, vol. X (New York, London: G. P. Putnam's Sons, 1899), 378.

7. Gaillard Hunt, ed., *The Writings of James Madison*, vol. IX (New York, London: G. P. Putnam's Sons, 1910), 245–46.

Inaugural Address, Jefferson said it this way: "Sometimes it is said that a man cannot be trusted with the government of himself. Can he, then, be trusted with the government of others? Or have we found angels in the form of kings to govern him?"[8] Jefferson laid the foundation by declaring, "We hold these truths to be self-evident." This parchment is our anchor, our foundation, of what we believe about ourselves and about sustaining our unalienable rights.

The close relationship between Jefferson and Madison certainly factored into Madison's design of the Constitution. The Declaration would spell out the philosophy of who we are as a people, as defined by our Creator. The Constitution would define *federal*—local and national—self-government through limited powers, and checks and balances, to protect us from abuse, from tyranny.

On the next July Fourth, on Independence Day, I hope that you will reread the Declaration of Independence and ponder this experiment upon the theory of human rights. When John Quincy Adams took office as president of the United States, he began his inaugural by stating, "I appear, my fellow citizens, in your presence and in that of Heaven to bind myself by the solemnities of religious obligation to the faithful performance of the duties allotted to me in the station to which I have been called ... and secure the blessings of liberty to the people of this Union in their successive generations."[9] Writing a letter to his son, he gave this advice: "You should form and adopt certain rules or principles for the government of your own conduct and temper.... [I]t is in the Bible that you must learn them."[10] John Adams, John Quincy's father, wrote: "Truth, liberty, justice, and benevolence are [the] everlasting basis" of law and government, "and if these could be removed, the superstructure is overthrown of course."[11]

---

8. Thomas Jefferson, "First Inaugural Address," March 4, 1801, *The Avalon Project* at Yale Law School, avalon.law.yale.edu/19th_century/jefinau1.asp.
9. John Quincy Adams, "Inaugural Address," March 4, 1825, *The Avalon Project* at Yale Law School, avalon.law.yale.edu/19th_century/qadams.asp.
10. *Letters of Mrs. Adams, the Wife of John Adams* (Boston: Wilkins, Carter, and Company, 1848), 430.
11. Charles Francis Adams, ed., *The Works of John Adams, Second President of the*

The Bible grounded and rooted the Founders of this nation in the source of Truth. They did not look to the government for their identity. Revisionists have rewritten America's history for state education and the mass media, but modern Christian scholars, such as David Barton, are helping to rebuild the foundations of America's providential Christian history—our true history. The Declaration parchment, so treasured throughout our history, will continue to be a lively,[12] guiding document if we claim it and live by its principles.

United States, vol. 3 (Boston: Charles C. Little and James Brown, 1851), 463.
12. Not *living*, as modern liberals, who would undermine the Constitution, intend.

THE BIRTH OF AMERICA'S EDUCATION

The Inheritance Belonging to America's Children

May 2016

In the introduction to Noah Webster's 1828 *Dictionary*, distributed by the Foundation for American Christian Education, Rosalie Slater chose to include some selections from Noah Webster's Master's Thesis from Yale College. Her selections in the preface carefully guide us in the use of this volume. Many people consider the 1828 *Dictionary* as the next most valuable book in the home library, second only to the Holy Bible. This writer certainly does. It contains the language of liberty. Its definitions relate back to Scripture, wherever appropriate.

Comments on the Declaration of Independence in the 1828 Dictionary

Writes Rosalie June Slater, in the introductory article "Noah Webster, Founding Father of American Scholarship and Education":[1]

> The Declaration of Independence, July 4, 1776, announced to the world the separation of the American colonies from Great Britain, their establishment as "free and independent states," and their "firm reliance on the Protection of Divine Providence." To this ringing declaration to faith in God was affixed the signatures of the fifty-six men who mutually pledged to "each other" their "Lives," their "Fortunes," and their "sacred Honor."

---

1. Webster, *Dictionary*, 9.

It took seven long years of the American Revolution to "dissolve the Political Bands"[2] which connected them to England, and six more years before the document detailing the Christian philosophy of American government took shape and form. But political separation alone would not suffice to keep the young republic on her Christian constitutional course. If American liberty was to be complete, all mooring from the old world must be cast off,... especially those that might bind her in alien philosophies of government, and hence to educational systems lending them support:

"This country must in some future time, be as distinguished by her literary improvements, as she is by the liberality of civil and ecclesiastical constitutions. Europe has grown old in folly, corruption, and tyranny. In that country, laws are perverted, manners are licentious, literature is declining, and human nature debased. For America, in her infancy, to adopt the present maxims of the old world, would be to stamp the wrinkles of decrepit age upon the bloom of youth, and to plant the seeds of decay in a vigorous constitution....

"It is the business of Americans to select the wisdom of all nations, as the basis of her constitution, to avoid their errors, to prevent the introduction of foreign vices and corruptions, and check the career of her own,—to promote virtue and patriotism,—to embellish and improve the sciences,—to diffuse a uniformity and purity of language,—to add superior dignity to this infant empire and to human nature."[3]

Rosalie Slater cited Webster from his dictionary and from his translation of the Holy Bible. God used his vision, his research, his writing, and his passion for America's uniqueness to prepare this one individual, one who would give birth to American education. God's providence used this amazing document, this American dictionary, to preserve Christian liberty until well into the 1900s. In our generation, He once more is using Webster.

---

2. The quotes in this section come from the Declaration of Independence.

3. "Dissertation...upon the universal diffusion of literature, as introductory to the universal diffusion of Christianity." Webster, *Dictionary*, 11.

The story of how God prepared Noah Webster for this monumental task is fascinating. He was a descendant on his mother's side of Governor William Bradford of Plimoth Plantation. Webster's great-great-grandfather served as governor of Connecticut in 1656. With such a devout and accomplished heritage, no one should be surprised that Webster would write: "The Christian religion is the most important and one of the first things in which all children, under a free government, ought to be instructed.... No truth is more evident to my mind than that the Christian religion must be the basis for any government intended to secure the rights and privileges of a free people."[4]

Webster was certainly not alone in his views. The Founding Fathers of the nation made clear the relationship of Christianity to American government and liberty. Their dream was to extend the blessings of liberty to all people through the liberating Gospel of Jesus Christ.

In recognizing the role of American civil government, Webster was careful to limit the jurisdiction of government when it came to education and the family. He wrote: "The foundation of all free government and of all social order must be laid in families and in the discipline of youth. The education for youth, [is] an employment of more consequence than making laws and preaching the Gospel, because it lays the foundation on which both law and Gospel rest for success."[5]

How fascinating to read how God prepared this young man for his life's work in the founding of America's distinctively "Christian educational system."[6] Growing up in Hartford, Connecticut, on a family farm, he and his siblings were happy, diligent laborers. They prayed together for good weather, because a good crop of corn harvested in good weather would provide for the winter months. They ate the corn they grew, of course, but primarily intended its export to England. However, when night came, while his brothers,

---

4. Webster, *Dictionary*, 12.
5. Webster, *Dictionary*, 11.
6. Webster, *Dictionary*, 25.

Abram and Charles, slept nearby, Noah could be found with his small candle burning brightly by his bed. Perhaps because books were scarce, words and a printed page always fascinated this young boy.

In 1771, though books were rare in the colonies, *everyone* had a family Bible. The local pastor likely possessed twenty or more books, most in Latin. On a weekly basis, a family might well see the newspaper from Hartford, and an annual *Ames Almanack* at Christmas time. The almanac brought weather information and tidbits such as moral maxims, poetry, and other matters of interest to a literate people. In the little schoolhouse by the church, again a scarcity of books prevailed. Yet the school usually had a speller from which the small child could learn his letters, a primer, and a Psalter. In 1764, at six years old, letters, words, and spelling already fascinated Noah.

At age thirteen, after harvesting the fields, Noah eagerly returned to the one-room schoolhouse. Boys usually did not continue their schooling after age fourteen. Yet they would have already received a fine basic education in literacy and math, sufficient to support most vocational endeavors, and the mental acuity necessary to the responsibilities of a free and just society. The New England colonists believed Biblical literacy essential to personal and societal life. For these last months in school, Noah walked four miles to attend. Without books for research, many of Noah's questions remained unanswered. In the following spring, a new minister came to town, Dr. Nathan Perkins. Dr. Perkins had graduated from Princeton and so possessed many more books than usual for this time. Dr. Perkins took great interest in the promising young Noah Webster. He welcomed him into his study and loaned him books—first, a Latin grammar. Novels and storybooks as we know them today hardly existed in Noah's childhood, certainly not in the colonies. The colonial New Englander desired instead the spiritual and practical knowledge necessary for a righteous and good life.

After serious study with Dr. Perkins over many months, Noah decided he must attend college. He discussed it with his pastor and his father. He found that Yale College had 2,500 books in its library. That added fuel to Noah's fire for college. After another year of preparation with his minister and his work in the Latin Grammar School, at almost age sixteen he determined to enter Yale in September. With parents willing to place a mortgage on the family property, Noah determined to prove the worth of his parents' risk of investment. Yale College had three buildings, old and not in good condition. On the edge of the Long Island Sound, New Haven was a lovely town of fine old trees and an atmosphere of quiet dignity.

Noah plowed into the academic life of Yale. One hundred fifty students occupied the academic halls, with forty boys in Noah's freshman class. Noah displayed leadership ability from the start. He was well aware of his responsibility. He attended on borrowed money. He must prove his worth to his beloved parents. During the summer months, he would be back on the farm with his hoe.

These mid-1770s were turbulent times. In 1776, with a great demand for liberty, particularly in New England, Thomas Jefferson took a pen and paper and wrote the formal statement that we know as The Declaration of Independence, adopted on July 4, 1776, by the Continental Congress. This development in the history of liberty thrilled Noah Webster, so that he now desired to learn everything he could about the fifty-six men who had signed the document. He learned that fourteen were lawyers, and twelve were jurists—really much the same thing. These facts stirred an interest in law as a possible career path. Over time, Noah would add law to his many accomplishments.

Due to the war, college would be in recess for months at a time, and Noah would be back on the farm, always reading, always studying. When Dr. Ezra Stiles was appointed president of Yale, he decided to bring back to the college those boys too young for war. The new republic would need truly and broadly educated men, and Dr. Stiles would see to it. The man for the job, he was extremely versatile and well educated.

Thirty of Noah's classmates returned to graduate. The others left for war. Noah's graduating address proved to be the most impressive of all. Returning home after his graduation, Noah learned that the war had ruined his family financially. His parents could not help him with law school. In a matter of just days, Noah received a position of teaching in the village school at Glastonbury, Connecticut, where his class at Yale spent a summer. The children loved him at the school, but the lack of books continued as a chief problem. Fifty children shared only one spelling book. In the cruel winter of 1779–80, Noah walked four miles to school. It made him think of General Washington and his troops at Valley Forge.

Nights found him deep into his law books. He passed the bar in April 1781. However, education remained his passion, especially to serve needy and deserving American children. His first published textbook, titled *The American Instructor*, was a spelling book. He filled it with inspiration for patriotism, courage, and Christian character. Noah included simple phonics as well. He took it to Philadelphia, and after a name change and a delay, the spelling book was published in 1783 under the title *A Grammatical Institute of the English Language*. Later, millions more copies would be published as *The American Spelling Book*. This first publishing effort established Noah Webster's career producing school textbooks. These, in turn, would form the foundation of America's unique education in all of world history.

One writer described Noah Webster as "the man on horseback" for all the travel he did from colony to colony promoting his speller and seeking copyright protection among the states. Among his travels, in 1785, George Washington entertained Noah at Mount Vernon. Webster encouraged General Washington to consider a national constitution, sharing with him a pamphlet entitled *Sketches of American Policy*. By this time, not only *The American Spelling Book*, but also a *Reader* had come into print.

He took a twenty-seven-day sailing trip from Baltimore to Charlestown, South Carolina, where he successfully persuaded adoption of his textbooks for the entire state. In addition, he had now written a history text that told of America's founding and early history. Over a period of one hundred years, a hundred million copies of Webster's dictionary and texts literally wore out from faithful use. From the pen of Noah Webster, American children, from north to south and from east to west, have learned "their letters, their morality, and their patriotism."[7] Noah Webster truly became America's schoolmaster.

When American colonies first settled, each immigrant group brought with them their old-world philosophies. Some were indeed Biblical Christians, such as the Pilgrims in Plymouth. Some were more cultural Christians, not necessarily orthodox in Bible terms. Some were humanists or advocates of other philosophies mixed together. Webster was keenly aware of the intellectual, ideological, moral, and spiritual threats from foreign shores. He made sure that his textbooks and dictionary addressed those threats. Thankfully, he lived to see much fruit from his labors. Prominent men, such as John Jay, offered support and encouragement.

Looking back over his remarkable life, and remembering the direct and divine operation of the Spirit of God, Webster wrote: "I could no longer question or have a doubt respecting the Calvinistic and Christian doctrines of regeneration, of free grace, and of the Sovereignty of God.... I was struck by the 26th verse in John 14, 'But the Comforter, which is the Holy Ghost, whom the Father will send in my Name, He shall teach you all things, and bring all things to your remembrance, whatsoever I have said to you.'" [8]

America's history is the story of individual liberty, as no other nation has ever known. It leaves a legacy to which every American child is entitled. God has blessed the Christian constitutional republic as He has no other nation in world history. God used one man, Noah Webster, to set the truth in textbooks for generations of early-America children. One hundred million copies of his textbooks circulated.

---

7. Webster, *Dictionary*, 13.
8. Webster, *Dictionary*, 20.

Noah Webster stressed that all begins in the family—family living out the Biblical mandates of Scripture. Do we have enough families today that embrace Biblical order in their home to cherish and live out once again "life and liberty," as generations of our forefathers dared to dream?

Education

2020 Definition of the Word *education* from *Merriam-Webster's Unabridged Dictionary*:

noun

1a: the action or process of educating or of being educated; a stage of such a process

  b: the knowledge and development resulting from the process of being educated

2: the field of study that deals mainly with methods of teaching and learning in schools.

1828 Definition of the Word *education* from Webster's *American Dictionary of the English Language*:

noun [Latin *educatio*.]

The bringing up, as of a child, instruction; formation of manners. *education* comprehends all that series of instruction and discipline which is intended to enlighten the understanding, correct the temper, and form the manners and habits of youth, and fit them for usefulness in their future stations. To give children a good *education* in manners, arts and science, is important; to give them a religious *education* is indispensable; and an immense responsibility rests on parents and guardians who neglect these duties.

CHAPTER 17

GOD & COUNTRY: CHRISTIAN SELF-GOVERNMENT WITH UNION—THE BIRTH OF AMERICAN FEDERALISM

December 2018

President Ronald Reagan and both houses of Congress united in proclaiming 1983 as the Year of The Bible.[1] The president and a Joint Resolution of the Congress undertook the dynamic purpose of embracing the influence of the Bible in the founding of our nation. Biblical teachings inspired our Founders to establish Christian self-government with union, and a nation of American Federalism. Our very U.S. Constitution rests on the Bible.

The Foundation for American Christian Education published the best book of all on the Bible and the Constitution, called, aptly, *The Bible and the Constitution of the United States of America.*

Regarding America and the Bible, I quote from the book:

> The history of the Bible and the history of American liberty are inseparable. The Bible is the source of individual liberty—salvation from sin through Jesus Christ. It is also the basis for external or civil government. As Noah Webster wrote: "It is extremely important to our nation, in a political as well as religious view, that all possible authority and influence should be given to the Scriptures; for these furnish the best principles of civil liberty, and the most effectual support of republican government."[2]

---

1. See "Public Law 97-280," *Prove the Bible*, provethebible.net/T2-Hist/ H-0901.htm.

2. Verna M. Hall and Rosalie J. Slater, *The Bible and the Constitution of the*

American Federalism combines essential local self-government with union in greater governmental spheres for the sake of community, justice, and the mutual protection of justice internally and self-defense against external enemies. Federalism would not have been possible without the Bible. Its root lies in the perfect individuality and union of love in the Holy Trinity of God. It thus also lies in the two commandments of Christ—love God and love your neighbor (Matthew 22:37–39; Mark 12:30–31; Luke 10:27; Deuteronomy 6:5; Leviticus 19:18). The two commandments indicate the horizontal peer relationship, and the vertical authority relationship. God's love and grace binds us to our neighbors. The Pilgrims, the Puritans, and all of our early settlers lived out Christian self-government and organized their homes, villages, and larger communities upon a Biblical order. Their character virtue of generous faith inspired volunteerism. Having taught history for nearly a half century, I can assure the reader that American Federalism is unique in the history of world governments. It is unique in the sense that local self-government is primary but combined and balanced with union. The presence and the power of the states and the nation must keep in balance.

So, how do we make sure that this constitutional form of government will work? It is in grave danger today, as we know. When we are fully Biblically educated into and practicing the two great commandments—to love God and love our fellow man, and so fulfill God's law—then our founding form of government will work. Solomon told us to get wisdom! We need time to relearn the ropes of Christian self-government. But if we commit to it, no doubt, our gracious God will give us the time we need to reverse the unholy trends we see today.

It is so interesting to read about John Wycliffe (1320–84) and his translation of the Bible into English. He was a leading theologian with the highest scholarly degree in England and an influential member of Parliament. Wycliffe saw the need for an English

---

United States of America (San Francisco: Foundation for American Christian Education, 1983), 4.

Bible translation in the spiritual decay around him. His translation began a long-lasting movement toward individual liberty—both civil and religious—culminating in the expansive and growth-oriented Elizabethan era. It is an encouraging example of individual contribution to history. One man or woman in the hand of God can change the world!

Thus, the American home must be the center for building Christian character in our nation, as an example to others. Today, the majority of American families have relinquished that responsibility to government schools. These schools have not embraced our heritage of American Federalism, the Bible, and the Constitution, but rather, in many if not most cases, they have worked self-consciously against them.

The failure to embrace, and instead reject, our civil and spiritual heritage became evident throughout the mid and later 1900s and has grown since. J. Edgar Hoover spoke frequently to national conventions about America's challenge. A longtime director of the FBI, Hoover said, with great passion:

> What has happened to the time-honored precepts of hard work and fair play which influenced the American scene during the all-important formative years of this great Republic? Where is the faith in God which fortified us through our past trials? Have our national pride, our moral conscience, our sensitivity to filth and degradation, grown so weak that they no longer react to assaults upon our proud heritage of freedom?[3]

In speaking of the communist influence in America, Hoover stated, "Foremost among their targets have been America's young people, for the aim of communism is world youth and the capture and corruption of that youth." These quotes are from a 1962 speech Hoover gave in Las Vegas to The American Legion. At the end of the passionate speech, he concluded, "We are a God-loving people.

---

3. J. Edgar Hoover, "An American's Challenge," *FBI Law Enforcement Bulletin*, October 9, 1962, Vol. 31, No. 11 (November 1962): 10.

This is our greatest strength. Let our national motto always be, '*In God we trust*.'"[4]

Today in our beloved nation, we experience continual attack that we can name as *postmodernism*.[5] We can identify at the heart of this attack a hatred of Biblical Christianity typical of inherently sinful man unwilling to accept God's grace. The colleges, universities, politics, and media widely accept postmodernism. Postmodern culture aims at rebellious immorality, particularly among the young. We must prepare our young people to face it in the schools of learning and the open marketplaces. Better, we must prepare our children to resist immorality—as it is integral to postmodernism—in the home, church, and in rigorous Biblical educational training in the knowledge, wisdom, faith, character, and skills necessary to restore God's Christian republic.

As Christians, we know that the absolute truths of the Bible cannot change. The God of the Bible does not change. He is the same yesterday, today, and forever.

Postmodern (PM) followers believe that every person constructs his own story or narrative. The PM term appeared in the 1970s. Right and wrong is a matter of personal opinion in their eyes. Many see the results of PM in the breakup of families, divorce rates, and overcrowded prisons. Some have identified these aspects:

1. **Deconstruction**: a tearing down of our past heritage, spiritual and religious.

2. **Moral Relativism**: the destruction of all moral absolutes.

3. **Pluralism**: diversity of morals and tolerance prevails toward all except those with Biblical morality.

4. **Existentialism**: in which feelings rule. "It is what I *feel* is right for me."

---

4. Hoover, "An American's Challenge," 12–13.
5. Upon increasing disappointment with hopeful modern humanist notions, postmodernism arose in its place. Postmodernists distrust historic unifying themes of larger meaning and purpose. Associated with the term *deconstruction*—a concept that declares that real communication is ultimately impossible—*postmodernism* is essentially *nihilism*—ultimate meaninglessness. Nihilism, of course, opposes the faith of Christ at every level. —Ed.

Dear Reader, let us stand against the attacks by affirming and reasserting our Christian faith, and living out our fellowship with the God of the Bible. Let us stand against the attacks on our Christian constitutional republic with Biblically informed action in the public square. Let us be passionate in our prayer life, loving our family and friends, and reaching out to our neighbors.

The decline of the family life in America is a national crisis. Let us pray that strong Christian women and men, with dedicated family life, will put us on course again.

> The United States, in Congress assembled ... think it their indispensable duty to call upon the several states, to set apart the last Thursday in April next, as a day of fasting, humiliation and prayer, that our joint supplications may then ascend to the Throne of the Ruler of the Universe,... that the religion of our Divine Redeemer, with all its benign influences, may cover the earth as the waters cover the seas. (Continental Congress, March 19, 1782)[6]

---

6. "Journals of the Continental Congress, 1774–1789," *Library of Congress: American Memory*, Tuesday, March 19, 1782, memory.loc.gov/ammem/amlaw/lwjc.html.

THE BATTLE FOR THE MIND

May 2013

Before the proletariat fights out its battles on the barricades, it announces the coming of its rule with a series of intellectual victories.[1]

—Karl Marx

Fifty years ago, I would have said that the colleges of America were the crucial battlegrounds in the most perilous ways in the modern world. In the college classrooms, the minds of the next generation will embrace and affirm freedom and individual dignity and worth, or become active combatants in opposing these treasured truths and virtues.

Today, in 2013, I would sound an alarm for *all* education in America, stressing the importance of what goes on in every classroom, from primary school throughout college. What is the battle? What are the issues? What is the result and who are the winners and losers?

What exactly took America by such surprise? How could we have kept ourselves in such lethargic sleep? America has abandoned moral absolutes, broken down the family, and worked hard to destroy the economy. Capitalism is unpopular, although it has provided the highest standard of living in the Western world. What became of the concept of God's decrees, the foundation of our republic, and the only possible one?

---

1. Franz Mehring, *Karl Marx: The Story of His Life* (New York: Covici, Friede Publishers, 1935).

America's unique blessing of civil and religious liberty is in peril. College professors, no longer even needing to hide behind tenure in the majority of colleges and universities today, wage the intellectual war against America. They have embraced godless, materialistic, and amoral collectivism as a philosophy, one that enables government to tyrannically dictate to all of society as a replacement god. Many professors, not in agreement with socialist ideals, have become silent and of negligible influence in their secular, and sometimes even in once-Christian, colleges.

The late Hon. Joseph S. Clark, former mayor of Philadelphia, writing in *The Atlantic*, July 1953, wrote:

> To lay a ghost at the outset and to dismiss semantics, a liberal is here defined as one who believes in utilizing the full force of government for the advancement of social, political, and economic justice at the municipal, state, national, and international levels.... A liberal believes government is a proper tool to use in the development of a society which attempts to carry Christian principles of conduct into practical effect.

He continues:

> The philosophy of the reformers in the universities becomes the action platform in the liberal politicians in the next generation.... Moreover, it is a potential leadership psychologically prepared to enlist under the liberal banner.... It is significant that what used to be called "history" is now "social studies." Spiritually and economically, youth is conditioned to respond to a liberal program of orderly policing, of our society by government, subject to the popular will, in the interests of social justice.[2]

Mayor Clark was correct in his warning. In the 1950s, state liberalism had won a monopoly in major universities in America. Today this philosophy has penetrated almost every college in America, except it usually carries no pretense of representing Christianity.

---

2. Joseph S. Clark Jr., "Can the Liberals Rally?" *The Atlantic*, July 1953, theatlantic.com.

The government-ordered curriculum in state classrooms from early education through higher education has become entirely secular and anti-Christian. In any supposedly open forum, tolerance for free expression and of differing views is extremely rare.

Another historic philosophy exists, one entirely different from the postmodern one, known as classical liberalism. Emerson described it.

> Society everywhere is a conspiracy against the manhood of every one of its members.... Society never advances.... All men plume themselves on the improvement of society, and no man improves.[3]

> [T]he wise and just man will always feel that ... he imparts strength to the state, not receives security from it.[4]

> The first rule of economy ... [is] that every man shall maintain himself.[5]

> The harvest will be better preserved and go farther, laid up in private bins, in each farmer's corn-barn and each woman's basket, than if it were kept in national granaries.[6]

Emerson continues:

> The less government we have the better,—the fewer laws, and the less confided power. The antidote to this abuse of formal government is, the influence of private character, the growth of the individual.[7]

> In all my lectures, I have taught one doctrine, the infinitude of the private man.[8]

3. Ralph Waldo Emerson, "Self-Reliance," *Essays* (Boston: James Munroe and Company, 1841), 41, 69.
4. Ralph Waldo Emerson, "The Young American," *The Dial* (April 1844).
5. Ralph Waldo Emerson, *Works of Ralph Waldo Emerson* (London: George Routledge and Sons, 1883), 414.
6. Bliss Perry, ed., *The Heart of Emerson's Journals* (New York: Dover, 1995), 193.
7. Emerson, *Works of Ralph Waldo Emerson*, 129.
8. Lawrence Buell, *Emerson* (Cambridge, MA: Harvard University Press,

Emerson held a fairly accurate memory of the Christian roots of true liberalism, though he represents the beginning of its secularization and the seed of its destruction. In representing the old classical liberalism—love of liberty—he distorts its Christian roots. Its essence does not lie in "infinitude of the private man," but in the Lord of heaven, Who by grace enables the best in man. Time has not been kind to true Biblical liberalism—due largely to mainstreaming of the Christian Pietistic movement where Christians increasingly withdrew into an essentially isolated personal faith.

Let's be clear. By early 1900, liberalism in many colleges had begun to distort Christian principles, such as compassion and charity, into an anti-Christian form. As a false substitute for true liberalism, all collectivist regimes—whether fascism, Fabianism, or communism—regulate, compel, prohibit, dictate, and confiscate. Hitler defined true idealism as "nothing but subjecting the individual's interests and life to the community."[9] Rather than a godly balance between the individual and the community, the materialist always denies the individual in favor of the collectivist state. The collectivist state must eventually become authoritarian and tyrannical, as the seed of godly liberty runs deep in the soul of man created in God's image. Man cannot tolerate subjection into essential slavery without destroying his soul. We bear witness to the zeal of community organizers over the past decades of American political life, carrying out the postmodern philosophy of contemporary classrooms.

This worldview is not new, but as old as sinful man himself, sometimes called "man's second-oldest faith." Quoting Whitaker Chambers:

> Its promise was whispered in the first days of the Creation under the Tree of the Knowledge of Good and Evil: "Ye shall be as gods." It is the great alternative faith of mankind. Like all great faiths, its force derives from a simple vision ... : the vision

2003), 59.

9. Adolf Hitler, *Mein Kampf, Complete and Unabridged* (New York: Reynal & Hitchcock, 1939), 411.

of God and man's relationship to God. The communist vision is the vision of man without God.... It is the vision of man's mind displacing God as the creative intelligence of the world. It is the vision of man's liberated mind, by the sole force of its rational intelligence, redirecting man's destiny and reorganizing man's life and the world.[10]

And so, the classrooms of modern America have expelled God and His Word. In government schools, they proclaim no eternal truth. Rather, all reason is relative, and morality is reduced to manners, or increasingly, simply selfish preference.

On the other hand, some dedicated people fight a battle today against further government control over Alabama education in grades K–12, through the defeat of the new Common Core standards. I hope that they succeed, but if so, it merely places a band-aid over a festering boil. No one openly debates today the underlying problems in education. Until free men stand up in the public square, debate the arguments for and against collectivism, declare eternal Truth as the basis for right reasoning, America will not receive God's blessing.

One wonders where the alumni of the once-godly institutions have gone. What about the trustees? Have they long evaded their responsibility? Are they *fellow travelers* with us, or part of the opposition? Do parents even know how to evaluate colleges before sending their precious children to them? Do parents read the books assigned to their children? I have lived to see four generations in my own family. Yes, my generation bears much responsibility for an educational and political system which now constantly undermines what was once a Christian constitutional republic, one with power well balanced among the branches of government to protect liberty through justice and just defense. Today, the educational system idolizes government power as the means for a benevolent life, attacks religious liberty, and conditions youth in the socialist worldview.

---

10. Whittaker Chambers, *Witness* (Washington, D.C.: Regnery, 1969).

Many people have given up the fight and believe that socialism and totalitarianism are inevitable. During my four years serving on the Republican National Committee (1968–72), I saw politicians weak in their defense of liberty. Many "got along by going along." Only courage of conviction can resist a power structure. Coming against a popular movement requires determination. It takes intelligence and conviction. It takes the study of good material, such as is readily obtained through the von Mises Institute in Auburn. No one has better resources for economics and the free market, and it is easily available.

However, for the will to do battle, it takes more than human strength and energy. It takes the leading of God Almighty, for human strength alone will never defeat this current power structure. The more Biblically and historically informed you become, the more you will realize that nothing is new under the sun, and the many facets of today's socialism are simply the revival of old dogmas at the root.

Paul's words are reassuring: "When all things shall be subdued unto Him, then shall the Son also Himself be subject unto Him that put all things under Him, that God may be all in all" (First Corinthians 15:28).

CHAPTER 19

THE BATTLE FOR THE MINDS OF CHILDREN: AMERICAN EDUCATION AT THE CROSSROADS

March 2014

Train up a child in the way he should go, even when he is old he will not depart from it. (PROVERBS 22:6)

This battlefield hosts not guns and swords, but spiritual warfare for the minds and hearts of children. The battle centers on the definition and purposes, methods, and content of education in America today. Sincere people, passionate about their own views of traditional education and of life, wage a bloodless war restoring the traditional American Christian heritage and therefore re-empowering education. Each group, and its several sub-groups, has a mission with dedication to fulfilling it.

Traditionalists embrace the Biblical Hebrew-Christian worldview. They inherited it via providential Western civilization, and in America particularly through the Protestant Reformation legacy. This educational philosophy sees children as created and owned by God, their Creator, and children as a holy stewardship of parents. Each child is born with a providential plan for his or her life, "'For I know the plans that I have for you,' declares the LORD, 'plans for welfare and not for calamity to give you a future and a hope'." (Jeremiah 29:11 NASB). The Creator of life has entrusted the child and responsibility for him with the parents through a covenant relationship described in the Scriptures. God obligates parents with responsibility for educating the child His way. Achieving the goals of this traditional education will transform lives into a Biblical worldview, enrich the life of a family, and be a wholesome influence in the community and beyond, even a testimony to the nations as numbers of traditionalists grow. A well-educated productive citizen has an assured outcome.

This group of citizens can be found in Christian and home schools, and some in traditional public schools. A majority of these families will have church affiliation, though not all. They will universally affirm the moral law and moral standards for individuals and civil society. They expect these moral standards affirmed in the schools. This fairly describes the traditionalist.

Another group, in stark contrast to the traditionalists, are the progressives. These too are very idealistic and sincere and have the good of students in mind as they earnestly have brought about stark changes in American education through their secular, humanistic worldview. If one wonders how so many people have aligned themselves with this progressive group, and abandoned the traditional Hebrew-Christian worldview, it really requires a study of the last century and a half in American education. It is a sinful progression in its rejection of God and its ways, yet it has required a devoted effort of two centuries to efface the powerful Christian heritage of the American founding.

It started when European humanist intellectuals, especially from Germany, came to our shores to join and expand the programs of America's universities in the first half of the nineteenth century. They have had a tremendous influence to this very day. Remember that the vast majority of colleges and universities in America were founded by orthodox Christian churches and early denominations to educate preachers.

Community classroom teachers never really championed in large numbers replacing the teaching of orthodox Christianity in American school classrooms. Rather, for centuries they chose their profession out of love and dedication to children and families, and they knew true education could only come with the help of the Holy Spirit in Christ. They delighted in God to teach in such a way as to "enlighten the understanding, correct the temper, form the habits and manners of youth, and fit them for their future stations" (1828 *Dictionary*). In all the years I have interviewed teachers, I have never known one who did not love children, and desire to teach, really teach, and mentor students on an individual basis, appreciating the individuality of each student. Teaching is a unique calling, and to me, it has been a sacred one.

We recognize the influence of the progressive outsiders, indeed radicals, via the transformation in education they created. Influential non-Christian philosophers such as Spinoza, Rousseau, Darwin, Huxley, Marx, and others eventually made headway, particularly through the colleges. But a key person for dramatic change in the twentieth century was our own John Dewey. Born in Vermont in 1859, he lived ninety-three years, dying in New York in 1952. He opposed any system of fixed values in any human arena. This position really created a problem for him regarding truth. His philosophy has been called numerous things, but is best known as *instrumentalism*. His theory of human nature and ideals of social change, etc., clashed with the Scriptures, and his view of the child and education initiated what we recognize as the progressive movement in America. With generations of Americans now schooled in this view, its influence has expanded far beyond the classroom. Imagine Christian pastors schooled from early childhood by parents who learned likewise. Under Dewey's influence, the effect has been to undermine even the pulpit over generations, weakening the entire Church.

Thus, rejecting Christianity, the state competes for its place, desiring to become god. Deism, a mere excuse for doing what is right in our own eyes, has become acceptable. Now, any nominal god will do, except for the God of Christianity, which must oppose the god-state.

This group, intent on removing moral absolutes from curriculum standards, maintains that religion is private and has no place in today's classroom. To remove religion from the classroom, they have reinterpreted the First Amendment to the U.S. Constitution to say that congress must inhibit Christian religion in the public sphere. All education is religious. The progressives replace one religion—Biblical faith—with the religion of materialism. Their goal for education is an economic goal, to equip the student for mere vocational readiness for a highly technical society, where our nation competes with other nations in the global economy. Less productive people become discarded serfs. The progressives have prepared their plans and possess the money to carry out the progressive ideals at the heart of the plan. They have already won the educational institutions, the media, and much of civil government. They propose an assembly-line approach of educators, principals, and teachers—a concept at least as old as Horace Mann. They have stripped classroom teachers of gifted individuality in their teaching. They likewise have stripped the content of recognized historic truth in solid-subject contents. They have cast out the moral law with its concordant character training of the child. The child is now little more than a soulless machine used to compete with the machines of other countries. Of course, as history reveals, these materialists always destroy the societies they intend to use. Where are Babylon, Rome, Hitler, the USSR?

One would think that American parents would not have been so easily deceived by bureaucrats empowered to enforce Obamacare, which literally redefined *health* in an authoritarian-government way, mandating that all employers support their view and program. It even forced services in clear violation of the First Amendment and right of conscience in choice. As if that were not enough, it assaulted Christian sexual morality in America's classrooms with sex-education classes that provide contraceptives and redefine human sexuality.

Everyone with children in schools today should become informed about the current battle for the minds and the hearts of the children. The propaganda of the progressives tells us over and over that we have an "eighteenth-century model to reach a twenty-first-century workforce."

My husband inherited the old Ames Bag Manufacturing Company in Selma, Alabama, at the end of World War II. It was the largest manufacturing plant in the area and had hundreds of employees who worked there for many decades. It had awards for the efficiency of the operation and for race relations, remarkable in those years. Not every business was mindful of race relations back then. The demand for cotton and burlap bags dwindled, forcing the company to close or to make a transition to other products. Space does not permit me to expound on this remarkable story related among corporate boards over the nation as an inspiration. Just let me say this: Our Selma and Blackbelt employees unanimously and with a good will desired to learn new and better methods of manufacturing. They remained true to my husband's business, as they learned new skills of making fiber and plastic containers of every kind imaginable. They made the first miniature Morton Salt and Accent cans, for one example. Jack Green, our on-sight engineer, designed in part the very first Wet Ones®. I never knew if he had his professional engineering credentials or not, but he certainly was a genius. This workforce made up of many without a complete college education learned fast-changing and demanding skills. They possessed a love of learning new things. They shared inspiring prayer and Scripture over the loudspeaker. They had an open door any time day or night to the boss's office. We all shared moral absolutes and family values. I prayed with many individual mothers who worked there. No racial concerns divided our company team.

I don't know one elementary teacher who would not welcome the Ten Commandments on the wall of his or her classroom. I don't know one who would not welcome a prayer at the beginning of the day. It would settle down the children and set the tone for the students to begin to learn that day.

Allow me to exhort you to embrace and self-consciously live out the Biblical worldview with a generational mindset, avail yourself of the resources we identify in this book, and join the battle for the minds and hearts of the children. May the Lord lead us all.

CHAPTER 20

How Do You Conquer a Culture?
Focus on a Nation's Children

... and Introduce Secular Sex Education

June 2016

Patrick J. Buchanan, author of *The Death of the West*, wrote about exposing the de-Christianizing of America:

> In the Great War of 1914–1918, Catholic France fought Catholic Austria and Protestant Germany fought Protestant England. Nine million Christian soldiers marched to their deaths. Yet, only Orthodox Russia succumbed to a communist revolution, and that was more coup d'état than mass conversion. A prominent Italian communist disciple of Marx, Antonio Gramsci, concluded that two thousand years of Christianity had made the soul of man impenetrable to Marxism. Before the West could be conquered for communism, its faith must be uprooted. But how could it be achieved?[1]

Marx's disciples were everywhere. Devotees worked hard on varied schemes to spread communism. One was the Hungarian, George Lukas, recognized as a Marxist theorist to rival Marx himself. Intent on overturning the values of a Christian culture, he instituted a radical sex-education program in Hungarian schools. He brainwashed children with instruction on "free love" and in the

---

1. Patrick Buchanan, *The Death of the West* (New York: Thomas Dunne Books, 2002).

"irrelevance of religion." He treated monogamy as "outmoded." His program promoted licentiousness among women to further destroy the core institution of Christianity—the home.

Antonio Gramsci, declared by scholars the most outstanding Marxist of the twentieth century, fled to Russia after Mussolini's march on Rome in 1922. He carefully observed the Russian people and came to the conclusion that Leninism had failed. While the people had obediently complied with the political power, in their hearts they were not committed to communism. Their homeland, their old faith, and their Mother Russia, still had their hearts. Observing all of this, Gramsci concluded that the only thing holding these people back from communism was their Christian faith. After all, the world had been saturated with Christianity for two thousand years, and many people had zeal for the Gospel of Jesus Christ.

Gramsci concluded that Marxism must destroy Christianity across the West. Yes, Marxists must de-Christianize the West. Hoping to lead the communist forces in his homeland, He returned to his Italy, but Mussolini imprisoned him. While in prison, he devised a plan, committing it to writing in his *Prison Notebooks*. His work amounted to a blueprint for the destruction of Western civilization. The cultural revolution, witnessed by this writer over a lifetime, could have come right from Gramsci's notebook.

Gramsci did not seek initially to seize military power in any nation. Rather, he believed communists could infiltrate and destroy culture from within. The nation would then fall into the communists' laps "like ripened fruit." To reduce a culture, he saw a long path ahead. He must go through culture's institutions—the arts, theater, schools, colleges, seminaries, newspapers, and magazines. Targeting them one by one, he would politicize them each into an agency of revolution. Over time, with a new education model for children, he saw them indoctrinated first to understand, and then to welcome the revolution.

Gramsci urged his fellow communists to find Western intellectuals who shared his contempt for Christianity and to generate a zeal for transforming educational institutions in the West. Lenin's reign of terror finally failed after seventy years. His regime collapsed without the destruction of Christianity. Meanwhile, Gramsci and his fellow communists set up the Frankfurt School in Moscow to promote his theories. A Communist Party director named Max Horkheimer began retraining communists in Western cultural terms, to infiltrate the institutions of family, schools, the church, and public squares. Discarding the old military battlefield manuals, the communists developed new action manuals to undermine the institutions that support culture. They certainly aimed at America as a prime target, but other Western nations as well.

Victory was assured if they could stamp out Biblical Christianity from within. Violence creates revulsion and pushback. Yes, their hopeful, gentler nonviolent plan would require time, patience, and determination, but would be more effective than direct oppression. They confidently asserted that they could capture the institutions through their trained allies, agitators, and agents of the revolution.

In the 1990s, the Frankfurt School came to America. With help from Columbia University, New York City welcomed them. They proudly affirmed their goal to undermine the culture of the country that gave them refuge. One particular weapon in their arsenal, a book published by the Frankfurt School, *The Authoritarian Personality* (1951), placed its emphasis on cultural determination. In this book ostensibly on the subject of prejudice, they targeted the patriarchal family and the middle class.

As we fast-forward from the beginning of this new revolution, we see the culture war with respect to the children. The sexual revolution destroys children and their future. Statistics on divorce, out of wedlock births, abortions, single-parent homes, child abuse, violent crimes, drug use, teen suicide, promiscuity, and falling test scores all paint a picture of tragedy for this generation of American children. Gramsci's revolution continues today in America's institutions and throughout the West.

One of the most successful and destructive communist instruments in America is the distorted human sexuality movement.

Protect America's Children, founded by Anita Bryant in Miami, Florida, hired me to assist combating the distortion of sexuality. In 1980, the ministry moved to Selma, Alabama, and Anita placed her children in our Christian school. I worked full time with Protect America's Children. The devoted their whole energy and purpose to protecting America's children from sexual and other abuses.

The most notable authority on human sexuality of the time was Melvin Anchell, M.D. Dr. Anchell was a brilliant physician with a long and successful career in psychoanalysis and general medicine. He wrote five books on subjects relating to sexuality, sex education, and pornography. Acclaimed by the National Association of Psychoanalysis and The American Boards, he served generously testifying in court as an expert witness, as well as speaking across the nation and abroad. Dr. Anchell graciously served as a consultant to Protect America's Children with great generosity and commitment to the cause of America's children, particularly the many families suffering abuse. He found great favor with those who heard his testimonies. Clearly, the grace of God prevailed through his testimony in court and in his writing.

The Hoffman Center for the Family, our own ministry in Montgomery, Alabama, published Dr. Anchell's 1991 book *What's Wrong with Sex Education?*[2] He views his subject from an accomplished, professional medical standpoint, and speaks from this podium. He sees no conflict between this position and his deep faith in the Scriptures of his Jewish heritage.

In discussing sex education, Dr. Anchell clearly articulates the "harm these classes cause the students and society."

He states three inherent truths applicable to all people throughout the world.

1. *Long established is that sex is truly an intimate affair.* Two people in love seek privacy. This is properly a marriage between one man and one woman, as God created and established.

---

2. Melvin Anchell, *What's Wrong with Sex Education?* (Montgomery, AL: Hoffman Center for the Family, 1991).

Dr. Anchell condemns modern sex education in schools. He writes, "Students are desensitized to the intimate nature of physical sex. In any classroom discussion of sexuality, students must openly discuss their most intimate sexual feelings, and at the same time, become involved with similar sexual thoughts of their fellow classmates." Such brutally open and blunt talk hardens the natural sensitivity toward the body as a holy thing before God.

2. *In humans, sexual instinct consists of two currents* — an affectionate current and a physical current. The affectionate (love) current is as important, if not more so, than the physical component.

For human sexuality to fulfill individuals, these two components must come together. The Creator intended this for marriage. Demoralized school classrooms emphasize the physical, while they damn everyone's affectionate needs by what Dr. Anchell called "faint praise."[3]

He further notes that the very teaching of sex education in the classroom "publicly coarsens and severely diminishes the affectionate nature of privacy."

3. *Instruction should not interfere with the normal progression* of development in the years before the child reaches adulthood. Planned Parenthood is a chief proponent of radical sex-education programs. Dr. Anchell states that their programs are "not in accord with normal growth processes of sexual development. Their proposed programs make it virtually impossible for the students to grow into sexually mature adults." He documents in his books the reasons he believes that today's Planned Parenthood programs cause irreparable harm to students. To fully expose Planned Parenthoods agenda—what their teaching manuals contain—is too shockingly obscene to reveal here, but well documented.

Many respected psychologists Dr. Anchell knew and quoted agreed with his positions. They agreed that sexual preoccupation in the lives of young children will cause sexual dysfunction in adulthood. Today, we see the truth of this assertion in the now-frequent

---

3. Anchell, *What's Wrong with Sex Education?*, 3.

news coverage of children adopting perverse sexual identities long before puberty.

In reviewing things of importance in the life of a six- to twelve-year-old, Dr. Anchell makes an interesting observation. "The educability of children is not all that is at stake when latency is disturbed by classroom sex interferences. For example, during latency, some redirected sexual energy is used for development of compassion. Compassion is essential for the control of cruelty in the human personality. Compassion is one of the elements that separates man from beast." The sex indoctrination hampers achieving self-government at all age levels. The teaching hampers social, cultural, and personal achievement.

For those of us who are Bible-based in our world and life view—as all should be for their own good—proper concerns for our children involve chastity, abstinence, virginity, all as a sacred and faithful trust awaiting marriage. Marriage means a covenant between one man and one woman—Lord us help us, amen—for a lifetime commitment.

The great theologian and educator, J. Gresham Machen, said long ago, "If you give the bureaucrats the children, you may as well give them everything else as well." He spoke of the moral and intellectual decline of the people as the national government continued to reach for more and more control of American education and of everything else. Look at the grave injustice to children, parents, and the future of liberty in our nation by the people's demoralization. If we will face the truth of historic, self-conscious sabotaging of our heritage of Biblical morality, perhaps many more people will wake up to the dangers, make their convictions heard, assert God's rightly ruling laws and grace, and thereby rescue God's children from this tragedy.

THE SURRENDER TO SECULARISM

Have We Forsaken the God Who Gave Us This Blessed Nation?

October 2017

The story of nations and the role of secularism in America is a story unique in many ways. America did not suffer in chains at birth, as did other countries. The Founders and Framers of our government and nation were men of historic faith. They inherited the moral law and the Bible from earlier generations, and they brought the concept, with its importance, of religious liberty with them across the oceans. We think of emigrants from England, Scotland, France, Germany, and other countries bringing the Gospel as a prime reason for crossing the oceans.

What a unique beginning. Many people in many countries bore chains for generation after generation until they received the liberating Gospel.

Through their strengthening Biblical morality, our Founders incorporated into our founding documents many barriers to damaging infringements upon our religious liberty by civil government.

Thomas Jefferson spoke of erecting a wall of separation between church and state in order to protect both. This was not to diminish the importance or authority of both church and state within their spheres. Each would have its providentially ordered sphere of power and influence in building our Christian constitutional republic. The God-given power to the Church is essentially educational and influential. Government protects the church through maintaining defense and justice in the protection of liberty. The church instructs the body of Christ, both individually and in voluntary union, to do the work of the ministry (Ephesians 4:11–12), including influencing and serving in civil government as godly stewards.

So long as men recognize that God is the Creator and that their rights come from Him alone, men can enjoy freedom. Why is it that so many nations have attempted and yet failed to recognize these truths?

During my long lifetime, I have seen our nation move from religious liberty in practice to selfishness, to secularism, to complacency, to socialism. As a teacher of American history for nearly half a century, I have made it my practice to try to understand how such a thing happened in America.

The very founding documents of our nation make Biblical references and refer to Divine Providence. The governmental structure of our three representative, separate-and-equal branches of government arises from our Biblical worldview (Isaiah 33:22).

It is evident that the entire globe is under siege with the primary goal of eradicating spiritual faith and replacing it with secularism, socialism, fascism, communism—whoever holds the chains.

In the 1960s, the Cardinal Mindszenty Foundation, in their booklet entitled, "The Surrender to Secularism,"[1] shared the experience and writing of a Catholic Bishop by the name of Father Cuthbert O'Gara, who was imprisoned by the communists in China for a number of years. A reprint is available today in its twelfth printing.

Having gone to China as a Christian missionary in the 1940s, Father O'Gara became widely known throughout China as the "Stretcher-Bearer Bishop," so called because he so often carried wounded to his mission hospital. When a stretcher was not available, locals would see him carrying the wounded on his back.

---

1. Cuthbert O'Gara, "The Surrender to Secularism" (St. Louis: Cardinal Mindszenty Foundation, 1967).

He was twice arrested, once by the Japanese, and later by the communists who took over China. In 1951, they took him before the altar of his church, stripped him of his robes, and cast him into prison, where he suffered every kind of inconceivable torture. After several years of suffering unbearable abuse, two priests managed to carry him to Hong Kong on a stretcher.

The insights of his writing are so appropriate for us to read and to ponder in America today. I quote some from his journal below and pray that we can understand the secular culture that dominates our present day.

From Father O'Gara's journal:

When the communist troops overran my diocese, they were followed in very short order by the propaganda corps—the civilian branch of the Red forces—an organization, if anything, more disciplined, more zealous, more fanatical, than the People's Army of Liberation itself.

The entire population, city, and countryside was immediately organized into distinctive categories—grade school and high school pupils and teachers, (Catholic, Protestant, and pagan), merchants, artisans, members of the professions, yes, and even the lowly coolies. Everyone, for a week or more, was forced to attend the seminar specified for his or her proper category, and there, willy-nilly in the servile submission, listen to the official communist line.

Now, what was the first lesson given to the indoctrinees? One might have supposed that this would be some pearl of wisdom let drop by Marx, Lenin, or Stalin. Such however was not the case. The very first, the fundamental, lesson given was man's descent from the ape—Darwinism!

This naturally shocked the Christians, (Catholics and Protestants), attending the seminars, and, as might have been expected, they reacted violently. The non-Christians, who constituted the majority in China, were equally antagonistic to the ape theory, because from time immemorial the Chinese people in a nebulous sort of way had believed in a Supreme Being, in a soul and in an existence after death.

Are you surprised that the Chinese communists chose Darwinism as the cornerstone upon which to build their new political structure? At first, this political maneuver amazed me. I had taken for granted that they would begin by expanding the economic theories of Marx. Later on when in a Red jail, the reason for this unanticipated tactic became very obvious to me. By that time, I knew very well that the primary purpose of the People's Government in Peking was to extirpate all religious belief and practice from China, particularly to destroy the Catholic Church. After two years of house arrest and suffering with my fellow priests and religious Sisters every manner of annoyance and humiliation, I knew only too well that the clause "Freedom of Religion" written into the 1948 Constitution had been inserted there to hoodwink foreign governments, and had no relevancy whatsoever within the territorial limits of Red China. The official policy, rigid and ruthless, was transparently clear: Religion *delenda est*: Religion must be destroyed.

Darwinism negates God, the human soul, the afterlife. Into this vacuum, communism enters as the be-all and the end-all of the intellectual human slavery that it has created. In the Red prison in which I was held, the slogan, "Bring your mind over to us and all your troubles will end" was hammered into the minds of the prisoners with brutal and numbing monotony. Nothing but a groveling holocaust of the human person can satiate the lust for dominance of Peking's Red regime.

So wrote Father O'Gara.

When he returned to America, he spoke warning to the American people about John Dewey and Horace Mann, and the impact of secularism in our American culture and in the schools. He saw America as surrendering to this secular way of life sweeping across the land.

Grieving over what he had observed, he warned us well, as God's Word is now banned from schools of the land and unwelcome in the public square. He reminds us:

Communism is an evil that menaces us from without; secularism is a deadly cancer eating at the very vitals of our national life. The corrosive influence of secularism has already made tremendous inroads into every phase of our national existence. Business and government, labor and education, religion, the arts, the sciences, all have felt its base impact. No department of our national life is immune.

Basically, communism and socialism are one; both are predicated on the same premise—the materialistic concept of life. They are one in their materialism, one in their pragmatism, and one in their atheism.

Thinking of the American school classroom, Father O'Gara wrote, "Within the borders of the United States, the same perfidious principles are being continually expounded before our American youth, that there is no God, no soul, no afterlife, no absolutes, no stable morality; that what the majority decrees and does, however outrageous to our Christian morality, or contradictory to the teachings of Christ, is the accepted standard of modern morals and good manners."[2]

Father O'Gara is right!

"In other words, we are nourishing in our breast at home the very viper whose head, with so much fanfare and sinister hypocrisy, we set out to crush in the far corners of the globe." How can we be so blind?

America was clearly established as a Christian constitutional republic, and only in recent decades have we departed from this foundation.

Those radicals, who called themselves *progressives*, rejected Biblical morality, justice, freedom, and order. Their goal is to replace creationism, Biblical morality, and law with Darwinism, evolution, and a march toward world government (globalism).

Will we accept their radical changes, their views, and practices relating to human sexuality, polygamy, Shariah law, jihad, and the

---

2. O'Gara, "The Surrender to Secularism."

evolutionary pantheistic godhead in the family? Will we accept their new definitions and debased social structures they call *family*?

Shockingly, "One federal judge declared in 1996, in a Texas court, 'Parents give up their rights when they drop their children off at public school'"[3]

We are in a war over God Himself and His Word. Our national motto is "In God We Trust." This is the line of battle. Our Founders stated the liberating truth:

> We hold these truths to be self-evident that all men are created equal, that they are endowed by their Creator with certain unalienable Rights, that among these are Life, Liberty, and the Pursuit of Happiness.

—Declaration of Independence, 1776

This was once the heritage and legacy of every family and every school child. The Northwest Ordinance provided, before and after the adoption of the Constitution, free land for the placement of schools. For many years, only Christian schools existed in America, and many families homeschooled their children as well. The second president of the United States, John Adams, with his wife Abigail Adams, homeschooled their children, including our sixth president John Quincy Adams.

Patrick Henry made it clear that the vital issue in life is liberty, and that the only ground for life and liberty is in Jesus Christ, through our personal Christian faith and practice. In his will, Henry charged to his own family that "the religion of Jesus Christ is the only inheritance that can make them rich indeed."

Early on, New England Puritans began to tax farms to ensure the support of learning in the communities, yet pastors and the local church typically sponsored schools. Unitarians and early socialists quickly usurped and appropriated this tradition to promote secular government schools supported by mandatory property tax. For decades Christians maintained local control of

---

3. James Becker, ed., *Schooling for a Global Age* (New York: McGraw-Hill, 1979), xiii, xvii.

essentially Christian schools. In the past hundred and fifty years or so, the materialists and pagans have gained the upper hand. For real changes in education today, Christians must relearn the Biblical basis of every subject once so widely understand in America. For example, we must replace modern social studies—promoting equality of cultural religions, norms, and ideals—with a true God-centered, providential view Christian history, including the importance of America's unique contribution to Christian liberty. Even mathematics, properly understood, is only possible viewed as a created reflection of the Holy Trinity. For math to realize its Biblical purpose and potential, we must devote it to Christ.

The modern U.S. Supreme Court outlawed prayer in school and defied the intent of the Declaration of Independence and the Constitution, undermining American morality in the children. So we ask the individual Christian believer who reads this chapter: Which way? Will we restore this Christian constitutional republic by our faith and practice? Or will we give the resolute Satan his victory by our dereliction?

CHRISTIANS, PULL YOUR CHILDREN FROM PUBLIC SCHOOLS

July 2017

Afew months ago, Dr. James Dobson, one of the nation's most influential Christian leaders and a former public school teacher, hosted a discussion on his national radio program about the dangers of secular, anti-God education. Dr. Dobson, on his nationally syndicated show *Family Talk*, broadcast on hundreds of stations across the nation, hosted Lt. Col. E. Ray Moore. Col. Moore is a retired military chaplain, pioneer in homeschooling and co-founder of the Exodus Mandate, a ministry devoted to urging Christians out of the state schools. No doubt millions of Dr. Dobson's fans heard this two-part interview, "The Current State of Public and Christian Education," focusing on the indoctrination of American children by the state for twelve or more years of their young lives.

When asked about the indoctrination of children, Col. Moore cited the research of the Nehemiah Institute and other sources. He explained that "students have been propagandized and given a philosophy that is in many cases against Scripture and what we believe." Moore cited evidence that the large majority of millennials—about 80 percent—are actively progressive and left wing leaning. In summary, as Christians, we are losing the next generation!

Col. Moore challenged Christian pastors and parents to provide Christian education for the flock—not just Sunday school, but Monday, Tuesday, Wednesday school as well.

In the second part of the interview, Dr. Dobson asked Col. Moore an interesting question. Would removing Christian children from the classroom deprive other children of the Christian influence? Moore was glad that the question came up, because you often hear that opinion.

He answered, "That is the light-and-salt argument, and it is the number-one objection that I get from people who don't support what I am doing." Jesus's reference to salt and light certainly didn't refer to children in the K-12-level in public schools, according to Moore. Children are not yet sufficiently mature or of established character to bear such a burden. Apostle Paul even warned adults, "Be not deceived: evil communications [cowardly or wicked conversations] corrupt good manners" (First Corinthians 15:33). God gave His moral law to Moses to purge evil from the midst of Israel (Deuteronomy 17:7). Evil is contagious, but with innate sin, good does not easily transfer, particularly among the vulnerable.

Col. Moore has heard that argument so often that he addressed it in his publication, *Salt and Light*, to emphasize that "we are putting children in harm's way in pagan and godless schools." As a scholar who has thoroughly researched God's mandates on rearing covenant children, he declares that God leaves us "no wiggle room on how we should educate our children."

What Christian could possibly disagree with the Bible mandate to educate our children in the fear and admonition of the Lord? We Christians should deem ourselves deeply indebted to Dr. Dobson for taking on this explosive issue. He is so right. There is no "wiggle room" on the Bible's requirements for the education of Christian children.

The Nehemiah Institute, led by Dr. Dan Smithwick, has conducted worldview testing on many thousands of students since the 1980s across the nation. The many years of research, readily available from the institute, show the results of testing for public, private, Christian, and Principle Approach® (Christian worldview) schools.[1]

---

1. The Nehemiah Institute is found at nehemiahinstitute.com.

PEERS stands for Politics, Economics, Education, Religion, and Society. In each area, Nehemiah Institute has scientifically identified high Biblical expressions in each area as against secular expressions, allowing for answers that also represent views somewhere in between. Scores thus range from Biblical theism worldview, moderate Christian worldview, secular humanist worldview, and socialist worldview.

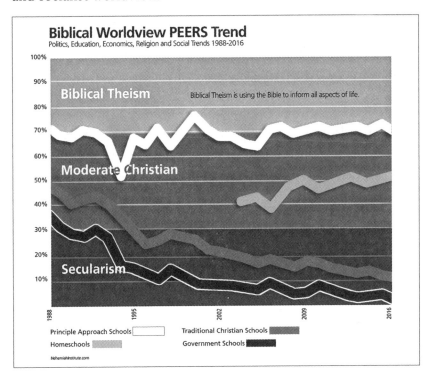

Through the years, Principle Approach® schools, sometimes called worldview schools, have consistently scored above other forms, specifically government schools, traditional Christian schools and home schools in general. A simple explanation: the historic American Biblical method of education.

This method inspired and informed our school ministry for fifty-two years, where we taught the Word of God as central in every subject. The method forms real Christian character in the children through reflective practice. Very young children learn how to read without duress. They learn how to reason, how to relate truth, and how to express it in word and in writing.

The Principle Approach® resulted from the pioneering research of Verna Hall and Rosalie Slater documenting America's Christian history and reidentifying its underlying Biblical principles. Schools self-consciously and specifically apply the Scripture to every area of human endeavor. In their research, the ladies rediscovered America's historic method of Biblical scholarship they called the 4 Rs: Research, Reason, Relate, and Record. Historically, it corresponds to the Christian scientific method, which itself resulted from the historic queen of the sciences: Biblical theology. The 4 Rs apply research of Scripture upon a carefully identified philosophical vocabulary, as from Webster's 1828 *Dictionary*, and the study of God's providence in history on the subject. History reveals the best expressions to emulate and the misguided ones to avoid. We know a tree, Jesus says, by its fruit. The learner then relates—applies—the complex of resulting data to draw conclusions for godly use—the science and art of the subject. Every subject carries the burden of God's intent for it. Every subject also requires something of the learner and practitioner, in Biblical faith, character, purpose to please God, skill, and wisdom.

The Foundation for American Christian Education continues its work as a great and primary source of information on the Biblical Principle Approach® to education. Its resources are available at the Foundation in Chesapeake, Virginia.[2]

In comparison to Principle Approach® schools, home schools have not done quite as well, but have done gradually better over time. Again, in contrast to Principle Approach® schools holding their own Biblically, government schools and traditional Christian schools show downward trends toward increasing secularism and socialism, with Christian schools consistently doing somewhat better.

The American colonies employed the Biblical method of scholarship, which, in turn, produced a Biblical method of education. This

---

2. The Foundation for American Christian Education is found at FACE.net.

worldview founded our nation. Our Founding Fathers embraced the impact of providence in our founding. They learned to reason from Biblical principles in every single subject, whether Bible, economics, government, literature, science, math, history, or art. Principles of Biblical Christian liberty in society and civil government figure prominently in the Principle Approach® curriculum toward self-government, liberty, and justice.

This nation was founded on the Biblical philosophy of history—Creation and the book of Genesis—providing the fundamentals of God's ways and purposes. The Creator—the omnipotent, omniscient, and Triune God—formed out of nothing the universe, time, history, man, and all created things. Therefore, we must accept everything in history in terms of God and His Word.

In contrast, modern education has created tales of process and many extremely long and environmentally determinant geological ages, an excuse to abandon the Triune God of the Bible.

No one disputes that modern man wars against the God of the Bible. Because modern man is thoroughly secular and humanistic, he casts Bible doctrine aside so that man can, assisting evolution, create his own social order. Turning from the Scriptures, man turned back to pagan thought and embraced natural law. Socialism, state education, government-run mental-health, and all social programs lead to more rejection of Scripture. The result must be the destruction of liberty, justice, blessing, and hope in the world. Man cannot oppose God without consequences.[3]

---

3. Contact information for Frontline Ministries, Inc.: Chaplain E. Ray Moore, (Lt. Col.), USAR Ret., President, Frontline Ministries, Inc., and the Exodus Mandate Project, PO Box 12072, Columbia, SC 29211, email: exodusmandate@ gmail.com, 803-714-1744, exodusmandate.org.
You can listen to the interview "The Current State of Public and Christian Education" with Lt. Col. E. Ray Moore on Dr. Dobson's syndicated show, *Family Talk* at drjamesdobson.org/Broadcasts, or by mail from 540 Elkton Drive, Suite 201, Colorado Springs, CO 80907, 877-732-6825.
Learn about the Principle Approach® and the 4 R method of scholarship in the *Christian History* series of books at the Foundation for American Education at FACE.net, and in the Nordskog Publishing title *Thy Will Be Done: When All Nations Call God Blessed* (nordskogpublishing.com).

As a history teacher of many decades, I see history as His Story. I find exciting Luke's account in chapter 1, verses 46–55. The Magnificat assures us that the Messiah will destroy all of His enemies. He will exalt the lowly. Calvin saw the Magnificat as a revelation concerning history also. Never doubt God's redeeming power.

The Magnificat
Luke 1:46–55 (NKJV)

The Song of Mary

> And Mary said: "My soul magnifies the Lord,
> And my spirit has rejoiced in God my Savior.
> For He has regarded the lowly state of His maidservant;
> For behold, henceforth all generations will call me blessed.
> For He who is mighty has done great things for me,
> And holy is His name.
> And His mercy is on those who fear Him
> From generation to generation.
> He has shown strength with His arm;
> He has scattered the proud in the imagination of their hearts.
> He has put down the mighty from their thrones,
> And exalted the lowly.
> He has filled the hungry with good things,
> And the rich He has sent away empty.
> He has helped His servant Israel,
> In remembrance of His mercy,
> As He spoke to our fathers,
> To Abraham and to his seed forever."

Good Books, Good Friends, Great Stories ... Never Forgotten

April 2014

Several years ago, the *Harvard Education Letter* published as its lead article "The Power of Family Conversation" (Vol. 24, No. 3, May/June 2008). It began:

> School matters, but literacy starts at home. Teachers armed with reading contracts and carefully worded missives have long urged parents to read aloud to their children. But now there is a second and perhaps more powerful message: Talk to your kids, too.

Mounting research proves that language-rich families with great communication correlate to school achievement and overall success in life. Shouldn't common sense tell us that? One interesting fact among many in the article is that children from age three to five are "ripe" for rich language learning. This fact prompts me to focus this chapter on reading, and not just reading to be reading, but reading good stories—good books that we remember a lifetime, and enjoy reading over and over again.

The little ones from ages three to five are truly sponges for knowledge. Read aloud every day to them. Read *Grimm's Fairy Tales* and Hans Christian Anderson's wonderful stories, and don't neglect *Mother Goose*. Even amid the ridiculous and the hysterical, you find lessons in reality. Jack falls down and breaks his crown, and Jill comes tumbling after. The king's men and horses couldn't put Humpty Dumpty together again. In the world of great children's literature, anything is possible. Young minds learn from the stories that the bad guy never wins, because light overcomes darkness. Good knights stand always ready to fight for right.

In nearly forty-eight years of teaching at home and at school, I believe the best moral education is through wonderful and moral stories. Yale president Timothy Dwight noted that the Bible

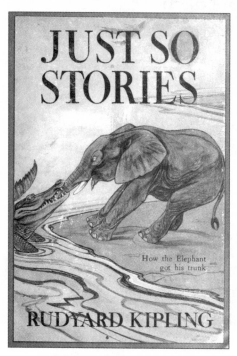

Illustrated by J. M. Gleeson & Paul Bransom, 1912

appeals principally to the imagination and not the intellect or emotions.[1] We must teach and train the principles of virtue—moral strength (Proverbs 22:6; Ephesians 6:4). We are all born with a sin nature, and no wonder the natural man from infancy sins so easily. Every home should possess and read William Bennett's *The Book of Virtues*. *Virtues* presents stories, poems, and essays from the annals of human history and great literature. It is a book for every age—child and adult alike. It treats every reader as though he or she is a proper moral agent. This book speaks to the mind and heart. It addresses the inner man, teaching virtues including compassion, courage, honesty, friendship, and faith.

Take time for humor, even for the ridiculous or the preposterous in good stories. Sometimes contrary things can teach a sublime lesson. Cherish the evenings that you read Kipling's *Just So Stories*.[2]

1. Verna M. Hall, *The Christian History of the American Revolution: Consider and Ponder* (San Francisco: Foundation for American Christian Education, 1976), 225.

2. Kipling pokes fun at Darwinistic evolution in these great children's stories.

Read these aloud to children before they can read themselves: "How the Camel Got His Hump," "How the Whale Got His Throat," "How the Leopard Got His Spots." And of course, also read Kipling's *The Jungle Book*. Share the adventure, hunger for courage, examples of loyalty, the challenge of a dare. And Kenneth Graham's *The Wind in the Willows* teaches the value of a friend and the absolute joy of life.[3] George McDonald's *At the Back of the North Wind* takes us to Scotland and expands our imagination, while tenderly treating human suffering and God's grace in it. The world is full of many more examples of true imaginative literature and culture for hungry hearts and seeking souls. And then in a few short years to come, your children can read the same stories back to you that you read over and over to them. Please build a home library with print books that they can hold, care for, and treasure.

Does reading aloud represent a challenge for very young children? Of course it does, and just what they need is to be challenged, to absorb beauty, truth, and courage. Literature gives the parent an opportunity to teach—vocabulary, thinking, speaking in whole thoughts, and understanding good and evil on God's terms. Everything becomes a teaching and learning opportunity. In literature lies an inner kingdom fortified with adventure, with bravery, with generosity and self-sacrifice, with love. We call this the kingdom the soul. And to strengthen both mind and heart, start very early with Bible stories. Don't read and teach the Bible as you do the fairy tales. From the opening of the pages, stress the difference in Bible stories from other stories. In the Bible, after all, our Heavenly Father tells us His stories through the individuals He chose to live them, and those He chose to write them down. These are true stories with true-life lessons. Unwrap these gifts regularly at special family times, hopefully at evening devotions.

---

3. However, Graham also teaches with friends' help, Mr. Toad's naughtiness receives no real consequence, and so no help toward repentance. Hence, we suggest explaining the good things and bad, here and in all literature, media, and life. Teach the children discernment and discretion (Proverbs 1:4; First Corinthians 12:10).

Elementary and middle school students should read Long-fellow's "Hiawatha," and "The Sage of King Olaf," Coleridge's "Rhyme of the Ancient Mariner," and *The Arabian Nights*. Each one challenges loyalty and courage—doing what is right. There are so many great authors from which to choose (with discretion and discernment): Nathaniel Hawthorne, Emily Dickinson, Lord Tennyson, Henry Louis Stevenson, Charles Dickens, Robert Frost, William Shakespeare, Robert Browning, Jack London, and so many others. We always had Thanksgiving at our grandparents' home, about a sixty-mile drive. We learned the meaning of *smorgasbord* when many contributed to fill two giant sideboards with tantalizing dishes of every kind to serve over sixty people, all family. Stories for children should be as varied as the family smorgasbord. The short stories should be well written, and great for character development of every age child, poems that tell a story but have music and rhythm in the beat. Good children's literature should not be dumbed down, childish, or condescending. Children love a mystery, providing that they can solve it. Excellent stories introduce the young child to imagery and figurative language. An example is Robert Frost's poem, "The Road Not Taken." How wonderful for a teen to grasp the meaning of Frost's poem:

> Two roads diverged in a wood, and I—
> I took the one less traveled by,
> And that has made all the difference.[4]

Another wonderful story, a bestseller in the 1970s, is *Jonathan Livingston Seagull* by Richard Bach. Most seagulls don't bother to learn anything but the simplest facts of flight—how to get to the food source and back. Flying is not all that important, only eating. Jonathan is a seagull of a different character. More than anything Jonathan loved to fly and wanted to learn more about flying, and

---

4. We suggest discernment once more. Yes, we should take courage to embrace unique experience according to God's individual gifts and calling. But we should also reject the conceited elitism of Ralph Waldo Emerson's philosophy of transcendentalism implied in the poem. This philosophy held the common man, the ordinary path, in contempt. Such a view is not Biblical (Romans 14:4).

about the world, about different altitudes, about different creatures, and the techniques that would lead to excellence. He loved science! Even his parents didn't understand his desire to be the very best that he could be. His determination led to his becoming the fastest seagull alive. Though he longed for the flock to benefit from his achievement, they did not choose to do so. His high-speed dive brought him the rare and tasty fish that schooled ten feet below the surface of the ocean. Jonathan believed that gulls had short lives because they were bored and lived in fear. He lived in perfect liberty and "lived a long, fine life indeed." Celebrate God's principle of individuality, and your child's uniqueness; build upon it.

In traditional schools, the middle- and high-school student studied real history, and usually the sequence of history of the ancient world, the Middle Ages, the Renaissance, and the modern world. History focuses on key individuals or communities representing either godliness and the moral and faithful line of Christ, or the sons of Noah falling in various degrees from Noah's knowledge of God. In a study of the ancient world, there should be a strong emphasis on the Old Testament, and please, do not neglect the psalms and proverbs. The great epics, Homer's *Iliad* and *Odyssey* deserve a careful study, these assumed to have been written about 850 B.C. They paint a memorable portrait of Greek culture—their debased pagan religion and moral concepts—but also their bravery and determination. Sea nymphs could marry mortals, as men accepted adultery then. Zeus was one of many gods, yet the most powerful of all. As with unsaved men, life for the gods was concerned with power and largely with selfish desires. Reading Homer is a test for one's imagination and hopefully well worth it. Most classes move to the Athenian democracy and study the history of the Peloponnesian War with the aid of Thucydides. Consider writers across the centuries, from 500 B.C. to Vergil (70–19 B.C.)— Sophocles, Euripides, Plato, Aristotle, Cicero, and others of note. Verna Hall and Rosalie Slater considered the classical era as the highest attainment of men apart from God, yet therefore falling very short and not sustainable.

Jesus's birth ushers in the New Testament period in history—His birth, ministry, death, and resurrection—with the Biblical epistles. In the early-Christian era also we find an opportunity to discover Augustine's *Confessions*, *The Song of Roland*, "The Saga of Hrafnkel, Priest of Frey," Dante's *Divine Comedy*, and especially Chaucer's *Canterbury Tales*. *The Canterbury Tales* brings us to the literary flowering of the English language. Sir Thomas Malory's (1485) *Le Morte d'Arthur* still ranks high with every history student I ever taught. How could anyone not love chivalry? The better parts of chivalry challenge every young man and thrill every young maiden who dreams of her own Prince Charming.

This brings us to the period we know as the Renaissance in both history and literature. Renaissance writers mirror the broad cultural and political characteristics of every previous age in their literature. By *renaissance* they meant a rebirth of classical Greek and Roman thought and life. Sadly, most philosophers in this period and the moderns concluded that reality reduces to a world of matter—essentially pantheism. To them, man is the measure of all things.

However, let us not neglect the importance of the overall literature of Western civilization, as that has, over centuries, formed our own culture. English drama, as all western European drama, had its origin in religious observance and rituals. There is no evidence that the early English adapted the Roman theatre's drama to their culture. But the epic, often complex, held high honor. Thankfully, John Dewey was not present in our historic formation to overrule the very complex narratives and expanding use of language. Though varied in form and content, English literature projects a strong, even fierce, masculinity. That is not an offense to me. In fact, God created man to be strong, to lead, to provide for his family. Scripture exalts the mighty men of valor of King David's era, yet also meekness—power restrained until needed to combat evil. Strong ethical principles weave into the Biblical stories. Sometimes they represent an appropriate pessimism over the sinfulness of the human condition. That is reality, and it is not an offense to acknowledge it. With an acknowledgment of the destructive power of sin, they also tell of God's ultimate moral victory in the earth through Christ.

Select a variety of English literature over the past centuries. Determine to read aloud at home. It will challenge, reward, edify, and connect the members of your family circle. It will also connect to the suffering, challenges, and victories of all those who have gone before us. By viewing it through the wisdom-lens of Scripture, let our reading self-consciously act to create or renew goodness and greatness within us.

CHAPTER 24

The Cost of Forsaking the Humanities
in Education

May 2014

In 1962, at the Southern Humanities Conference at the University of Alabama, N. Floyd McGowin, president of the W. T. Smith Lumber Company, served as keynote speaker. He addressed the topic, "Can the Humanities Be Dispensed with in an Age of Crisis?" He opened his talk:

> I assume that we are using the word *humanities* today in its original and true sense, and that we shall have nothing to do with the sly distortions of meaning that were insinuated into our language when John Dewey and other peddlers of revolutionary novelties called themselves humanists. The confusion of meaning in our time has become so great that such a newspaper as *The New York Times* has dared to describe as a humanist such a barbarian as Fidel Castro.

If good men will preserve the English language as a means of communication between rational men, we must protect our words from semantic sabotage and use them carefully in their proper, traditional meanings. In his 1828 *Dictionary*, Noah Webster defined *humanity* in part as "the kind feelings, dispositions, and sympathies of man, by which he is distinguished from the lower orders of animals; kindness; benevolence; especially, a disposition to relieve persons in distress, and to treat with tenderness those who are helpless and defenseless; opposed to cruelty." He also defined *humanist* as "one versed in the knowledge of human nature." In the best sense, we use the word *humanities*, therefore, to designate elements of human culture—of the mind and spirit, and their outworking in the community. We sharply distinguish this from mere pragmatism, from every kind of technical skill possibly acquired by a workman, artisan, or practitioners of professions as a means of livelihood. Our English word historically holds the higher meaning. It derives from the Latin. The Romans called this word *humanitas* in the firm belief that the study of literature and kindred arts made them men *humaniores*—more human, in the sense that they had more fully realized in themselves the highest capacities of human beings through the cultivation of mind and spirit that would otherwise remain latent. The Romans thus concentrated their interest not only because they understood in every society a few must lead and many follow, but they also realized that the greater a man's talent, the greater is his potential for harm as well as good. The Latin heritage of humanities is significant but incomplete. It omits the fact that full human realization only occurs in Christ, a problem typical in non-Christian history. Nonetheless, the word serves us, given proper qualification.

Returning to Mr. McGowin's address, he outlined many crisis situations in our history, but he saw in the 1960s a crisis in education, and that question regarded changes to the study of the humanities. What impact will it have on the fight for survival of Western civilization and Christianity? Remember that this address came fifty-two years ago at Alabama's leading university, where today humanities studies are in sharp decline, just as they are in colleges and universities all over the nation.

He viewed the crisis America faced then as proof of cultural and educational weakness. He believed that a modest exertion of strength by the civilized nations of the West could have broken and destroyed the communist empire. Our present danger, in his view, is that we created it by our folly. He said:

> It is a proof of a dangerous lapse of our mental powers—not one of our technical skills, but a lapse of our capacity to use them, for clearly we have failed to protect ourselves because either

we lacked the moral perception that would have recognized evil when it was paraded before us or the intellectual ability to devise the simple means necessary for dealing with it.... The twentieth century has been a period of great scientific and technical advance, and of what is generally regarded as material progress, has also been a time of progressive weakness of our national intelligence and practical judgment—a time of fatuous illusions and stupid blunders, that have, in their effect, been almost suicidal. It may not be a coincidence that it is also the time in which the humanities have been progressively eliminated from our educational system. Bergen Evans in his recent *Dictionary of Contemporary American Usage* can say that *humanist* is almost as vague and confusing a word [as] there is.

Before the birth of Christianity, a sovereign God dispensed common grace[1] in the ancient world to protect sinful, rebellious man from complete destruction. Remnant traditions in the ancient world, from the time of godly Noah and his sons through Old Testament times, eventually formed the classical Greek and Roman cultures. We can hardly conceive what the world would have been like without the classical foundation of culture. From the Renaissance to my own childhood in the 1930s, no educated person would have dreamed of discarding classical education and depriving an essential part of our heritage to the rising generation.

When we think of depriving students of understanding their heritage, Mr. McGowin reminds us that:

The supreme value of life lies in the excellence and worth of the individual mind and soul. It makes us aware how completely the fundamental ideas of our civilization have been leached away and replaced by alien and barbarous notions. We realize that many of our supposedly educated contemporaries blandly

---

1. Common grace is that limited, but great and undeserved, favor God shows to all men, including unbelievers, while we live this probationary life in anticipation of eternity. The Scripture, "He maketh His sun to rise on the evil and on the good, and sendeth rain on the just and on the unjust" (Matthew 5:45), well summarizes this theological concept and conclusion. —Ed.

assume that the function of society is to see that the people are fed, clothed, housed, and amused with a minimum of effort on their part—which by the way, is precisely what the savage asks of life—that is to say, satisfaction of those appetites which man shares with animals.

He continued the speech by addressing two issues, both impacting the subversion of our society: the decline of the teaching of the humanities in education, and the matter of private property in our economic system. Motivation for the attacks on our culture, according to his study, grew out of:

A rabid determination that no man shall be morally and culturally above another—that no man shall be permitted to violate the new and yet tacit dogma that the satisfaction of animal needs and animal appetites is the whole end of man. I suspect that upon close analysis we shall find that the attacks upon private property are in their source not economic at all, and do not arise from an envy of material possessions. They are primarily cultural and motivated by resentment of the self-cultivation that economic security of private property makes feasible.

Obviously, Mr. McGowin saw socialism on the march in America, and he saw it as a cultural worldview. The only way to fight it is with a contrasting worldview, one that requires the moral and spiritual dedication to fight the prevailing enemy by faith, with dependence on God's help. We face a crisis in America. National and state departments of education, through ever-more-centralized control, further threaten the elevated human mind and spirit through Common Core and no doubt future planned programs. Centralized planning is certainly not the only threat in education, but one we must constantly deal with. God has uniquely created each child at his school desk. God endowed him with a body, mind, and spirit, all three requiring nourishment and nurture. God created the child in His own image with hope of eternal life for the next world, not as an animal to be trained to behave in particular ways. Each child possesses great potential. When properly developed, God will use that potential both to prepare the child for eternity, and to use him in this life to contribute to the eternal preparation of others (Matthew 28:19–20).

Let's be clear. If the universe is merely physical matter, we must reject non-material values and all meaning. Ultimately no purpose or desire to live will remain. Unchecked sin is suicidal. "But he that sinneth against me wrongeth his own soul: all they that hate me love death" (Proverbs 8:36).

A true teacher delights in the potential of the student. The teacher ministers to felt need, works to awaken latent ones, and desires above all to help the student climb to his highest potential. The teacher assists the young person to face the big challenges, to know God, to discover what is man before Him, and what are his gifts and callings. How does the student live rightly before Him?

What American educators are discarding is what made us the envy of the world. Think of Tocqueville's envy of America.[2] He valued our liberty and equality above French aristocracy.

If any humanities course at a secular university included the Bible in its studies, it would surely be to deny the Bible's claims or better declarations. Allan Bloom, in his book *The Closing of the American Mind*, offered the following insight. Handlers treat the Bible

> in one of two ways: It is subjective to modern "scientific" analysis, called Higher Criticism, where it is dismantled, to show how "sacred" books are put together, and that they are not what they claim to be. It is useful as a mosaic in which one finds the footprints of many dead civilizations. Or else the Bible is used in courses in comparative religion as the one expression of the need for the "sacred" and as a contribution to the very modern, very scientific study of the structure of "myths."... A teacher who treated the Bible naively, taking it at its word, or Word, would be accused of scientific incompetence and lack of sophistication.[3]

2. Alexis De Tocqueville, *Democracy in America* (Cambridge: Sever & Francis, 1863).

3. Allan Bloom, *The Closing of the American Mind* (New York: Simon &

Dr. Bloom appeals to the education world, "Our problems are so great and their sources so deep that to understand them we need philosophy more than ever, if we do not despair of it, and face the challenges on which it flourishes.... This is the American moment in world history, the one for which we shall forever be judged. Just as in politics the responsibility for the fate of freedom in the world has devolved upon our regime, so the fate of philosophy in the world has devolved upon our universities, and the two are related as they have never been before."

We know that the Bible condemns vain humanistic philosophy. Here we speak of a Biblically grounded philosophy or worldview. Noah Webster defined *philosophy*:

> Literally, the love of wisdom. But in modern acceptation, *philosophy* is a general term denoting an explanation of the reasons of things; or an investigation of the causes of all phenomena both of mind and of matter. When applied to any particular department of knowledge, it denotes the collection of general laws or principles under which all the subordinate phenomena or facts relating to that subject, are comprehended. Thus, that branch of *philosophy* which treats of God, etc., is called theology; that which treats of nature is called physics or natural philosophy; that which treats of man is called logic and ethics, or moral philosophy; that which treats of the mind is called intellectual or mental *philosophy*, or metaphysics.
>
> The objects of *philosophy* are to ascertain facts or truth, and the causes of things or their phenomena; to enlarge our views of God and his works, and to render our knowledge of both practically useful and subservient to human happiness.
>
> True religion and true *philosophy* must ultimately arrive at the same principle.[4]

True philosophy means assuming the truth and authority of God's Word, and then finding internally consistent principles by which we can faithfully translate its content into obedient life.

Schuster, 1987), 374.
4. *American Dictionary of the English Language*, s.v. "philosophy."

Just about the time that Allan Bloom's *The Closing of the American Mind* went into publication, David Barton published his first book *America: To Pray Or Not To Pray*.[5] The book was a statistical look at what has happened to American education since prayer was ordered out of public schools. In June 1963, by a court decision, schools forbade thirty-nine million students and two million teachers to pray in school. Since that time, David Barton has documented the changes in American education. He has continued through the years to collect and document research that further proves the damage of that fateful decision when the government outlawed corporate public prayer. Using graphs, the book shows the decline of student morality, the increase of sexual activity, teen pregnancies, sexually transmitted diseases, divorce rates, single-parent families, the decline of student achievement and test scores, rising violent crimes among the young, increased alcohol consumption, illegal drug use among the young, and illiteracy. His website wallbuilders.com is a great and trusted resource.

We share all these things in hopes of inspiring readers to inform and involve themselves, to re-strengthen the Hebrew-Christian worldview under attack and subversion. Prayer represents a good first contribution to the spiritual battle. Pray specifically for every official at every branch of our state and national government (First Timothy 2:1–2). Please pray for the millions of children in government schools. They may never read Ben Franklin, as social studies has replaced history in government schools. However, these are his words, reflecting his knowledge of Psalm 127:1 and his love for our country. "We have been assured, Sir, in the Sacred Writings that 'except the Lord build the House, they labor in vain that build it.'"[6]

---

5. David Barton, *America: To Pray Or Not To Pray* (Aledo, TX: WallBuilder Press, 1989).
6. Farrand, ed., *The Records of the Federal Convention of 1787*, vol. 1, 451, available online at *Online Library of Liberty*, oll.libertyfund.org.

CHAPTER 25

Sustainable Freedom for the American
Future, or a Free People's Suicide?

November 2012

This is the subject of an excellent new book by noted scholar Os Guinness (D.Phil., Oxford), author or editor of more than twenty-five books, including *The American Hour: A Time of Reckoning and the Once and Future Role of Faith*.[1] Born in China and educated in England, Guinness now lives near Washington, D.C. He has long been associated with the Brookings Institution, the Woodrow Wilson Center, and founded the Trinity Forum. He reveals remarkable insight into the problems we face in preserving our constitutional republic, and thereby, our freedom to practice individual self-government.

He begins the book by asking the question, What kind of people do you think that you are? The question holds profound implications. The day of reckoning for America is here, a time of critical testing for our nation. Who can ignore the political crisis we face over the debt ceiling, the consequences of the economic crisis, the continuing unemployment, and the mounting moral decay and social problems?

Internationally, we face the possible ending of Western civilization as we have known it, and the emergence of an Asia-led world with worldviews at war with everything America stands

---

1. Os Guinness, *The American Hour: A Time of Reckoning and the Once and Future Role of Faith* (New York: The Free Press, 1993).

for. Os Guinness puts it plainly: "In short, the state of the union is at stake."

"Freedom Is the Special Glory of America"[2]

Freedom is our birthright and, until recently, our highest virtue. How to sustain it is the question, the problem we must solve in this generation, or America and its liberty are lost. Guinness claims that the greatest enemy of freedom is "freedom." Here is a paradox to ponder. To sustain freedom, societies must maintain freedom at two levels, at the level of the nation's constitution and at the level of their citizens' convictions. As a mother and Christian educator, I loved his sentence: "If the structures of liberty are well built, they last as long as they are properly maintained, whereas the spirit of liberty and the habits of the heart must be reinvigorated from generation to generation."[3] He compares the nation's constitution to a covenant, remaining strong only if the citizenry upholds their side of the covenant.

Freedom always faces a fundamental moral challenge. And that is a heart issue, isn't it? The character of our representative leaders and the character of the citizens are a matter of heart and conscience. Therefore, at this moment in America, our greatest danger may be internal dangers where the people have lost our way.

Guinness says of the financial crisis of 2008 and following, "These two events were of world significance because they created the first global crisis in history that was caused principally by the United States, and they raise major questions for the republic."[4] Contrast contemporary encouragement of debt-levered consumerism against our forefathers' stress on hard work, savings, thrift, and delayed gratification. Lack of strong character and its sinful self-indulgence have bred household, government, and international debt. Our dependency on foreign sources of energy, our debt

---

2. Os Guinness, *A Free People's Suicide: Sustainable Freedom and the American Future* (Downers Grove, IL: InterVarsity Press, 2012), 17.
3. Guinness, *A Free People's Suicide*, 19–20.
4. Guinness, *A Free People's Suicide*, 24.

to foreign investors, and sadly, disapproval of the United States from all over the world are realities of our failures.

The book is realistic about our failings, but it offers hope for the future. Os Guinness chastises us rightly, as our friend. He refuses to picture our future as a utopia. Rather, he foresees continued conflicts, with ongoing tyranny and evil in the world. He quotes Samuel Johnson: "We continue every day to show by new proofs, that no people can be great who have ceased to be virtuous."[5]

Guinness presents a challenge: "Let your choice be made, and let it be known. Remember that free societies are rare and transient, that the American republic is neither ancient nor stable and that its nature as a great experiment may not survive the abandonment of the foundation of its founders.... It is far better to rise to the challenge of generations past and generations yet unborn, and choose freedom and the faith it requires with all their stern requirement as well as their sweet gifts."[6]

I must praise Os Guinness for his insight. The rule of law remains essential to America. As free people, God binds us to His revealed law. Our founders established under God the entire right of freedom of conscience and religious liberty in this land. Humanist authorities have removed ultimate truth from the schools, along with moral absolutes. In a spirit of arrogance, policy makers have craftily imposed many policies beyond just and true law. Lack of morals in the family and then in the public square has bred insecurity, further family breakdown, and all manner of vice. Washington, Adams, Jefferson, Madison, and the entire body of Founders understood the importance of Christian self-government as the one essential virtue in preserving liberty.

Guinness understands that covenant—our accountability to the Creator in relationship with Him and each other—is foundational to restoring freedom. Guinness loves America, enough to tell the painful truth. If we will only avail ourselves, the scope of his

---

5. Robert Lynam, ed., *The Works of Samuel Johnson, LL.D.*, vol. 5 (London: George Cowie and Co, 1825), 359.
6. Guinness, *A Free People's Suicide*, 204–5.

knowledge and understanding of history, philosophy, education, and the entire political scene internationally should add to our education, our resolve, and our effectiveness in upholding our part of America's covenant. May the Lord lead us to see our failures and correct them before it is too late for America.

CHAPTER 26

EVERY CULTURE EXPRESSES A RELIGION: WHAT IS THE RELIGION OF AMERICA TODAY?

March 2013

Where is the voice of the church?

Hillsdale College, located in Hillsdale, Michigan, has an amazing outreach throughout America with its monthly newsletter *Imprimis*, which reaches over 2,600,000 readers monthly. Some days ago, a friend came to my home with a copy of *Imprimis* in his hands. "Have you read this?" he asked. Actually, it was by my bed in the stack of "must reads," with the stack ever growing with each incoming mail. The newsletter adapted a speech given on September 20, 2012, entitled "Man, Sex, God, and Yale," by Nathan Harden.[1] In it he discusses the themes of his book *Sex and God at Yale: Porn, Political Correctness, and a Good Education Gone Bad*. Harden, a 2009 graduate of Yale, edits *The College Fix*, a higher-education news website.[2] He has written for numerous publications, including *National Review* and *The Weekly Standard*, both great reads. The *Imprimis* article focused on William F. Buckley's experience at Yale, but also how the anti-Christian sexual revolution continues unabated and is apparently growing beyond anything Buckley could have imagined.

William Buckley, a graduate of Yale, published his first book in 1951. *God and Man at Yale* described two ideas Buckley brought

---

1. Nathan Harden, "Man, Sex, God, and Yale," *Imprimis* vol. 42, no. 1 (January 2013), imprimis.hillsdale.edu/man-sex-god-and-yale/.
2. Online at thecollegefix.com.

with him to college, ideas that governed his worldview. Buckley often wrote of his active faith in God and in Christian principles, which he believed were the primary influences for a good life. He devoted himself to free enterprise and limited government, as they had served America well and would so in the future. Buckley wrote of the antagonism he encountered at Yale to those very basic ideas. The teaching he encountered at Yale revealed hostility to religious faith and promoted collectivism over a free market. He declared that Yale waged war against the faith and principles of the alumni and the parents of students enrolled. Contemporary teaching violated even the fundamental, original college charter, which remains in force, at least on paper.[3] Yes, for Buckley and since, Yale represents open hostility to the historic faith of the Bible and its principles. And now it is much, much worse than in Buckley's time.

While this attitude grew across the entire nation in education, it remained quiet and underground for a short while. Then came a new battle cry for secularized education. It appeared first in the most prominent universities, followed by others, under the alias

---

3. "The Yale Corporation Charter and Legislation" begins:
"ACT FOR LIBERTY TO ERECT A COLLEGIATE SCHOOL, 1701
By the Govrn, in Council & Representatives of his Majties Colony of Connecticot in Genrll Court Assembled, New-Haven, Octr 9: 1701:
An act for Liberty to erect a Collegiate School:
WHEREAS several well disposed, and Publick spirited Persons of their sincere Regard to & Zeal for upholding & Propagating of the Christian Protestant Religion by a succession of Learned & Orthodox men have expressed by Petition their earnest desires that fully Liberty and Priveledge be granted unto Certain Undertakers for the founding, suitably endowing & ordering a Collegiate School within his Majties Colony of Connecticot wherein Youth may be instructed in the Arts & Sciences who thorough the blessing of Almighty God may be fitted for Publick employment both in Church & Civil State.
To the intent therefore that all due incouragement by Given to such Pious Resolutions and that so necessary & Religious an undertakeing may be sett forward supported & well managed."
(New Haven, Published by the University, 1976), yale.edu/sites/default/files/files/University-Charter.pdf.

of academic freedom. This is what makes Nathan Harden's book so telling. These secular educators refashioned America's culture through the education process over the last hundred years or so. Who were they? And what was the agenda? We could start in Great Britain with Charles Darwin and his theory of evolution. Or we could start with John Dewey in America, with his degrading of reading instruction by removing phonics, or his progressive education philosophy. His influence was great enough to create new curriculum philosophy and the retraining of teachers and school administrators. Current educational theories and practices continue to perpetuate his evolutionary and humanistic principles.

Nonetheless, let's begin our focus on 1933, when educators became more organized, publishing their agenda in the form of the *Humanist Manifesto I*.[4] In the minds of the thirty-four humanists who signed the document, including John Dewey, the time had come to spell out the religious and philosophical worldview, which would defeat orthodox religion and dogmatic positions of the past. To them, science and economics held the keys for establishing the good life in the twentieth century. These would not be the science of history, or the economics of liberty that the framers and Founders knew.

The first articles in the *Manifesto* proclaim the universe to be self-existing (pantheistic, as in Hinduism) and not created. They go on to state that man is merely a part of nature, emerging as the result of a continuous materialistic progress. The fifth article states that humanism represents and asserts the nature of the universe depicted by modern science, making unacceptable any supernatural or cosmic values. The sixth article states that the time has passed for theism, deism, and modernism. Throughout, the document denies the existence of the supernatural. Rather, with man as god, to realize social well-being and social justice, the *Manifesto* calls for cooperative effort. They declare religious humanism as the religion for the twentieth century, and claim the enhancement of human life as its purpose. Unstated is the obvious implication that to

---

4. Kurtz, *Humanist Manifestos I and II*, available online at americanhumanist.org.

empower accomplishment of their goals, humanists, as they always do, must acquire coercive political power—authoritarianism—to achieve cooperative effort.

In the forty years since they signed the first *Humanist Manifesto* and successfully promoted it widely across all of academia, wars, totalitarian states, struggles for human rights, prevailing poverty challenges, and racism all have arisen. In turn, such problems resulting from practical humanism then called for solutions. Christian cultures always look to the Holy Scriptures for solutions to societal problems—because God is faithful. Instead of recognizing that their secularizing views created or exacerbated these problems, the humanists penned a new manifesto, The *Humanist Manifesto II*, signed by 114 very determined leaders, was intended to guide mankind into the future. Their worldwide ambition dreamed of a one-world community "where disproportions in wealth, income, and economic growth should be reduced on a worldwide basis" (*HM II*, fifteenth article). Does this sound familiar to anyone?

The second *Manifesto* states the humanist position on religion, ethics, the individual, democratic society, the world community, and humanity as a whole. "We believe that traditional dogmatic or authoritarian religions that place revelation, God, ritual, or creed above human needs and experience do a disservice to the human species" (*HM II*, first article). It further states, "Promises of immortal salvation or fear of eternal damnation are both illusory and harmful. They distract humans from present concerns, from self-actualization, and from rectifying social injustices" (*HM II*, second article). They warn again that economic and political theory stemming from traditional religious beliefs is nothing more than wrong-headed ideological dogma.

Addressing the life of the individual, the manifesto reads, "In the area of sexuality, we believe that intolerant attitudes, often cultivated by orthodox religions and puritanical cultures, unduly repress sexual conduct. The right to birth control, abortion, and divorce should be recognized" (*HM II*, sixth article). The document advocates for "sexual proclivities" and "lifestyles" built as individuals desire—that is, sexual anarchy.

The *Manifesto II* also advocates for the right to suicide and euthanasia.

And who were these 114 individuals who signed the document and the thousands of others who embraced the document and the agenda? Professors at leading universities, such as Columbia, University of Pittsburgh, Harvard University, University of Michigan, University of Minnesota, University of Chicago, Union Graduate School, Ohio State University, Emory University, California Polytechnic, Indiana University, Syracuse University, University of Florida, and many more in America and in Europe. Unitarian ministers and churches signed as well. Many leading editors of humanist publications signed, including Paul Kurtz, editor of *The Humanist*. Also, note Alan Guttmacher, Planned Parenthood executive, was a signer. Of no small significance was the influence of B. F. Skinner, and his ideas of behavioral psychology.

These radical humanists completely united to further their radical agenda to refashion America's culture through education and politics. This they have largely done. Nathan Harden's book relates past and current activities at Yale that William Buckley could hardly have dreamed of. He writes of a Yale professor who openly praised Hamas and Hezbollah. He writes that the social agenda promotes promiscuity, and he describes the hosting (with Yale's approval) of a "Sex Week"—a festival of sleaze, porn, and debauchery. His book describes things you can't force yourself to believe actually took place, but the author insists that it did—with administration approval. Though I was relieved to read that many students took offense and objected to the "Sex Week" activities, a host of educators nonetheless publicly committed themselves to gay rights, feminism, and supposed academic freedom. The tragedy of this movement is that such debauchery has become widespread and mainstream in higher education across the nation.

Yale University has educated U.S. presidents and Supreme Court justices. We who love liberty have permissively taken too much for granted in these changes. We have perhaps not guarded our own hearts and minds. We have left unprotected too many children. Unprepared for the universities of today, unprepared to defend their faith, too many young people have walked away from the church and faith of their youth.

Too many Christians of earlier generations, monastically insulating themselves from world, made themselves ignorant of the real influence of Dewey, Darwin, and others. When they expelled God from the public schools, very few sounded the alarm. The churches remained empty all week, when they could have been filled with self-consciously Biblical Christian schools training Christian warriors for Truth. And now America, including much of the church, has lost her hunger for the liberty which only Christianity can offer: liberty from the bondage of sin, liberating of the mind to dream Christ's thoughts after Him, and by His Spirit to soar to the heights. True liberty supports building Christian character to make loyal commitments to marriage, family, faith, and one's neighbors. Have we even forgotten that religious liberty is not possible without civil liberty? Did we never study the desolated and dead legacy of Greece, Rome, and all the pagan, God-hating ancients? Did we never really learn the lessons of history?

All worldviews must find a foundation in man (as god), or in the true and living God. Apparently, humanism holds the majority vote today at the ballot box and in the public square. Yet, as you travel America, in or close to nearly every public square, if you look up, there is a church steeple, tall and white, shining against a blue sky, calling us back to the faith that built this nation, calling us back to Biblical Christianity. Immigrants flocked here for freedom in early America. They left their past with no regrets. It was that faith and persistence that gave America the greatest liberty and prosperity that the world has ever known—that shining city on a hill that we read about.

Did God ever need a majority to prevail? Of course not, and He doesn't today. The Scripture says God laughs at the wicked. (Psalm 2:4; 37:13). But His people, who are called by His name, must be able to reason from moral absolutes toward right choices by faith. This imperative always sends us back to search His Word for guidance, beginning with repentance in the homes and in the churches.

As a history teacher, I grieve over the rewriting of history since the early 1900s, and I urge parents to seek sound Christian education for children and grandchildren. Historical understanding is necessary for understanding liberty—how to achieve it and how to retain it. Those professors leading students into religious humanism are like those pictured in Second Timothy Chapter 3, Verse 7, "ever learning, and never able to come to the knowledge of the truth." Psalm 33:12 declares, "Blessed is the nation whose God is the LORD."

CHAPTER 27

ROE V. WADE CONTINUES TO IMPACT ... MORE THAN 54 MILLION ABORTED BABIES![1]

February 2013

A year after the United States Supreme Court handed down the Roe v. Wade decision, a group of pro-lifers prepared a March for Life in San Diego, California. On January 22, 1974, they placed an ad in the *San Diego Union* newspaper of a picture of the tiny feet of a ten-week-old unborn baby. That picture haunted my dear friend, Virginia Evers, and her husband, Ellis, living in San Diego and already activists in the pro-life movement.

The authentic photograph had quite a story behind it. Dr. Russell Sacco and a pathologist who shared his lab kept unborn babies (fetuses) in formaldehyde lined up on a shelf in the lab. Virginia wrote that Dr. Sacco, father of four children, had become acutely aware of the highly developed state of the very tiniest of these unborn babies. As a photographer, he realized the impact that these photos could make in awakening the American people to the fact that these babies were human beings from conception. Ginny told her husband, "These precious little feet should be the pro-life movement's symbol."

---

1. Since the publication of this article, the number continues to skyrocket at a gut-wrenching rate. National Right to Life reports 60,942,033 total U.S. abortions since 1973, "based on numbers reported by the Guttmacher Institute (GI) 1973–2014, with projections of 906,308 for 2015–18, based on -2.05% drop seen by CDC from 2014–15. GI has estimated possible undercounts of 3–5%, so an additional 3% is factored into the overall total [as of January 2019]." From "Abortion Statistics: United States Data and Trends," *National Right to Life Educational Foundation*, nrlc.org/uploads/factsheets/FS01AbortionintheUS.pdf.

Virginia and Ellis Evers made arrangements to have a model made of those precious feet, in exact size and shape, and ordered lapel pins to distribute along with literature. This educational endeavor took place in their home in the beginning, and the distribution grew nationally, and then internationally. Ginny and Ellis's passion for the unborn members of the human family was contagious, and the demand for their travel for speaking mushroomed. Five years later, in Dublin, Ireland, in January of 1979, the "Precious Feet" were designated as the international symbol of the pro-life movement. Millions of the pins have touched hearts worldwide, speaking through a symbol, where language barriers might exist.

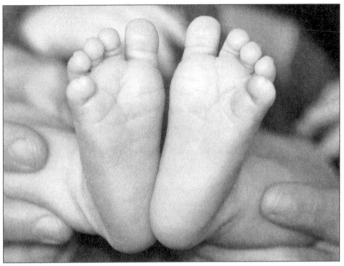

Image by Ben Kerckx from Pixabay

Ginny Evers was never idle. She was a great friend of her state governor Ronald Reagan. She urged him to run for president. I have had the joy of reading his letters to her over the many years of their friendship. Ginny introduced us personally to Governor Reagan, and later to his daughter, Maureen, whom we entertained in Alabama. Ginny also introduced us to Walter and Ruth Brennan (Walter, famous for his acting career and service to country), our friends for years. They also visited us in Marion, Alabama, to endorse Christian education. We loved visiting them in California as well.

In Ginny's many speeches, she often began with, "The Holy Bible tells us that to whom much has been given, much will be asked. The endless blessings we enjoy as Americans, through no merit of our own, are unprecedented in the history of mankind. Therefore, we have a moral obligation to oppose that which threatens our blessed land." She added this important point, "The world's problems are all interrelated. We can only influence other people if we are able to give intelligent reasons for the positions we take." Ginny's beginning point was always the sacredness of life.

The Everses sponsored homes for unwed mothers, using the proceeds from the "Precious Feet." The most successful, and the model for the others, was run by her daughter, Dinah Monahan and husband, Mike. Today Mike and Dinah run the Heritage House '76 ministry from Snowflake, Arizona. Ginny and Ellis retired nearby. Heritage House has everything you could possibly need to establish an effective a pro-life ministry and crisis pregnancy center.[2]

Two years ago, I flew to Arizona as one of many who were paying tribute to the life and ministry of Virginia Evers on her ninetieth birthday. She has enriched my life, introducing me to so many wonderful patriots. In coming to Marion, Alabama, she encouraged us in the ministry of our school and affirmed our mission for a Christ-centered education for all of life. Her influence truly spans the world. It all started with a single photo of a ten-week-old unborn baby's footprints. After one image touched one couple over one life, through one family, that photo continues dynamically to save many babies all over the world.

Jeremiah 1:4–5 says it best: "Now the Word of the LORD came to me saying, 'Before I formed you in the womb I knew you, and before you were born I consecrated you" (NASB).

Why is this so relevant today? Roe v. Wade struck down state laws protecting the life of the unborn. Justice Harry Blackmun ignored biological evidence and declared the unborn not fully persons, but merely potential persons with no legal standing as human

---

2. Heritage House '76, at hh76.org.

life. The Supreme Court decision struck down all abortion laws regardless, showing total disrespect and contempt for state laws, but more importantly, contempt for the living God whose children the aborted babies are.

This is the primary issue at hand today. What is the unborn? Don't be misled. This is the issue. And the answer is obvious. The unborn is fully human from the moment of conception. He is a member of the human family possessing the right to life. Many distractions seek to lure people into side issues. The Alabama Supreme Court has confirmed the personhood of the unborn in recent rulings, the latest court document, issued January 11, 2013, can be found in public records, for the October Term, 2012–2013, No. 1110176.[3]

Disregard for life is inherent in the Affordable Care Act. It provides access to abortifacient "morning-after" pills and such things to minors. The government threatens companies such as Hobby Lobby with heavy fines if they refuse to go along.[4] Today abortion providers perform some abortions remotely by webcam, with the physician and the patient in different rooms!

If they will, Christian schools are free to teach a Biblical worldview and lifeview across the curriculum and live out the sanctity of life before their students. If they will, pastors may freely preach the Biblical view of human value—based on God's image in His children—on controversial subjects such as abortion, embryonic stem-cell research, and cloning. Churches and pastors should actively support crisis pregnancy centers and other positive solutions to these cultural problems. Every Bible-believing church

---

3. Pete Williams, "Supreme Court won't hear appeal to restore Alabama abortion law," *NBC News* (June 28, 2019), nbcnews.com/politics/supreme-court/supreme-court-won-t-hear-appeal-restore-alabama-abortion-law-n1024516. In 2019, Alabama continues to lead the forefront, passing legislation banning an abortion procedure commonly used in the second trimester of pregnancy.
4. The Supreme Court ruled in favor of Hobby Lobby in its suit against the morning-after pill requirement, though the decision limits companies able to decline providing the pills. Burwell v. Hobby Lobby Stores Inc., *Legal Information Institute*, law.cornell.edu/supremecourt/text/13-354.

should be engaged in teaching apologetics, like we had at First Baptist Church, Montgomery, January 19 and 20, 2013. Some of the top apologists in the nation were right here to provide the tools for speaking effectively in the marketplace of ideas. Teachers offered their wisdom without charge to the community. It was a great service.

Western culture suffers attack in many places, but the first and most destructive is the denial of moral relativism and of the moral law (The Ten Commandments)—which is the basis of Western civilization—denial encouraged by Christian inertia.

CHAPTER 28

CHRISTIANITY, EDUCATION, AND THE GROWING POWER OF THE STATE

September 2013

A great theologian educator J. Gresham Machen said long ago, "If you give the bureaucrats the children, you might as well give them everything else as well."[1] He was speaking of the moral and intellectual decline as the national government continued to reach for more and more control of American education. Let's look at the moral and intellectual decline in the culture and the attack on the minds and hearts of American children through a thoroughly secular school system. Let's look at the grave injustice to children, parents, and the future of our liberty. By facing the truth, perhaps people will wake up to the dangers of today.

Faith and Culture

In early America at the time of the American Revolution, the literacy rate was astoundingly high, probably higher than any other place on earth. Americans honored labor and treasured liberty. Community groups banded together to form community schools. These typically met in churches or neighborhood schoolhouses erected for that purpose. Schools in churches were common in every colony. In New England, Pilgrim and Puritan communities chose the older and wiser women, those already successful in their

---

1. J. Gresham Machen, in testimony before Congress, *Proposed Department of Education: Joint Hearings Before the Committee on Education and Labor, United States Senate, and the Committee on Education, House of Representatives, Six-ty-Ninth Congress* (Washington, D.C.: Government Printing Office, 1926), 103.

own families and often widows, to lead the "Dame Schools." The solidly Christian culture across all the colonies embraced the Genesis account, and faith in one God, the Jehovah God of the Old and New Testaments speaking through His Word. What He spoke He accomplished, sending His Son to redeem His fallen humanity.

Education began with a focus on this one God, who brought all things into being, the Creator God, the source of all things. Children learned of their dependence on Him, their accountability to Him, how He made them in His image, and how He loves them. No wonder New Englanders didn't suffer self-esteem problems.

About 150 years ago, mainstream understanding and teaching of origins dramatically changed. Charles Darwin's book *The Origin of the Species* and its concept of evolution soon not only impacted the teaching of biology and all of the life sciences, but sabotaged the teaching of Biblical Creation in all public schools. In so doing, they effectively undermined belief in the Biblical and true God. Sadly, teaching unprovable and scientifically deficient evolution as true science to unsuspecting children has now destroyed the faith of generations of Americans.

In turn, this teaching has most astoundingly damaged our American, Christian theory of government, as politicians now view all levels of government as evolving as well. This led to the currently and largely accepted view of a "living constitution." Today, the concept of law is not fixed as historically understood by the framers of the Constitution, by their forebears for over 170 years before, and by their children for one hundred years afterward. Now all three branches of our national government ignore the checks and balances so carefully crafted into the Constitution. Likewise do state governments. The states have made themselves absolutely dependent on the national government merely to receive their thirty pieces of silver.

We are encouraged that many people today are reawakening to our very evident, self-inflicted problems. Yet many citizens have never read the Constitution, nor otherwise have any idea how to solve the onslaught of socialism and Atheism. Whom will we elect with the conviction and stamina to reverse the violations of our Constitution? Who will take courage for the battle? Who will prepare himself with historic Biblical wisdom and skills to govern? We have not focused on true American, Christian history or its justice and liberty in public schools since the late 1920s and early 1930s. I was there, and I was in one of those schools. John Dewey, with the help of other atheists, developed a methodology for the early teaching of humanism, training future teachers and school superintendents at New York's Columbia Teachers College. For centuries, the godless have waged siege upon the fundamental principles of civil and religious liberty, but never has the attack been so swift and sophisticated as in the postmodern world of today. More powerfully and efficiently than any enemy's sword, the monopolistic system of education controlled by the State now crushes the rights of parents and the rights of Christian liberty. Yet, the current gang of John Deweys and NEA leaders does not speak for every teacher in every classroom in America. They never have. Not every member of the NEA or local teacher unions approves the agenda. Tyranny never received a popular vote of approval. Though it would sneak up from behind until too powerful to combat, it is not so powerful today in America. With a well-envisioned, equipped, motivated, and active constituency, these people can be stopped.

Most articles on education are necessarily short. They seem to peer through a small window, displaying bits and pieces. However helpful and informative they might be, they rarely reveal the vast panorama of the demise in the culture. The battle has many fronts. Add, then, to the incalculable result of teaching evolution, constant attacks on religion by the secular philosophers who have produced enormous change. These include Immanuel Kant, Søren Kierkegaard, Friedrich Schleiermacher, Friedrich Nietzsche, Karl Marx, and the Romantic Movement. In our new century, add the pragmatists, the existentialists, the positivists, the neo-orthodox, and the just plain liberals (illiberal, really). This wishful, fanciful, humanistic anti-intellectualism brought about the failed mediocrity in modern education in America we now know so well, but also the demise of Western civilization in Europe.

These pagan philosophers achieved a deadly result. They deceptively but effectively separated faith and knowledge in public education, from state-supported elementary and secondary schools through the state-supported colleges and universities. In fact, everything has a religious foundation. Man cannot separate knowledge, or anything else in life, from religious presuppositions. The only question is whether knowledge rests on a pagan or a Biblical framework. The denizens of modern campuses ridicule Christian faith and practice, while blithely ignoring the rickety philosophical base of their so-called science and rationalism, denied even by their own philosophers. The anti-intellectual climate reminds one of Pilate's question, "What is truth?"[2] The ridiculous pedagogic theories of the modern university would take a column by itself. Let it be said that the liberal arts of Western civilization have vanished from most American university campuses.

For close to two centuries, on classroom walls hung the Declaration of Independence, U.S. Constitution, and the Ten Commandments. There was very little conflict between Christianity and culture, between knowledge and piety. We accepted that true knowledge must rest on the foundation of absolutes found in the Bible.

Government bureaucrats in education circles have attempted to teach character without reference to God's moral law. Attempting to train the mind without the moral law of God is to educate into a moral collapse of our country.[3] Creation and evolution are mutually exclusive worldviews regarding origins. These are dramatically conflicting approaches to how our children view themselves, their purpose in life, and the reality of eternal life. Now a government

---

2. John 18:38.
3. Furthermore, sin cannot resist sin by itself. It is helpless. We need empowerment of the Holy Spirit by faith. This is a fundamental of the Gospel. Bad education is a huge impediment to the Gospel. Train up a child and he will not depart from the training—good or evil. —Ed.

has the power to remove truth from the curriculum and replace it with moral relativism. No scientific evidence can prove any facet of evolution. It is not science. It contradicts fundamentals of science such as the second law of thermodynamics—the law of entropy—which declares that all things naturally tend toward lower energy states and disorder. True science does not contradict the Bible. The anti-intellectualism of the age is blind—willfully blind. The Institute for Creation Research and Answers-in-Genesis freely provide true scientific documentation on origins, geologic history, etc., true to Scripture.

Not only has the executive branch of government overreached, but the Congress and United States Supreme Court typically grievously overstep beyond sound Constitutional action. Just one court case involving Alabama is the Prayer Case of 1982–1983 in Mobile. The United States Supreme Court dealt a deadly blow to the First Amendment. Some readers may recall the landmark case in Mobile County, where Ishmael Jaffree filed against the schools to forbid simple prayer in school: prayers such as, "God is great, God is good, let us thank Him for our food." Judge Brevard Hand made a constitutional ruling in line with the First Amendment religious rights, but the United States Supreme Court overturned his ruling and built its own Wall of Separation theory for the new interpretation of the First Amendment. The Supreme Court has since rendered many such cases on this new so-called interpretation of the *living* constitution, as they proclaim it. The Supreme Court has taken jurisdiction over church-state matters at will, it seems to this writer. Will the states be strong enough to band together to amend the Constitution to restore the original intent of the Founders for a Supreme Court limited to individual cases?

Senator Jesse Helms summarized unconstitutional actions by the Supreme Court as falling into two categories.

1. The Court invades the prerogatives of the legislative branch by amending national statutes.[4]

---

4. See Bob Jones University v. United States, 461 U.S. 574 (1983).

2. It alters the Constitution without a constitutional
   amendment.

Today American liberty is being destroyed. The love of liberty
was taught so diligently to my mind, that the love of liberty lives
in my heart. My husband and I dedicated ourselves to pass on that
love of liberty to our children. We understood that liberty is not
preserved by ink on a page, but by that love written on the heart.
We may be called on to pay the price that the Scottish Covenanters
paid in the 1600s, when they, at great sacrifice, preserved religious
liberty for the faithful.

There can be a revolt against the tyranny that is upon us, such as
the French Revolution. That would be a tragedy. There is another
way, and that is for every person in the nation who embraces the
God of Truth to become involved in taking back Christian self-government, and in doing so, restore the Constitution.

Christianity is a worldview, but it is also a system of government
that worked for us for a long time, and with God's help we can
restore it. Only in this manner will truth prevail and will we once
more enjoy a just, free, productive, and generous society.

CHAPTER 29

AMERICANS PAY FOR THEIR OWN DESTRUCTION THROUGH EDUCATION & GOVERNMENT BUREAUCRACY

July 2013

D r. Francis Schaeffer wrote over forty years ago, "We are on the verge of the largest revolution the world has ever seen—the control and shaping of men through the abuse of genetic knowledge, and chemical and psychological conditioning. Will people accept it? I don't think that they would accept it if they had not already been taught to accept the presuppositions that lead to it and if they were not in such despair. But many have accepted the presuppositions and they are in despair. Many of our secular schools have consistently taught these presuppositions, and unhappily many of our Christian lower schools and colleges have taught the crucial subjects no differently than the secular schools."[1]

What are these presuppositions that are so basic as to dethrone God and elevate man's interests and values as supreme? From the early primary grades, the schools teach children evolution. Just as proposed in the *Humanist Manifesto*, the public school textbooks teach evolution as truth. It teaches:

1. The universe is self-existing and not created.

2. Man is a part of nature and has emerged through a self-generated, gradual, continuous process.

---

1. Francis Schaeffer, *Back to Freedom and Dignity* (London: Inter-Varsity Press, 1972), 44.

3. A merely materialistic view of life, rejecting the traditional view of mind, body, and soul.

4. Interaction with his natural environment and social heritage shapes man's culture, rather than any supernatural faith.

Teaching evolution as fact is necessary for secular humanism to prevail in education. A leading scientist of fifty years ago wrote, "the Theory of Evolution itself [is] a theory universally accepted, not because it can be proved by logically coherent evidence to be true, but because the only alternative, special creation, is clearly incredible."[2]

Secular humanists have been winning the battle for the minds and hearts of the children of America through government schools, which most Christians continue to attend. The evolution hypothesis (it ought not to be elevated to theory since it is empirically such a poor one), falsely accepted as scientific fact, has destroyed the basis for theistic education that solidly grounded early America and continued until around the beginning of the 1900s. It cannot be disputed that John Dewey had more to do with the retraining of educators to a materialistic belief system, such as regarding origins, than any other single man. The amazing thing is that they did so with few questioning materialistic assumptions and with a shocking lack of real science behind them.

Dr. Henry Morris and Dr. John Whitcomb sounded the alarm in their early books, *The Genesis Flood* and *The Twilight of Evolution*. Dr. Morris wrote:

> The evolutionary origin of the universe of life, and of man, is taught as scientific fact even to elementary school children in probably most public schools.... The Biblical record of origins is ignored, sometimes allegorized, or even ridiculed. Such concepts as Creation, the Fall, the Curse, Sin, Redemption, etc...., which really are the most basic facts of science and history ... are taboo.

---

2. D. M. S. Watson, "Adaptation," *British Association for the Advancement of Science Report of the Ninety-Seventh Meeting* (London: Office of the British Association, 1930), 95, available online at archive.org/details/reportofbritisha30adva.

This is a remarkable phenomenon in a nation founded largely on Christianity and the Bible. Undoubtedly, many factors have contributed to this …, but it is highly probable that the introduction of the 19th-century doctrines of evolutionary optimism is back of most of it.[3]

Presuppositions and principles guide all education, just as Biblical principles guided us at Emerald Mountain Christian School, and all Principle Approach® schools associated with the Foundation for American Christian Education curriculum. Just as Biblical principles guide all subjects in the curriculum, humanist principles guide the education of secular humanism. Pagan religious secular humanism represents a set of morals and faith opposite of the Biblical view. What are some of these pagan tenets? Above all, they do not believe in God, the Bible, the supernatural, or eternity. They believe that such faith matters are irrelevant, even harmful. They believe in the supremacy of human reason, denying the original sin of Adam and Eve, and the Fall. Using evolutionary theory and Darwin's social and cultural application, they believe in the inevitability of progress and higher and higher forms of life. (Everyone loves to think of himself personally as the highest form—god.) They view the government as a saving institution. If that means that totalitarianism becomes necessary in government to enforce solutions, then so be it. The materialist can justify anything to himself.

They place much importance on their unique view of science, psychology, and sociology. Rather than emphasize the conscience and responsibility of individual self-government, students must learn social responsibility, that society must collectively—not as

---

3. Henry M. Morris, *The Twilight of Evolution* (Grand Rapids, MI: Baker, 1963), 19–20. Note, this was written over fifty years ago. Dr. Morris ably pointed out in his books and many winning debates with evolutionists that organic evolution denies one of the most fundamental and well-established scientific laws—Newton's second law of thermodynamics. This *law of entropy* states that all energy tends to move from a higher state to a lower state—from organization and meaning to disorganization and uselessness. Evolution requires the opposite. —Ed.

individuals—take responsibility for man's actions. Whether considering crime or deviancy, social environment is causative. Man is merely a victim of his social or environmental circumstances, and so has every excuse for his degeneracy. Denying the Biblical premise that through Christ God changes us fundamentally in our being, materialism superficially depends merely on manipulating behavior. Modern atheistic psychology is antichristian to the core.[4]

Friends, are we not more than a bundle of behaviors determined by the environment? Do we live by situational-ethics morality with no absolute standards? Is this the way we want our children and grandchildren to live? Anything goes?

Decades ago, Barbara Morris wrote a book *Change Agents in the Schools*.[5] She explained how the university teaches progressive teachers to undermine and convert the beliefs, attitudes, and behaviors of students, without the knowledge or consent of parents. The big push for "values clarification" meant that students should be liberated to choose their own values rather than the admonition of parents and grandparents. She pointed out how helpless young students are as captive victims in the classroom. Her book challenged parents to help them be "worthy of the blood shed to obtain religious liberty for us."

To add to the poor job public schools do, their mandatory attendance rules provide no ground for agreement between home and school. Children must attend. Yet parents cannot choose their teacher, curriculum, or methods. Teachers have no institutional

---

4. Rarely do materialists honestly deal with their religious presuppositions. They ignore the fact that they have no rational basis for believing in a self-existing universe out of nothing. Nor do they have a rational basis for meaning, love, mind, goodness, or any other element of moral or material life. Their own philosophers fail them. Thus, Jean Paul Sartre says take a leap of faith. Live in God's world and its laws, but deny Him and any but materialistic laws. This nihilism is closer to Buddhism than to a rational philosophy. It is decidedly religious—anything but purely rational. Meanwhile, the applied faith of Christ founded in Scripture produces a robust rationality, bringing understanding to all important things in life. —Ed.

5. Barbara Morris, *Change Agents in the Schools* (Ellicott City, MD: Barbara M. Morris Report, 1979), 257.

incentive to support the home. The home has no relational incentive to support the teacher or school. The resulting prevailing condition is an adversarial one between home and school. As public schools moved from local to state control, the situation worsened.

Humanists and communists have much in common. They both deny the supernatural and divine revelation. They promote world government in hopes of improving the human race and society. They seek to prevail with their worldview by eliminating other worldviews. They claim to believe in individual autonomy for man to choose his own values and life styles—situational morality. Make up your own mind about sex, drugs, etc. Sex-education programs teach a radical view of attitudes and values, as public schools distribute condoms to teens. They have discarded abstinence sex education.

The Silent Majority in America is about to wake up. We must listen once more to our heritage of moral values. We must speak out, though Christians and Jews in America may face a plight similar to that faced by Christians in the Roman Empire. To make your voice heard requires more than just church membership. It means we must inform ourselves about the dangers we face, about the destruction of our nation as a Christian constitutional republic. We must learn and understand what God requires of us from Scripture—Biblical wisdom. Unless the Silent Majority become warriors for religious liberty, we will indeed pay for our own destruction, and our grandchildren will bear the brunt.

In this chapter we have dealt with abusive government education, and not covered other abuses of government, the root of those things that threaten us politically. Next, we deal with other abuses that threaten our liberty, civil and religious.

On March 23, 1775, Patrick Henry rose from a pew in St. John's Church in Richmond, and said, "Is life so dear, or peace so sweet, as to be purchased at the price of chains and slavery? Forbid it, Almighty God! I know not what course others may take, but as for me, give me liberty, or give me death!"

CHAPTER 30

UNBELIEVABLE BUT TRUE:
OUR MOST FUNDAMENTAL AND CHERISHED
FREEDOMS ARE IN DANGER

People of Faith Must Wake Up and Sound the Alarm

August 2013

Who has inherited more life than I, or fallen heir to better things than these: THE WORD, The Word, the word, a spirit and a mind to know them all, and human voice speaking to the three.

—Betsy Barber Bancroft, Alabama Poet

The WORD that Betsy points to is the WORD that inspired the passengers on every ship that sailed to the early settlements, every colonial charter of the colonies, every colonial constitution, every recognition and setting apart of the Lord's Day, the purpose of the first chaplains, the circulation of over 250 million Bibles in the first century of our national life, the *why* of the Declaration of Independence and the *how* of the United States Constitution. This WORD points to how to build a Christian nation.

These facts are all thoroughly documented in American history, with written words arising from the holy WORD referenced in Betsey Bancroft's poem—namely the Bible. We find them in original source documents. Sadly today, another vocabulary of words has come to dominate our postmodern world. Many words have taken on meanings that purposely distort the history of our country. Students in public schools have not learned the truth of their own heritage of religious liberty with its significance. The truth of history teaches the legacy of God's providential leading our forefathers, and the founding fathers of our Christian constitutional republic. God is the Great Creator of reality.

Corrupt views of history focus instead on men, magnifying every kind of fault and failing among us. Men then use those personal failings to condemn whole eras and movements, to displace them in the minds and hearts of the current generation. Then they rewrite history to indoctrinate with a new narrative to replace the old one. This is exactly what the humanists do. Rather, when we focus on God's providence, we are thankful and instructed by His workmanship in and among fallible men. God creates these better expressions in history. He instructs men in His Bible and then enables them by His Holy Spirit. This is the providential view of history.

The truths of the Bible composed the overriding influence in America's founding, growth, and blessing. In the Christian era, solemn oaths to that Supreme Being referred specifically to the God of the Old and New Testaments. The Founders included such in constitutions, statutes, and instruments. Oaths in court promised honest testimony from witnesses who feared the Mighty God and His judgment. Early Americans established no charter or constitution in the colonies or the United States either infidel or anti-Christian, and certainly with no pretense of moral neutrality. However, in our nation today exists, by government regulation, a hostility—even a repudiation of Christianity. Many of these attacks imposed upon the American people come by those appointed to high positions of power, not elected by "We the People." We have allowed godless men to replace our original common-law government of laws, with subjective rule by sinful bureaucrats bearing much power with few constraints on them.

The book, *No Higher Power*, by Phyllis Schlafly and George Neumayer,[1] documents many attacks on our freedom of conscience. Many in the fields of health care are aware of the dangers of Obamacare through the Health and Human Services (HHS) mandate for all employers to pay for contraceptives, sterilizations, and abortion-inducing pills for all employees.[2] Ever-more employers are trying to opt out of the program, understandably.

Cardinal Timothy Dolan, NYC, addressed the problem this way: "In effect, the President is saying that we have a year to figure out how to adjust our conscience."[3]

The battle with people of faith is not new. Karl Marx saw faith as the "opium" of the masses.[4] As typical among godless sinners, the leaders of the French Revolution were intent on the destruction of traditionally religious people from the face of public life. They must silence God's voice in the public turmoil. Today, the godless must again silence our voice in the public square. Since 2009, pro-life nurses and doctors no longer have protection at nationally funded hospitals to opt out of performing acts they consider morally wrong. Dr. Albert Mohler, president of the Southern Baptist Seminary, speaking of this administration regulation, called it "a tyrannical trampling of individual conscience by the power of the state."[5]

While national law demands that the president of the U.S. call for a national day of prayer, the Obama administration dropped the practice of holding this revered event in the White House, although President Obama attended other observances associated with the National Day of Prayer.[6]

---

1. Phyllis Schlafly and George Neumayr, *No Higher Power: Obama's War on Religious Freedom* (Washington, D.C.: Regnery Publishing, 2012).
2. Schlafly and Neumayr, *No Higher Power*, 2–3.
3. As of mid-2019, the Trump administration has essentially exempted conscientious objectors to the program, but the HHS mandate continues to be a political football.
4. Karl Marx, *Critique of Hegel's 'Philosophy of Right'* (Cambridge: Cambridge University Press, 1982), 131.
5. Schlafly and Neumayr, *No Higher Power*, 22.
6. Once more, thanks to the Lord, President Trump has revived active observance.

The Obama administration dropped the voucher system allowing children in the inner city of Washington, D.C., to attend the Catholic schools that offered a superior educational opportunity. There is no way to estimate the value of Catholic hospitals, assisted living institutions, children's homes, and other social-service networks which reach out to those in need. Are nuns, bishops, and priests expected to lay their faith aside and contribute to contraceptive-driven promiscuity? Would they require me—an administrator of a Christian school primarily existing to teach the orthodox, Biblical Christian faith—to lay aside our primary purpose and reason for our very existence these past forty-nine years? Would I knowingly contribute to the fornication of young people by passing out contraceptives and calling it a constitutional right?

Some Christians have long objected to secular schools and their teachers taking over the responsibility for comprehensive sex education, void of moral admonitions, and accepting of safe-sex premises.[7] One report in July 2010 reported that the Department of Education spent $190 million dollars on the newly created comprehensive sex-education curriculum that replaced the abstinence-based sex education.[8] The authors of *No Higher Power* bring the question to the front: "If traditional religious or moral values are not to guide law, what is to guide it? If the secular state is to impose its values and deny the people's 'belief liberty,' on what will the state base its values? This is the real revolutionary thrust of modern liberalism and of the Obama administration."[9] Men and women are in place to execute these sweeping changes.

Will the "hate crimes" legislation, passed in 2009, be interpreted in such a way that opinions will become "crimes?"[10]

---

7. Too many continue to send their children to schools of indoctrination, instruments of centralized government power. Published historic estimates typically indicate that up to 90 percent of Christians continue to send their children to public schools.

8. Schlafly and Neumayr, *No Higher Power*, 27.

9. Schlafly and Neumayr, *No Higher Power*, 32.

10. Schlafly and Neumayr, *No Higher Power*, 33.

The Justice Department abandoned the Defense of Marriage Act long before the Supreme Court did. In 2011, the administration ordered the Pentagon to authorize same sex marriages on military bases.

Problems with the faith issue in the military are numerous. For a time, it was forbidden to mention the name of Jesus Christ at burials in the Houston national cemetery, but the ban was lifted, after complaints.[11] In 2011, regulations instructed that Bibles were not to be given out at Walter Reed Hospital, but that ban was lifted after an outcry.[12] Imagine a soldier, who fought to defend the Constitution at the risk of his life, having his First Amendment right taken away as he is recovering on a hospital bed.

Also, in 2011, the Air Force dropped the long-time support of the Operation Christmas Child charity that sends needed gifts to children all over the world.[13] The ministry, led by Franklin Graham of the Billy Graham Association, is probably the greatest, most effective and best-run international charity for children. The millions of shoe boxes packed with needed items are hand delivered by people of faith to children of all races, faiths, and heritages, worldwide.

Having a husband and two brothers who proudly fought in World War II, each one testified to their faith and the faith of their comrades as helping them survive the terror. To have our military remove the logos and other signs of the recognition of God, in any context, is a detriment to the men and women in uniform, men and women to whom we owe our safety.[14] Can you imagine what will happen to the morale of the military if it is secularized, with no place to share faith and practice? When it comes to assignments and promotions, what will be the course for those chaplains and soldiers who have strong Christian convictions? One admiral is

---

11. Schlafly and Neumayr, *No Higher Power*, 37.
12. Schlafly and Neumayr, *No Higher Power*, 38–39.
13. Schlafly and Neumayr, *No Higher Power*, 39–40.
14. Schlafly and Neumayr, *No Higher Power*, 44–45.

reported to have said of chaplains, "If you cannot get in line, resign your commission."[15]

Muslims in America have a different reception, it seems. The approach to Islam is one of tolerance and accommodation. The Justice Department hoped to give a civilian trial to the planners of 9/11. Ramadan has been celebrated in the State Dining Room of the White House.[16]

Schlafly's book gives great attention to the influence of those who mentored President Obama—Saul Alinsky and William Ayers. These men place importance on mass organization for power, the ideology that drives it—an ideology that views our country as oppressive and racist—and the majority of our citizens as victims of an unjust economic system. The goal is the leveling of society.[17] There is no doubt that the social-justice agenda is achieved by the redistribution of wealth by the State, made necessary by "past mistakes in our history." I have had so many former students meet this mindset in colleges and universities they attended. These leftist ideologues push their indoctrination. They say that Christianity has brought oppression, and they must condemn and destroy the resulting lifestyles of "privilege." The challenge we face above all is that so many of our Christian homes, churches, and schools do not confront the issues this radical agenda raises against us. We often do not teach young people to defend their faith. Many have not learned to recognize the issues that threaten their future. Are young adults still adolescents by choice? Or have we neglected to inculcate godly wisdom?

We can accept the pagan agenda we see before our eyes, or we can turn back to the founding principles of our Christian history. Above all the evils of the postmodern world, the greatest threat is against the institution of family. The State will gladly take over your family. Faith in the State to care for all needs is the goal. Cradle-to-grave government.

---

15. Schlafly and Neumayr, *No Higher Power*, 119.
16. Schlafly and Neumayr, *No Higher Power*, 100.
17. Schlafly and Neumayr, *No Higher Power*, 63.

Goal: Remaking Education: Almost Completed

The authority of parents is already undermined, and children are viewed as wards of the state. Children are cared for by "the village" at younger ages, for more hours, for longer school terms. No-fault divorce, deviant lifestyles, and ideological feminism shatter families. The dreadful economic policies of the twentieth century drove both parents—not just one parent—into the workplace full time, making the long-enjoyed traditional family life the exception rather than the rule in America. Again, we say, the State will eagerly take over and fill the spiritual vacuum Christians leave.

Goal: A Secularized Society

Statistics regarding numbers of families in church show a decline every year for more than a decade. Most people would stammer if you asked them to articulate their world- and lifeview, their underlying philosophy of life and reality—their motive in life. God's Word gives us the framework for daily living, not a life without problems, but a living faith and practice to overcome the problems we must face.

A Secularized Society?

We should live our whole life in response to truth. For the people of Biblical faith, no secular division in life exists. "Whether therefore ye eat, or drink, or whatsoever ye do, do all to the glory of God" (First Corinthians 10:31). Even table manners matter! Moreover, we ought in all things we do to bring "into captivity every thought to the obedience of Christ" (Second Corinthians 10:5). Our Creator, our Heavenly Father, is indeed Lord of all. He is the Governor of His created universe. Men and nations are blessed as they live in harmony with the foundational propositional truths of God's revelation. Jesus said, "Ye shall know the truth, and the truth shall make you free" (John 8:32).

Friends, if we want to confront the cultural and moral tragedies, the injustices in society, the attack on morality and conscience, there is one way to a life of liberty, peace, grace, mercy, and forgiveness. We must get out of our comfort zone and enter the worldview debate in the public square, in the defense of truth. Jude, warning from history regarding the ungodly, writes, "Beloved, when I gave all diligence to write unto you of the common salvation, it was needful for me to write unto you, and exhort you that ye should earnestly contend for the faith which was once delivered unto the saints" (Jude 3).

CHAPTER 31

The Lord Hath Done Great Things for Us; Whereof We Are Glad (Psalm 126:3)

Individual Religious Liberty in Practice

November 2013

We will repeat the tragic lessons of history if we remove history from our nation's memory as we have done for several generations. Social studies replaced America's providential Christian history in public schools nearly a century ago. How many adults know what sacrifice and triumph brought about our uniquely American holiday tradition of Thanksgiving?

Through brief bits of the story here, let's look at this American legacy, our own American heritage. Then let us embrace that heritage to fuel a true Thanksgiving celebration this year. Go back with me to the Pilgrim Fathers of 1620, as they embarked on the adventure of colony planting with no experience and no skills for the task, only seeking freedom of worship and self-government.

Picture the wild land and the wild sea, the bitter cold winter of 1620, and the illnesses costing half of their lives the first year. The mercenary shareholders who contracted with the Pilgrims to capitalize on their adventure required them to practice communism in labor and supply. This imposition denied them private property rights and other incentives.

If communism would ever work, it should have worked for this colony. A deep religious faith, conscience, and love for one another compelled them. Likewise, they possessed a superior work ethic.

Governor William Bradford took over the leadership of the colony upon the death of Governor Carver in the first year. Bradford governed almost continually for thirty-seven years, until his death. His literary gift left us a detailed and documented history that is a treasure for every lover of history and every seeker of truth.[1] The lesson of the Pilgrims rejecting communism can be valuable today and help us to come against another similar "Pernicious System," as they called it. That system is strong in our postmodern world today.

After abiding by the terms of their contract for two years, seeing that communism had brought the colony to the verge of starvation and ultimate ruin, Governor Bradford "had the courage and wisdom to cut the knot he could not untie."[2] He divided the land among the families, and placed every single person into a family unit. Attitudes changed. Now, mothers with children would go willingly in the fields to help their husbands. Wives were pleased to wash the clothing of their family rather than collectively. Working their own field, laboring together as a family, brought peace and incentive, and Bradford wrote: "Any generall wante or famine hath not been amongst them since to this day." Every adult shared in the responsibility to ensure the investors suffered no loss, and through private ownership and free enterprise, a successful and profitable fur trade developed. Commerce, industry, and brotherly love combined for success.

Yes, abolishing communism may have been a violation of the contract, but Governor Bradford saw that the system as pernicious (destructive). The colony suffered a life-and-death struggle for survival. He made a defining decision to institute free enterprise.

---

1. William Bradford, *Of Plimoth Plantation, from the Original Manuscript*. This book has had numerous publications, e.g., (Boston: Wright & Potter Printing Company, 1899). It is also available online from numbers of sources, such as gutenberg.org. We highly recommend this fundamental document of American history. —Ed.

2. Edward Eggleston, *The Beginners of a Nation: A History of the Source and Rise of the Earliest English Settlements in America with Special Reference to the Life and Character of the People* (New York: D. Appleton and Company, 1896), 180.

Why do we remember this little colony, with never more than a few thousand people? God's providence is dramatically shown in their story. In their own words, they prayed to be "stepping stones for others" to migrate, and indeed they were. They were the forerunners of the great Puritan migration of the 1630s. History documents their profound influence on the Puritan Bay Colony. For example, the Puritans abandoned their unworkable Presbyterianism with session in England, for Congregationalism in their churches. In later years, Puritan masters would migrate throughout the colonies to educate the children, spreading the love of Christian liberty. Upon the Pilgrim heritage of the love of Biblical literacy applied to all of life, Massachusetts and Connecticut established Harvard and Yale seminaries.

When the Mayflower ship returned to England, not one Pilgrim went aboard. That little band of believers introduced a powerful new force on this continent—that of individual religious liberty in practice. Unable to reform the Church of England, now they could walk with God. They could raise their families in a church congregation guided by God's Word alone, not dictated by the king and not by the civil magistrate.

The glories of Christianity in England are to be traced in the sufferings of confessors and martyrs in the sixteenth and seventeenth centuries; and it was under the influence of Christian principles, imbibed at this very period, that the Mayflower brought over the band of Pilgrims to Plymouth.... We should never forget that the prison, the scaffold, and the stake were stages in the march of civil and religious liberty which our forefathers had to travel, in order that we might obtain our present liberty.... Before our children remove their religious connexions ... before they leave the old paths of God's Word ... before they barter their birthright for a mess of pottage—let us place in their hands this chronicle of the glorious days of the suffering Churches, and let them know that they are the sons of the men "of whom the world was not worthy," and whose sufferings for conscience' sake are here monumentally recorded.

—John Overton Choules, August 12, 1843

Looking at that simple first Thanksgiving, one dynamic rises above all others. This small group of survivors labored to bring glory to God for His providence. They had survived hunger, disease, native attacks, unreasonable demands of their shareholders, and the deaths of spouses, children, and best friends. Living in a wilderness, they utterly depended and faithfully relied on God to sustain them. They rejoiced in freedom of worship and in the civil liberty of Christian self-government. They had been successful in establishing a covenant relationship with their Indian neighbors, who were present at the first Thanksgiving. Can you not see the hand of God using those first seeds, which brought forth for us individual liberty of conscience, Christian self-government, and ultimately a Christian constitutional republic? May it be restored today. A day of Thanksgiving has continued as beloved tradition in our nation. *The Journals of the Continental Congress* record a proclamation by the United States Congress assembled on Saturday, October 18, 1783. These words are a portion of that proclamation:

Whereas it has pleased the Supreme Ruler of all human events, to dispose the hearts of the later belligerent powers to put a period to the effusion of human blood, by proclaiming a cessation of all hostilities by sea and land, and these United States are not only happily rescued from the dangers and calamities to which they have been so long exposed, but their freedom, sovereignty and independence ultimately acknowledged.... The interposition of Divine Providence in our favor hath been most abundantly and most graciously manifested, and the citizens of these United States have every reason for praise and gratitude to the God of their salvation. Impressed, therefore, with an exalted sense of the blessings by which we are surrounded, and of our entire dependence on that Almighty Being, from whose goodness and bounty they are derived, the United States in Congress assembled do recommend it to the several States, to set apart the second Thursday in December next, as a day of public thanksgiving, that all the people may then assemble to celebrate with grateful hearts and united voices, the praises of their Supreme and all bountiful Benefactor, for His numberless favors and mercies.

The Proclamation further leads in offering prayers for forgiveness, for wisdom to be granted, for prosperity in every good work, for peace among the nations, for blessings in the labors of the people, for commerce and navigation, for education and the seminaries and all means of education, for true religion to flourish, and that the world be filled with His glory. It was done and witnessed on October 18th, 1783.

John Hancock, governor of Massachusetts, called for a Day of Thanksgiving to be established, in a proclamation dated November 8, 1783. In his proclamation, he praises the Lord for the "Unanimity and Resolution to adhere to our just Rights." He refers to God as our "powerful Ally to assist us in supporting" those just rights. He pleads to continue in "the light of the blessed Gospel, and secure to us, in the fullest Extent, the Rights of Conscience in Faith and Worship." And so much more is in his proclamation. We see pure Biblical Christianity expressed strongly here, and in the virtue of the character of these Founders.

This Thanksgiving season, as a family and as a blessed nation, let us have a true celebration of praise and thankfulness to the Lord Who has done such great things for us.

One excellent source for these proclamations is *The Bible and the Constitution*, published by the Foundation for American Christian Education of Chesapeake, Virginia. I urge readers to go to their website and learn of their publications on America's Christian history (FACE.net). Also, they publish the Webster's 1828 *Dictionary of the English Language*, which assembles the language of liberty.

The Mayflower Compact, by Jean Leon Gerome Ferris, 1620

The Mayflower Compact (1620)

In ye name of God, Amen. We whose names are underwriten, the loyall subjects of our dread soveraigne Lord, King James, by ye grace of God, of Great Britaine, France, & Ireland king, defender of ye faith, &c., haveing undertaken, for ye glorie of God, and advancemente of ye Christian faith, and honour of our king & countrie, a voyage to plant ye first colonie in ye Northerne parts of Virginia, doe by these presents solemnly & mutually in ye presence of God, and one of another, covenant & combine our selves togeather into a civill body politick, for our better ordering & preservation & furtherance of ye ends aforesaid; and by vertue hearof to enacte, constitute, and frame such just & equall lawes, ordinances, acts, constitutions & offices, from time to time, as shall be thought most meete &

convenient for ye generall good of ye Colonie, unto which we promise all due submission and obedience. In witnes wherof we have hereunder subscribed our names at Cap-Codd ye 11. of November, in ye year of ye raigne of our soveraigne lord, King James, of England, France, & Ireland ye eighteenth, and by Scotland ye fiftie fourth. Ano:Dom. 1620.

John Carver	Edward Tilley	Degory Priest
William Bradford	John Tilley	Thomas Williams
Edward Winslow	Francis Cooke	Gilbert Winslow
William Brewster	Thomas Rogers	Edmund Margeson
Isaac Allerton	Thomas Tinker	Peter Browne
Myles Standish	John Rigdale	Richard Britteridge
John Alden	Edward Fuller	George Soule
Samuel Fuller	John Turner	Richard Clarke
Christopher Martin	Francis Eaton	Richard Gardiner
William Mullins	James Chilton	John Allerton
William White	John Crackston	Thomas English
Richard Warren	John Billington	Edward Dotey
John Howland	Moses Fletcher	Edward Leister
Stephen Hopkins	John Goodman	

AMERICA'S INVASION BY SOCIALISM: THE ROAD TO DESPOTIC POWER!

April 2016

The polity and government of these United States are original. Let us say it again—original and peculiar. It has two great elements of divisions of power:

a. That of the states (with their lesser jurisdictions) exercising local self-government, and

b. That of the nation, formed by a voluntary union of states.

The motto on the Great Seal of the nation highlights that origin: *E pluribus unum*, confirming that we find our beginning in the thirteen colonies and their voluntary union. Let us not forget that they based their union on that idea of local self-government as primary. In expanding spheres of less and less intrusive power over the local, the state developed, with the concept of union. These ideas formed the nation.

For early Americans, the individual citizen ought to be totally free to pursue the opportunities of his life within just law. In modernism with its prevailing centralization, we completely lose recognition of this concept. American liberty is unique in history.

Ruling monarchs through history, and even to the present age, have typically deprived people of the power of local rule, creating much suffering. A small, powerful, and wealthy elite ruling class creates a vast serfdom of poor people, often merely slaves. In some cultures such as ancient England, and a few others with historic Biblical influence, a tangible dream of local self-rule and liberty inspired them. In practice, only a few representative assemblies could frame laws under which they might realize this dream, as for a time with the Anglo-Saxon witenagemot.[1]

While many continued to dream of liberty and just laws, Christians, in particular, had the basis of the Word of God to justify their dreams and considered their aspirations as not only the advancement of the Christian faith, but as the honor due to the king and queen.

The Pilgrim story is one of the most revered of all in American history, and justly so. Their covenant signed aboard the Mayflower ship provided for a code of laws, a public authority, a local government. In early New England, the local political life grew in terms of towns, while in Virginia, in counties. In Virginia, political life had a distinctly aristocratic makeup, and in New England, a more democratic makeup.

Our ancestors built a system of government on the rule of law based in a Biblical Christian morality. Not every citizen professed and practiced Christian faith, but the vast majority realized that no government could be secure, nor could citizens be safe, without moral absolutes in practice, codified in the rule of law.

It is interesting that the early citizens of Connecticut created a little republic by the federation of independent towns, with primary sovereignty remaining with each town. It is perhaps our earliest model of what would become a republican form of government.

The Founders and Framers of our independence and Constitution shared the love of liberty above all else, with the passion and drive to protect it. The cause of liberty and justice surpassed any and all obligations to the king and queen of England. Their concepts of justice came from the Bible.

Moving ahead from the 1800s to the twentieth century, we are stunned at the changes in our culture. Our losses of liberty and justice are a mystery to many citizens who do not yet recognize the

---

1. John A. Eidsmoe, *Historical and Theological Foundations of Law*, vol. II (Ventura, CA: Norsdkog Publishing, 2016), 821–23.

seriousness of the disease of socialism invading our nation. We can trace modern socialism back to the days of the French Revolution in the mid-1800s, the Russian Empire of 1917, China in the 1940s, and Cambodia in the 1970s.

Since the mid-twentieth century, socialism has reared its head in many Western nations. In America, we first heard it introduced as progressivism. Progressives work within the system to gain their programs one at a time—whether universal health care or free government education for all, from kindergarten through high school and beyond. While Europe largely welcomed socialism, it rejected its first cousin communism. When Marx first published *The Communist Manifesto*, it obviously targeted Christianity and morality as its enemy. Communism must overthrow the social and political order birthed by that faith.

The *Manifesto* lists ten planks to advance communism:

1. Abolition of property in land and application of all rents of land to public purposes.

2. A heavy progressive or graduated income tax.

3. Abolition of all right of inheritance.

4. Confiscation of the property of all emigrants and rebels.

5. Centralization of credit in the hands of the State, by means of a national bank with State capital and an exclusive monopoly.

6. Centralisation of the means of communication and transport in the hands of the State.

7. Extension of factories and instruments of production owned by the State; the bringing into cultivation of wastelands, and the improvement of the soil generally in accordance with a common plan.

8. Equal liability of all to labour. Establishment of industrial armies, especially for agriculture.

9. Combination of agriculture with manufacturing industries; gradual abolition of the distinction between town and

country, by a more equable distribution of the population over the country.

10. Free education for all children in public schools. Abolition of children's labour in its [then] present form. Combination of education with industrial production, etc., etc.[2]

Already implemented in America are the following:

Note No. 2 from *Manifesto*: Our now heavy progressive income tax in America

Note No. 5 from *Manifesto*: Our Central Bank, monopolistic, created in 1913 through the Federal Reserve Act

Note No. 6 from *Manifesto*: The radical changes in control of communication, transportation, and media

Note No. 10 from *Manifesto*: Government schools are educating about 97 percent of our children with school-to-work being a high priority of socialists, as well as Common Core and its national mandates.

Progress toward government land ownership has also reduced landowners to tenancy through property taxes, where default results in confiscation. Likewise, socialists have achieved a partial confiscation of inherited wealth through inheritance taxes. With a few companies dominating communications and the Internet, and with government regulation, we are only a step away from government control. U.S. cities are increasingly adopting the United Nations' Agenda 21 designed to limit residential locations, contributing to Note No. 9 of the *Manifesto*.

Yes, we can acknowledge that socialism has come to America. The socialist agenda is clear. They oppose the ideals of America's founding and oppose constitutional government as was created in our nation. Full Soviet communism is only a step away from the socialist agenda.

In the lifetime of this writer, progressives have managed to invade every aspect of what we traditionally call the private sector.

---

2. Karl Marx and Frederick Engels, *Manifesto of the Communist Party* (Chicago: Charles H. Kerr & Company, 1906), 45–46.

Today's socialist candidates believe that socialism can be achieved by popular consent. Gradually over the past decades, they have achieved the forty-hour workweek, the minimum wage, national control over banking, agriculture, manufacturing, health care, and government subsidies for college. They are well on their way to proclaiming victory.

Socialism as an economic order is a failure. It is retrogressive, not progressive in any positive sense, because it defies God's commandments protecting individuals from the ravages of sinful men. Examples of failures include Medicare, Medicaid, and Obamacare. All stifle free enterprise.

The positions of the socialists against morality include an attack on the nuclear family. For example, they advocate sexual license, abortion, homosexuality, gender fluidity, and the sexualization of children.

An excellent writer and researcher on socialism, Charles Scaliger, quotes Alexis De Tocqueville, a French legislator at the time of the French Revolution. This legislator gave worthy advice following the overthrow of the royals. He identified socialism and warned of three key ideologies of the movement invading France.

1. The "appeal to the material passions of man."
2. An attack on the principle of private property, believing that it "is the origin of all the ills of the world."
3. "Opposition to personal liberty and scorn for individual reason, a complete contempt for the individual."

Tocqueville told his fellow legislators that socialists "call, in fact, for the forfeiture, to a greater or less degree, of human liberty, to the point where, were I to attempt to sum up what socialism is, I would say that it was simply a new system of serfdom."[3]

Tocqueville was popular in America due to his travels here and his praise for our Christian constitutional republic. People on both sides of the Atlantic Ocean highly regarded him as a political philosopher. We would do well to heed his words today.

---

3. Alexis De Tocqueville, "Tocqueville on Socialism" (1848), trans. Ronald Hamowy, available online at *Online Library of Liberty*, oll.libertyfund.org.

Tocqueville Observed Reverence for the Rule of Law in America

With 227 years of living under the Constitution and Bill of Rights, God has blessed us as no other nation on earth. We must be vigilant, however. Much has changed in the Constitution, and not all amendments to the Constitution have promoted liberty.

For example, the Seventeenth Amendment stripped political power from the state legislatures, which had selected the U.S. senators for each state. This undermined relational, representative government and Federalism. The Sixteenth Amendment gave the government power to tax personal incomes directly and has led to the present-day IRS. The Federal Reserve Act and the private bank, operate beyond the limits and control of elected officials. Money issued by government fiat produces unending inflation, which means no wealth is safe from loss over time. In turn, this produces non-stop get-rich-quick speculation.

The American Constitution and the Bill of Rights served us well until socialism invaded our land. Those foundational documents, based on the philosophy of the 1776 Declaration of Independence, assert that God grants our rights. Governments are instituted to secure these God-given rights. When the government fails to secure these rights, the people possess the right to take action to alter or abolish the form of government.

The U.S. Constitution is the rule of law for America. It was and is based on the Declaration of Independence. Thomas Jefferson said, "If a nation expects to be ignorant & free, in a state of civilisation, it expects what never was & never will be."[4] In turn, Ronald Reagan declared, "If we are to guard against ignorance and remain free, as Jefferson cautioned, it is the responsibility of every American to be informed."[5] Today is the day to be informed and

4. Thomas Jefferson, "Letter to Charles Yancey, 6 January 1816," *National Archives*, Founders Online, founders.archives.gov/documents/Jefferson/03-09-02-0209.
5. From President Ronald Reagan's statement during National Library Week 1981, referenced in *Departments of Labor, Health and Human Services, Education, and Related Agencies Appropriations for Fiscal Year 1983* (Washington, D.C.: U.S. Government Printing Office, 1983), 174.

involved in restoring the Constitution as the rule of law. It is the day to cherish and restore religious liberty to our land. Now is the time to become active in the public square, to be a responsible, informed citizen in the voting booth, and to diligently pray for revival and for the restoration of our beloved nation.

So Help Us God!

For more information and understanding of the U.S. Constitution, we recommend *The Christian History of the Constitution*, published by the Foundation for American Christian Education, in Chesapeake, Virginia, and on the web at FACE.net. The writings of researcher Charles Scaliger on socialism can be found through *The New American*, P.O. Box 8040, Appleton, WI, 54912 and online at thenewamerican.com.

CHAPTER 33

America Is at a Crossroad: The Agenda to Erase America

October 2015

All Is Not Well in America

The enemy of God is targeting Christianity, and doing so through attacking political and religious liberty. They threaten pastors and chaplains, even chaplains in prison systems where they are so badly needed. They remove crosses because they consider them offensive. Such a thing would have been unthinkable when I was a child. Public schools have not only removed teaching of the Bible as absolute moral truth, but have redefined gender, if you can comprehend such a thing. Some are even removing the words *girl* and *boy* from bathroom doors.

Many arriving on our shores come to destroy our country, doing so through their influence over our people. From January to October 2015, authorities arrested over fifty U.S. citizens for terror plots, according to Todd Starnes of *Fox News*. The ISIS strategy includes the use of the Internet for propaganda to recruit young people to join their efforts. They recruit individuals to engage in lone-wolf terrorist operations in American and European cities. Terrorist attacks on American cities have occurred in multiple states.

Five thousand Westerners have gone to Syria to aid ISIS. Most of these people have high-tech skills, according to Todd Starnes, acclaimed reporter and author of the recently released *God Less*

America.[1] They support radical Islam. In the Minneapolis-St. Paul area alone, the Obama administration brought in one hundred thousand Somali Muslims. Very few people are aware that in America, the U.S. government has targeted city after city for Islamic nations refugee resettlement. Jim Simpson, author of the book *The Red-Green Axis*,[2] alerts the nation to this mass immigration, which the mainline media seems to be ignoring. The faulty faith of Islam, with its supposedly eternal reward for jihad, drives terrorism. On the other hand, Jesus Christ, the authority of His Word, salvation by His grace through faith for all who believe, and the promise of eternal life drive all His children.

America is at a crossroads today. The faith of Christ, which made our country what she has been in the past and can be again tomorrow, has compromised in the areas of civil government, law, the political system, and in innumerable personal choices. Weakened pulpits weaken the churches and families of our nation. We all have a choice today as we stand at the crossroads.

In the founding of our nation, the vast majority of citizens were patriots in the most loyal manner. As Christian patriots, that vast majority practiced virtue in their private and public lives. When you read the writings of the Founding Fathers, you read the political philosophy of the Orthodox Christian Protestant Reformation. The Biblical doctrines of the Reformation inspired their ideals and high standards, compelling strong admonitions to fellow citizens from the pulpits and in ordinary correspondence.

The resulting new ideas concerning Western civilized culture, in turn, brought innovation to the world stage of action. In America, these Christian patriots founded Harvard, Princeton, and Yale as Bible colleges. These institutions committed themselves to educate pastors and a citizenry to oversee a just republican government. From the colleges and universities to the smallest common schools, students learned this Christian worldview. Godly patriotism grew.

---

1. Todd Starnes, *God Less America* (Lake Mary, FL: Charisma Frontline, 2014).
2. James Simpson, *The Red-Green Axis: Refugees, Immigration and the Agenda to Erase America* (Washington, D.C.: The Center for Security Policy, 2015).

They cherished it. Americans could truly call all education Christian education at that time.

God's providence early planted a cherishing of Scripture in certain people of certain times. The resulting articulation of Biblical principles became embedded in every document: the Magna Carta, the Articles of Confederation, the Declaration of Independence, and the Constitution. For these to be maintained, citizens must learn the Word diligently. They must study providential history, duty, honor, virtue, citizenship, obligations, and willing obedience to the law.

As a history teacher for many decades, I love true history. Yes, I weep over our failings and try to learn from them. I love the South. The Southern states of the American Union provided nine of our first twelve presidents. They provided 80 percent of the national budget during that period. They birthed statesmen that blessed the entire Union. They did not welcome radicals.

At a time of moving away from America's Biblical roots, the French Revolution came to have undue influence on our shores. Many strayed in their ways away from and contrary to God's Word. What we today refer to as secular humanism advanced in the marketplace and then into the educational mainstream. It became rampant in the Northern states before the South discerned it creeping into the Southern culture as well. Expediency took the place of duty, and pragmatism replaced virtue. The Enlightenment really only constituted a rebellion against God. Not in every family, of course. The sovereign God of the universe keeps His remnant with Him always (e.g., Isaiah 28:5).

We live in a postmodern age which is anti-Biblical and therefore, non-Christian. I trust that those reading this essay are professing Christians, and recognize that we are the remnant of God. We must restore as our goal our heritage of true, Biblical Christian culture. Included in the heritage, we must restore civil and all relational government to its Christian foundation.

What would this mean? If restored, what would the government look like?

Let us repeat, because it is crucial: colonial education, including the colleges and academies, supported the Biblical view of culture, law, and political affairs. Almost all educational institutions began as Christian. This heritage continued in many places long after the signing of the Constitution, including the law and legal education. Every colonial charter was a Christian document. The Bible was the single most cited reference, as the most respected authoritative source of political writers. Modern pastors would do well to read the sermons from the pulpits of America from the colonial period well into the early nineteenth century. Political sermons addressed the military, governors, legislators, government officials, and Congress. Widely reprinted and distributed, some remain in print even today. We badly need these inspiring messages in our time.

Our documents leave no doubt about the identity of our God. The Articles of Confederation call God the "Great Governor of the World."[3] Understanding of the sin nature of man inspired America's framers to embed checks and balances against the centralization of political power, and the rule of law against the arbitrary rule of man. Separation of powers, checks and balances, and representative government all stemmed from the teaching of Scripture concerning the Fall of man, and the resulting sin nature in every man, with his greedy lust for power at the expense of his neighbor.

What do we mean when we say a Christian view of the world? Very simply, we mean a Biblical view of God, man, life, politics, culture, and eternity. The Framers thus gave us law and a political system incorporating that view. However distant we are now from a religious consensus, at that time the Christian worldview naturally gave birth to our system of government.

John Jay, writing in *Federalist*, no. 2 reminds us of those days, "Providence has been pleased to give this one connected country to one united people— a people descended from the same ancestors, speaking the same language, professing the same religion, attached to the same principles of government."

---

3. "Articles of Confederation" (1778), Library of Congress, online at guides. loc.gov/articles-of-confederation.

James Madison, writing in *Federalist*, no. 51 wrote: "If men were angels, no government would be necessary. If angels were to govern men, neither external nor internal controls on government would be necessary. In framing a government which is to be administered by men over men, the great difficulty lies in this: you must first enable the government to control the governed; and in the next place, oblige it to control itself."[4]

The Framers saw the danger of one-man rule. They further saw the need to protect the minority as well as any majority. The mixed form of our government protects everyone. One man, able to act decisively, heads the executive department. Some components of majority rule operate in the House of Representatives. The Framers provided protection to the minority through power balances in the Senate and courts. Moreover, America's relational form of representation, American republicanism—as against democratic direct primaries, for example—provided further minority protection. This system kept a direct line between the most local and the greatest spheres through election of representatives by representatives face to face in caucus.

The political principles outlined the preamble to the Constitution came from the Bible. They affirmed God's created system of what we call *natural law*. Almost all the Framers had studied and internalized Blackstone's *Commentaries* on the laws of England. They affirmed that God is the Supreme Judge of all His Creation (e.g., Psalm 67:4). "Righteousness and justice are the foundation of Your throne" (Psalm 89:14 NKJV).

The Constitution was intended to ensure justice in the culture. This should not surprise any of us since the Ten Commandments are a summary definition of justice. I challenge the reader to read the Commandments to verify this definition. As wonderful as our Constitution is, it cannot change the hearts of the American people. It cannot restore a broken family or restore domestic tranquility in this broken culture. So how do we secure the blessings

---

4. John Jay, Alexander Hamilton, James Madison, *The Federalist Papers*, available online at congress.gov/resources/display/content/The+Federalist+Papers.

of liberty for ourselves and our posterity? God has told us that "where the Spirit of the Lord is, there is liberty" (Second Corinthians 3:17).

It comes down to the remnant, doesn't it? If America will be born again, restored, and well again, the remnant is essential. Where are we today, when we are needed so badly? The citizens in our state and nation are diverse. Millions have not come from the Protestant Reformation tradition and have never understood its background or heard the Gospel. Their schooling denied even our own citizens the true story. Millions more are not even comfortable with the English language. They have come to these shores for multiple reasons, but many with hope for a better life. It is up to us as Christians, to identify what a better life is—eternal life, through the Gospel of Jesus Christ. And with a growing Christian testimony on the whole counsel of the Bible comes an understanding of justice, equality, opportunity, and domestic tranquility.

God clearly sets before us an obligation to our fellow man as true Christian Americans to bear witness to the liberating power of the Gospel through the person of the Lord Jesus Christ. Christ must win back men and women to Himself. They must embrace His love for them. Only then can America become a beacon of light in a very dark world. We have the Message: everything good is a person—Jesus Christ, the Savior of mankind, the only hope for America.

Our Constitutional Republic Is at Stake

Liberty or Socialism for All?

August 2016

The publication of the pamphlet *The Communist Manifesto* in the mid-1800s may have attracted little notice at first, but it has emerged as the most influential publication of the century. The influence of the view of history promoted in that pamphlet has been felt across the world, even in the United States and to this day.

German natives Karl Marx and Friedrich Engels wrote the *Manifesto* while employed in England. The document asserts that all human history is the story of class struggle—where men establish themselves and their fortunes at the expense of others. In earlier history, many nations lived through class struggles, whether in medieval Europe or the Roman Empire. In Rome, the struggle occurred between the *patrician* (aristocrat, of the ruling class), the *plebeian* (common people), and the *slave*.

At the time of Marx's writing, England enjoyed growth in the manufacturing industry. Trading networks expanded, raw materials grew more readily available, and a growing and prosperous middle class emerged. Marx and Engels observed that uneducated and unskilled laborers comprising the working class (*proletariat*) served in those factories. These poor laborers were necessary to maintain assembly-line production. With increased industrial expansion came prosperity for the elevated middle class (*bourgeoisie*).

The Marxist communist sought to bring about revolutions between the classes, ultimately putting control of all production in the hands of the State—a communist state. With state control over the means of production, they could supposedly eliminate the problems they saw inherent in private property. They could create a workers' paradise. They saw all of history as the history of class struggles. And, yes, Hegelian social chaos would help accomplish their determined end.

Problems with communism should be obvious. At some point property must become private. When I take a bite of food, I can no longer share it. Two people cannot wear the same garment or occupy the same space. And when does an explosion (chaos) by itself ever create a better order?

A study of communism—its history and pattern of revolution—reveals its influence throughout the declining European nations and now its increasing influence over our own America.

We read in a much earlier time, the French Revolution's *Liberty, Equality, Fraternity*.

The French National Constituent Assembly in 1789 drew up and adopted the *Declaration of the Rights of Man and of the Citizen*, asserting that "all men are born free and equal in rights." It listed essential rights such as the right to liberty, private property, personal safety, and freedom from oppression. The French people had endured the absolutist rule of Louis XVI. The Declaration did not call for a democracy but did contain a plea for liberty. There was at least a dream of liberty among the French people. Yet with sinful humanism at its root, it could not materialize. Instead, it led to a bloody, vindictive revolution.

Contrast the French Revolution's principles with those of the Magna Carta of 1215. Among all the ancient charters, the Magna Carta has had the most lasting influence. The ideals in this document helped shape the Constitution of the United States among a people of a more virtuous faith and character. It provides an example of the legal principle and practice that the Constitution would contain. Consider:

No freeman shall be taken [arrested], or imprisoned, or disseized [have his lands taken away], or outlawed, or exiled, or in any way harmed,... save by the lawful judgment of his peers or by the law of the land.

Would this not stand today as a very fundamental judgment of justice?

When the English became fascinated with the idea of New World colonization, a group of investors founded The London Company to bring it to pass. Only 4 percent of the investors belonged to the ranking nobility. Capitalism was very much alive and active. A full 96 percent of the investors were tailors, skinners, salters, bakers, grocers, cloth workers, fishmongers, and other tradesmen or merchants.

Capitalism worked well, as it always does, when combined with integrity, compassion, and wise judgment. Every story of our founding seems to have an inspired message, whether that of Captain John Smith erecting a wooden cross on the shore of Cape Henry, or the founding of Plimoth Plantation in Massachusetts. The colonists could acquire their own property and earn due wages for their willing work. The citizens elected representative delegates for their assemblies and made their own laws through legal process. After Plimoth's initial experiment with communism imposed by their investors miserably failed, almost no sign of communism or socialism in the function of government would remain the New World.[1] A constitutional republic birthed the exercise of the sovereign power lodged in representatives elected by the people.

Early Americans recognized that virtuous public morality must undergird free institutions. Noah Webster wrote: "It seems to be

---

1. We say "almost" here because of the few examples of statism in colonial history, including in Connecticut, where the government meddled in church affairs, and Puritan price fixing killed the first American steel manufacturing business. In Philadelphia, Benjamin Franklin turned over several successful, private-subscription-driven public services—library, hospital, street maintenance—to the city for government control and financing through taxation. Godless temptation afflicts even the righteous. —Ed.

a political axiom that republics should be founded on an equality of rights, or so constructed as to preserve that equality."[2] John Adams wrote, "The foundations of national morality must be laid in private families. In vain are schools, academies, and universities instituted, if loose principles and licentious habits are impressed upon children in their earliest years."[3] Benjamin Rush certainly was in agreement. He wrote, "Without religion, I believe learning does real mischief to the morals and principles of mankind."[4]

Moreover, Americans understood the spiritual battle inherent in godly freedom and the need to defend it. One of America's most prominent women, Mercy Otis Warren, wrote, "It is necessary for every American ... to stop the dissemination of principles evidently destructive of the cause for which they have bled. It must be the combined virtue of the rulers and the people to do this, and to rescue and save their civil and religious rights from the outstretched arm of tyranny, which may appear under any mode or form of government."[5]

Thus, a complete education, including the acquisition of real skills and godly wisdom, played a central part in the foundation of America. It was solidly based on a specific worldview, which combined the fundamentals of Christianity and republican government, framed carefully to protect individual civil and religious liberty.

As we have already seen, in *Federalist* 51, James Madison wrote, "What is government itself, but the greatest of all reflections on human nature? If men were angels, no government would be necessary." However, not only do we not have angels governing men,

---

2. Noah Webster, "Letters to a Young Gentleman Commencing His Education," *Rudiments of America's Christian History and Government: Student Handbook* (San Francisco: Foundation for American Christian Education, 1968), 24.
3. Adams, *The Works of John Adams*, vol. 3, 171.
4. Benjamin Rush, "Letter to John Armstrong, March 19, 1783," *Letters of Benjamin Rush, 1761–1792*, vol. 2, ed. Lyman Henry Butterfield (Princeton, NJ: Princeton University Press, 1951), 294.
5. Mercy Otis Warren, *History of the Rise, Progress, and Termination of the American Revolution*, vol. 3 (Boston: Manning and Loring, 1805), 413–14.

we have progressives who deny the existence of God, and without His guidelines (the Ten Commandments) we end up with anarchy.

Christians—true Christians—are in such pain today. We look at the government educational system and realize that they indoctrinate evolution and other immoral curriculum content as truth to students. They have created a total vacuum of moral absolutes, as relativism has replaced truth. Progressives designed long ago to replace true history with social studies. They deprive children of their rightful American heritage. The legacy of John Dewey and Horace Mann and their followers has won the day—at least for now.

When we study the progressive agenda, another name for socialism, we see the call for more government controls over our everyday lives. They determine to create social chaos with the legalization of abortion on demand, gender selection, and same-sex marriage. Some judges even presume the right to determine what is in "the best interest of the child" or the "greatest public good." Government has no right to make any such determination apart from criminality in the parent.

This chapter intends to call Christians to prayer for families and for our country. We become rightly alarmed when we scan the numbers, constantly on the increase—babies born out of wedlock, babies aborted, single parents rearing children alone, and children in failing schools through no fault of their own!

We can all look back over our own family life and see our mistakes, but we can make a new determination this very day. Our country has no future without a moral base. To bring morality back will take more than one election, as important as that is. We may not have the perfect candidate, but where will we be if Christians are not involved and don't make their voice heard and their vote count? It will take families committed to each other, with a faith-based commitment of parent to child, child to parent, and sibling to sibling. For unity in the family, God made the provision for family life. We Christians must become once more societal and civil salt and light upon the wisdom of God's Word and by His power through faith.

"God setteth the solitary in families." (Psalm 68:6)
Hopefully, families who have neglected church attendance will locate an area church to meet spiritual needs that honors the Word of God, where the pastor preaches the Truth boldly without compromise. Hopefully, more grandparents will take the time to enrich the lives of grandchildren, especially if both parents work. This writer hopes that Kingdom-conscious Biblical home schools and Christian day schools will increase as more parents become informed as to exactly what is happening to our culture and its politics. Looking at the political process, it doesn't look inviting, but where will we be if Christians do not involve themselves? Nehemiah's wall builders carried a trowel *and* a sword. America's future as a Christian constitutional republic is at stake. God's Word holds the answer.

> "Where the Spirit of the Lord is, there is liberty."
> (Second Corinthians 3:17)

CHAPTER 35

THE UNITED STATES CONSTITUTION AND EDUCATION, THEN AND NOW

October 2013

The great debate in American education today centers on the role of the national government in education. The very foundation of national American government is the U.S. Constitution. Nowhere in the Constitution can we find the word *education*. The Constitutional Framers provided for enumerated powers. Education is missing from those powers delegated to the national government by the Framers.

In the last century, when selfish politicians replaced statesmen, many found a way to dream up programs and new powers in the name of the Constitution's "general welfare" clause. James Madison and the Founders would have never fallen for such abuse of the Constitution. In fact, Madison addressed such a possibility and spoke these words before the House of Representatives on February 7, 1792:

> If Congress can employ money indefinitely to the general welfare, and are the sole and supreme judges of the general welfare, they may take the care of religion in their own hands; they may appoint teachers in every state, county, and parish, and pay them out of their public treasury: they may take into their own hands the education of the children, establishing in like manner schools throughout the union; they may assume the provision for the poor, they may undertake the regulation of all roads other than post roads; in short, every thing from the highest

object of state legislation, down to the most minute object of police, would be thrown under the power of congress; for every object I have mentioned would admit of the application of money, and might be called, if congress pleased, provisions for the general welfare.[1]

Madison's sarcasm may have seemed laughable to his hearers in 1792, hearers who no doubt took their oaths of office to uphold the Constitution much more seriously than do modern members of the Congress. Yet his satiric laundry list of would-be national powers under the term *general welfare* has now long functioned as national policy.

You, America's taxpayers, have paid over one trillion dollars on failed educational policies since the creation of the national department of education. Under Democrat and Republican administrations alike, the education bureaucracy has increased money spent with no measurable, demonstrable academic progress. The Bush administration's No Child Left Behind program, intended for reform, based continued funding on test scores. President Bush requested massive funding and received it. In November 2008, Reading First Impact Study Final Report addressed the failure of the program: "There was no consistent pattern of effects over time in the impact estimates for reading instruction in grade one or in reading comprehension in any grade. There appeared to be a systematic decline in reading instruction impacts in grade two over time."

The report continued to reveal that: "There was no relationship between reading comprehension and the number of years a student was exposed to Reading First [a part of No Child Left Behind]."[2] This in spite of an 80 percent increase in spending by the Bush administration—well intended, but with sad results.

---

1. Jonathan Elliot, ed., *Journal and Debates of the Federal Convention, Held at Philadelphia, from May 14, to September 17, 1787*, vol. IV (Washington, D.C.: Jonathan Elliot, 1830), 237.

2. Jo-Anne Wilson-Keenan, *From Small Places: Toward the Realization of Literacy as a Human Right* (Rotterdam, The Netherlands: Sense Publishers, 2015), 52.

The Obama administration promised to continue—even accelerate—the national education policies through national programs and national funding. In March of 2009, Secretary Arne Duncan announced $44 billion stimulus funding from the American Recovery and Reinvestment Act. This was in addition to the tens of billions in regular education national funding.

American parents share the President's goal of seeing that every child has an access to a good education, but how to achieve it? In our research, we have found no evidence that the national government programs have achieved increased academic performance in the least. National test scores have not had any significant increases through the years. Mean scores have remained at or below the 1960s levels. The College Board has even adapted scoring to accommodate the decline.

So, what have educators and parents learned from the No Child Left Behind initiative and the programs following? One dedicated teacher in North Carolina, speaking of her experience with No Child Left Behind, said, "It left no teacher standing up."

Alabama and most other states have now accepted the newer Common Core standards. The Alabama legislature has an opportunity to repeal it. Accepting the national funds and standards will further nationalize education in America. Texas appears to be standing firm against it, but most states have fallen in line with the unions and the national dollars.

Many foundations and independent think tanks have examined the standards and found cause for alarm. A top-down educational model aimed at conformity for all schools and all students is cause for alarm.

Standard testing organizations will revise national testing to conform to the standards. The standard testing will lock teachers into teaching to the tests. The great Liberal Arts with its the historic undergirding of Western civilization will suffer under Common Core. Instead, Common Core standards will displace much of the former thoughtful education with informational readings. An example is a reading from the Environmental Protection Agency, titled *Recommended Levels of Insulation*. Another is *Strengthening Federal Environment, Energy, and Transportation Management; Executive Order 13423*. Obviously, such readings are designed to displace the arts of liberty with mere utilitarian, technical, and vocational data. This is social engineering.

The low, misplaced history standards deprive students of any depths of true American history and constitutional study. Brilliant math professors declare the math standards weak. The curriculum will now present Algebra One in the ninth grade instead of eighth grade—not a good strategy toward college readiness. When we hear the term "internationally benchmarked," should we infer that we are moving toward more U.N. one-world goals and cooperation?

Teachers and parents alike oppose the centralization of education in America. Parents are not willing to turn over the minds of their children to a faceless, faraway, national bureaucracy. The Department of Education was created by an act of Congress is 1979 and signed into law by Jimmy Carter. Since then, state and local control over education has eroded by degrees. Designated funding established by public/private partnerships of unelected people behind the scenes redirects education to achieve political ends. The Left hails all as improving standards and bringing education reform. The Melinda and Bill Gates Foundation, and the Carnegie Foundation of New York have made the largest contributions toward the Common Core agenda. It is all in place. Publishers' catalogs are already in the mail. They hail their textbooks as conforming to Common Core. The situation rests now with the Alabama legislature. The Republicans have the majority votes to do their will on the matter.

Citizens should hold state boards of education responsible for the content and curriculum taught in public schools. Better, we should oppose the mandatory attendance laws and property tax funding that urge Americans into unholy State classrooms—or at least we should reclaim local control. In addition to opposing Common Core, we trust that the people will oppose the data mining that accompanies Common Core and is pushed on the schools.

At least forty-one states have accepted grants for expanding data collection on students and families. Is there any justification for a national student database? How would your family feel about such a violation of privacy?

Serious problems haunt education in public schools. Educational challenges are best handled locally, by teachers and administrators who know and love their students, who personally understand the advantages and the disadvantages that students bring into their classrooms. Teachers occupy those classrooms also to teach and to deal with personal needs of the students, things that affect the students' ability to learn. Alabamian and many other good teachers desire to produce a moral and literate student who will be a lifelong learner. This is easily achieved with a child from a loving, stable family. It is difficult for the many children today who suffer from brokenness and other disadvantages. The teacher in your neighborhood school understands more about the needs of the students than the faceless architects claiming control of local and state education content. Godly education is relational by nature. Institutionalism creates a relational nightmare.

Parents have every right to face their elected school board and state house members to confront them with these concerns. For the sake of the children and the future of this state and nation, keep the control of education at least at the state level—better still, the local one. Protect and maintain the moral base required for liberty to prevail. Uphold the Constitution, which leaves education outside national government and in the hands of parents and community.[3]

---

3. More recent efforts to repeal Common Core (CC) in Alabama, as of August 2019, have stalled. According to the Edcite Blog, seven states have since rescinded approval of CC standards, and only one state implemented the full CC Partnership for Assessment of Readiness for College and Careers (PARCC) program. Meghan Thompson, "The Common Core #10YearChallenge: Only 1 State to Continue Using PARCC Test," *The Edcite Blog*, 16 February, 2019, blog.edcite.com.

Deconstruction of Truth to Postmodernism

September 2014

Our forefathers crossed the Atlantic Ocean not only to found America, but to overcome the ecclesiastical, political, and social ideas of the past. The great Puritan movement opposed the idea of church or clerical infallibility. They opposed its hierarchy. They rejected the supposed sovereignty of both pope and king. They rejected tyranny in church and state because they accepted the infallibility of the Scriptures and the Scriptures' God. Second Timothy 3:16 declares, "All scripture is given by inspiration of God, and is profitable for doctrine, for reproof, for correction, for instruction in righteousness." First Peter 1:19–21 likewise states, "But with the precious blood of Christ, as of a lamb without blemish and without spot: Who verily was foreordained before the foundation of the world, but was manifest in these last times for you, who by Him do believe in God, that raised Him up from the dead, and gave Him glory; that your faith and hope might be in God." The church in America would be Biblical, local, and self-governing.

In the past, men measured social status by rank or authority in the ruling hierarchy. Americans considered themselves equal as created by God, before His law—personal, criminal, and civil. God grants liberty, and so it is inalienable. This was America, and it was indeed a new world. Welcome to the new world of man and government under God. Americans lived in voluntary union with others, in liberty of conscience under God's law. First John 1:7 affirms, "But if we walk in the light, as He is in the light, we have fellowship one with another, and the blood of Jesus Christ His son cleanseth us from all sin."

The blessings of the first two hundred years of our history came from Americans living the Christian principles of Christian self-government and Christian character. Our forefathers applied the commands and principles of Scripture to form our representative government and the constitutional safeguards protected liberty for all. This was the blessing of the Christian modern age.

Postmodernism

If we had to define postmodernism, we could safely say *it is an attack on Biblical Christianity*. Since the 1960s and 70's a major change in the culture has occurred because of this philosophy. It penetrated the universities and institutions of learning throughout America. The majority of Americans did not even realize the massive movement or the first decades of infiltration. Now, it prevails in the public square as the mainstream thinking of Western society.

Dear Christian parents and grandparents: you must recognize the danger postmodernism poses today. Recognize the dire danger it represents to your family and to American personal liberty. We must equip our children and young adults to resist it, and understand its ever-present danger. Immorality lies at the heart of it, as postmodernism ridicules the Bible. They target family faith and morality.

In speaking of postmodernism, Dr. Martyn Lloyd-Jones viewed today's culture "as lost in sin today as Adam and Eve were in the day that they fell." As Adam, postmodern man still hides from God.

Postmodern man believes that each person constructs truth for himself. British theologian and pastor Rev. Erroll Hulse wrote extensively on postmodernism in a very understandable fashion.

He explains:

The Jewish Holocaust, Solzenitsyn's revelation of the Stalinist regime's horrors and the Gulag Archipelago, genocide in Africa, Cambodia, Yugoslavia, the ecological crisis, global warming, the Aids epidemic, and the abuse of political and military power all bring deep-seated disillusionment. No belief system is to be trusted. Indeed, one belief system seems as valid as the next. This attitude has encouraged relativism and bred a fixed aversion to claims of absolute truth. Simply stated, the essence of postmodernism is that *there are no fixed absolutes*.[1]

When I studied with Dr. Francis Schaeffer, he spoke of *post-Christianity*. We recognized its evidence as we traveled through Europe with him. Post-Christian culture has now come to America as postmodernism. It prevails in the multiplying humanistic statutes of our land. Our own Alabama Supreme Court is one of the few places we can see a faithful, historic, and legal interpretation of the rule of law.

Evolving statute law in general in America is antinomian to its core. It is against law as we knew it in the past. Bypassing Scripture, we construct new truth to eradicate true Biblical morality. We pass unlawful statutes to legalize immorality and make it socially acceptable. Examples include abortion, euthanasia, no-fault divorce, shifting sexual identity, and self-serving governmental indoctrination of school children. Does it make us wonder how different we will soon be from Marxist-Stalinist USSR if this continues in our nation?

What are the battle lines for believers in Biblical Christianity? How may we arm ourselves to combat the immorality of postmodernism? Dr. Erroll Hulse urges believers first to be informed. "The enchantment of modernity is characterized by technological messianism, enlightenment idealism, quantifying empiricism, and smug fantasy of inevitable historical progress."[2]

---

1. Erroll Hulse, "Postmodernism: Attack on the Heart of Biblical Christianity," *Reformation Today Series* (Pensacola, FL: Chapel Library, 2007), 6.
2. David S. Dockery, *The Challenge of Postmodernism* (Grand Rapids: Baker

The enemy of God intends to deconstruct our Biblical worldview and substitute a moral relativism, completely blotting out absolute Biblical Truth. Pluralism guarantees that all religions have an equal and level playing field, except Christianity. A supposed tolerance is crucial to postmodernism. There must be no final authority in that worldview, as anything goes.

Existentialism forms the heart of this view. At its heart, feelings reign supreme. Teaching can easily reach the heart of a student at any age for good or evil, but given the sin nature, especially for evil. One of many curriculum-outline examples encourages attitudes (feelings) rather than acts regarding the Declaration of Independence. You will recall these words and probably can repeat them by heart: "We hold these truths to be self-evident, that all men are created equal, that they are endowed by their Creator with certain unalienable Rights, that among these are Life, Liberty, and the pursuit of Happiness."

Rather, for example, a postmodern deconstructionist lesson might ask:

1. Does the language exclude women? Are only men created equal?

2. Thomas Jefferson penned these words, but didn't he own slaves?

3. We hear about equality and justice, but what about women and minorities? Is this document hypocritical?

Can you see how this discussion appeals to a student's feelings rather than a principally educated and discerning mind?

What can we do to combat postmodernism in our churches? Pastors have the pulpit and may freely and boldly preach propositional revelation. The writings of Dr. Francis Schaeffer and Dr. Carl F. H. Henry's *God, Revelation, and Authority* held firm to the Scriptures. These writers delved into the problems of humanism

---

Academic, 2001), 24, in Hulse, "Postmodernism," 7. We would add that true progress belongs to God, for the Kingdom comes without observation. That is, God brings about His kingdom sovereignly, behind the scenes, through many diverse individuals filled with His Spirit (Luke 17:20; Psalm 110). —Ed.

before many others understood our shift from the modern world to the postmodern. Dr. Henry, speaking of the Bible's relevancy in our modern age said, "Unless the study of theology finds its rightful preeminence among the priorities of modern learning there will be no authentic rescue or salvation for modern society."[3] His writing stresses that no modern thought can replace the loss of the Biblical God, a loving Father, who is both above His creation, and at work within it.

Dr. Erroll Hulse counsels us:

> We were created to relate to each other, to have fellowship with the Father, the Son, and with other believers—the assembly of believers who reflect the love of our Triune God (1 Jo 1:1–4). Christians are by virtue of their union with Christ brought into the heart of the Trinity, a heart which is love ("God is love"). The Father loves the Son eternally and perfectly: the Son loves the Father and proved it throughout His life on earth. The Holy Spirit infinitely and comprehensively loves the Father and the Son. Jesus referred to our union with the Father, and in that context prayed fervently for the complete unity of His Church. This unity is one of love which, when witnessed by the world, proves to be a tremendous drawing factor.[4]
>
> Let us stand against postmodernism by proclaiming the wonderful, unchanging truths of God's Word, and by faithfully loving others with Christ's love.

The true God rules in sovereign control. His church is alive in over 220 nations and His Word appears in over one thousand languages. God is not dependent on the United States of America. Should we become the United Socialist States of America, God will be constant, though we will have lost our way. The Bible is God's Word without error. It is the absolute Truth of all time. Wouldn't it be appropriate for every pastor to teach a series on the moral law of God and the dangers of postmodernism? I love the

---

3. Carl F. H. Henry, *God, Revelation and Authority*, vol. VI (Wheaton, IL: Crossway Books, 1999), 8.
4. Hulse, "Postmodernism," 20.

English Puritans and their focus. Had they not understood the last judgment, they would not have been so passionate about preaching the glorious Gospel. They knew nothing of shallow thought and feel-good preaching. Let's say it again. Bold proclamation of God's moral law and all Scripture is the answer to postmodernism. John 8:32 declares, "And ye shall know the truth, and the truth shall make you free."

We strongly recommend the authors featured in this chapter. Also, *Rebuilding Civilization on the Bible* provides a powerful armament to combat postmodern thought.[5]

---

5. Jay Grimstead and Eugene Calvin Clingman, *Rebuilding Civilization on the Bible: Proclaiming the Truth on 24 Controversial Issues* (Ventura, CA: Nordskog Publishing, 2014).

CHAPTER 37

The Restructure of America through School Choice in Education

February 2015

The restructure of the public educational system is reaching far more than the schools. Its aim is no less than the restructure of society through education. A careful investigation reveals that it is international in scope and entirely socialistic in philosophy. It is promoted by the United Nations, and already, numerous European countries have implemented similar methods.

Choice in education sounds wonderful. However, the choice offered by the government is not the grassroots choice of parents seeking the best for their children.[1]

This choice originated with the Department of Education in concert with the New American School Development Corporation years ago. All school systems dependent on national tax dollars will eliminate a true "choice" for parents, because they must conform to a national curriculum.

School will expand to include to four-year-olds, perhaps three-year-olds, with families increasingly monitored by government agencies.

---

1. The government's choice in education we present here may be changing in some degree. The Trump administration under Education Secretary Betsy DeVos emphasizes additional alternatives, including truly private schools and home schooling, which may lead to a small deflection from the deceptive school-choice program under the No Child Left Behind Act. See Valerie Strauss, "What 'School Choice' Means in the Era of Trump and DeVos," *The Washington Post*, 22 May, 2017, washingtonpost.com. —Ed.

Components of this philosophy have been evident for many decades. However, the system itself—thoroughly socialistic and without moral absolutes—has been in place as a cohesive system since Goals 2000 went public. President Bush released the Goals 2000 plan in 1991. With its own task force, Goals 2000 intended a complete restructure of community standards toward national educational goals, with a determined conformity in all local public educational systems. Now, Common Core expands that agenda's goals.

Make no mistake in understanding the primary and overall goals:

1. Global education
2. World-class citizens
3. Choice in education
4. Greater government controls
5. Greater responsibility on the part of government to watch over and teach (indoctrinate) pre-school children

The plan is to accomplish all of this by means of a national curriculum, national testing, a national database, outcome-based education, and state-based decision making conforming to national standards.

In Alabama, Christian schools are exempt from conforming to government regulations such as Common Core. But the feds are hoping that those schools will use a voucher plan or take tuition tax credits, and thus force non-public schools into the framework of the government plan.

From President Bush, to Carter, and to Obama, we hear much about "world-class" standards in every school, and at the same time, they promote choice in education. It can be confusing, can't it? Choice aims to increase the government's stronghold and eventually control non-public schools as well. Deceiving parents is part of the plan.

The Alabama legislature in its last session mercifully protected by law Christian, private, and home schools from government regulation. Nonetheless, many legal experts sound a warning to Christian schools. To take government assistance is inevitably to waive your right to teach and function as a Christian school, including holding the Bible as infallible, inerrant, and authoritative.

To expect national funds to flow without any control is to be ignorant of the law, and more importantly, of its deceptive, authoritarian abuses. For example, in the Excellence in Education Act of 1991, the bill states: "From funds reserved under section 3(b), the secretary shall conduct a national evaluation of the activities under this Act." This would include implementation of the program, etc. Justice Blackmon acknowledged that the government may call on the recipients of subsidies to relinquish some of their constitutional rights. (May 23, 1991).

Parents who have opted out of public schools have been paying their taxes to keep public schools operating in addition to paying tuition for their Christian and private schools. It will be tempting to see "choice in education" as a means of increasing enrollment in the Christian schools. If the matter were left only to the states or communities, we might expect a differing strategy.

However, the national government, which has no constitutional authority over education at any level, has proven hostile to Christianity, especially in recent years.

Christians already suffer a grave problem with college-age students leaving the church after attending Sunday school and church all their young lives. Families are in distress in America as never before in her history. The Left attacks religious liberty across America. The glorious light of the Gospel shines brightest against the backdrop of attacks, but only when Biblically informed Christians carry the armor of God into battle.

Rev. James Patrick, a thorough researcher and able writer, made this thoughtful observation:

> The United States seems to be drifting away from more than a sound foreign policy. It is drifting away from everything of any value, politically, economically, spiritually, and educationally.

We are a nation adrift with neither an anchor to hold us, nor a rudder to guide us. Many writers have proposed various reasons for their drift away from our country's original moorings, and I suppose that each has touched upon some aspect of the truth. But let me propose a different view. Could it be that we are adrift because of the deliberate actions of the enemy from within? Is it possible that a Trojan horse was left at our gates, and we, in a moment of security, opened the gates to the very enemy we oppose?[2]

For nearly two hundred years in America, local classrooms across the United States upheld Noah Webster's definition of *education*. *Education* is "the bringing up, as of a child, instruction; formation of manners. *Education* comprehends all that series of instruction and discipline which is intended to enlighten the understanding, correct the temper, and form the manners and habits of youth, and fit them for usefulness in their future stations. To give children a good *education* in manners, arts and science, is important; to give them a religious *education* is indispensable; and an immense responsibility rests on parents and guardians who neglect these duties."[3]

Will we now allow the United Nations to redefine the content and methods of education to produce a socialist and pagan nation?

May God forbid!

---

2. James Patrick, n.d., from author's library.
3. *American Dictionary of the English Language*, s.v. "education."

CHAPTER 38

Attacks on Faith, Family, and Freedom

March 2015

When America's constitutional republic providentially birthed as a Christian nation, the entire culture reflected moral absolutes. While true that not every citizen was what we call a *born-again* Christian believer, everyone enjoyed the blessings of liberty brought to our shores, the fruit of moral absolutes. Our republic emerged as a result of the Protestant Reformation, with its Biblical mandate. Devotion to Scripture through many trials formed in us a courageous character.

Education was of central importance from its inception. From the home school around the open fireplace, to the first New England "dame school" in the most humble village, parents and teachers taught a Biblical view and practice of life. By the turn of the next century, Noah Webster arose as the foremost schoolmaster in America. His influence remains to this day. From the training of pastors, to the teacher of reading, to the foundations of science, his American English language definitions are unmatched for clarity and truth.

As we have discussed earlier, his definition of *education* includes these words: "*Education* comprehends all that series of instruction and discipline which is intended to enlighten the understanding, correct the temper, and form the manners and habits of youth, and fit them for usefulness in their future stations. To give children a good *education* in manners, arts and science, is important; to give them a religious *education* is indispensable; and an immense responsibility rests on parents and guardians who neglect these duties."[1] In speaking of manners and habits, he defines these as the "course of life: in a moral sense." Webster's reference to religion always means historic Protestant Christianity. He relates it to every subject.

In the early twentieth century, changes entered America's textbooks. Secular educators cast aside the long-proven method of intensive phonics as the best way to teach reading, replacing it with many inferior and unproven experiments. The glorious history of providence was cast aside for the new concepts evident in social studies. Even in the late 30's and 40's, the *Dick and Jane* readers distressed parents. They were boring and inferior compared to school methods of twenty-five years earlier. Having taken away sound foundational phonetic tools, the new Sight-Say reduced children to merely guessing at words. Also missing were the moral teachings of Bible stories, stories which had helped form character for hundreds of years in education. By this time, science had introduced evolution, first as a *theory*, and then, unscientifically, as *fact*.

What could be more damaging to children than to instill in them the idea that they are an accident? Darwin's theory—that all life has developed accidentally over eons of random interactions with chemicals and gases with no life purpose other than to survive—has taken hold in the academic world. As preposterous as it seems, the leading universities in this once-Christian nation embrace this atheistic philosophy.

By the time I attended college in the late 1940s, this arrogant philosophy had infiltrated every academic discipline. Children spent many more hours in school than awake at home, or in church or synagogue. Is it any wonder that children from Christian homes were and are confused? And nearly a hundred years later, is it any wonder that bewildered young people from Christian homes have walked away from the church in masses?

In 1964, the Sex Information and Education Council of the United States (SIECUS) formed in New York as a tax-exempt

---

1. *American Dictionary of the English Language*, s.v. "education."

health non-profit. This organization had a revolutionary plan to change all of education through their program of sex education for all children and youth.

The executive director, Dr. Mary Calderone, focused on radically invasive and presumptuous sex-education teaching materials for all schools. She had previously acted as medical director for Planned Parenthood. For years, her husband Dr. Frank Calderone, operated as chief administrator of the World Health Organization. The pair was known as "ultra-liberal one worlders." Dr. Mary Calderone proudly believed that "everything that science knows about sex and sexuality our children must have access to."[2] She did not intend for teachers to be allowed to inject the "restraints of old-fashioned morality."[3] The government made national funds available to promote the agenda, as she traveled the states teaching educators. Some of the people associated with SIECUS had earlier been identified with the communist party, according to the records of the House Committee on Un-American Activities (as early as 1955 and up to 1968).

Promoters presented many of the programs for schools as "family life education." Parents complained that their very young children were targeted with lewdness and desecration of the most intimate sexual experiences. We cannot describe the slide presentations here out of respect for children.

Let it be known that the lessons openly invited children to experiment with sex. The textbook contents have grown increasingly obscene over the last decades. These one-world propagandists look upon parents who hold to moral absolutes as totally out of date and unrealistic. They worked passionately throughout the 1960s on their agenda. The Congressional Record of June 26, 1968,

---

2. John R. Rarick, *Congressional Record: Proceedings and Debates of the 91st Congress*, vol. 115-part 5, "Sex Education: Teaching, Moralizing, or Terrorizing?" (12 March, 1969): 6315.
3. Stewart E. Fraser, *Sex, Schools, & Society: International Perspectives* (Nashville, TN: Peabody International Center, George Peabody College for Teachers, 1972), 173.

mentions Dr. Albert Ellis, Director of the Institute for Rational Living, Inc. He wrote *Sex Without Guilt* and *The Case for Sexual Liberty*. Among the participants in the drive for new sexual freedom for America's youth, you will find the names of Dr. Isadore Rubin, the editor of *Sexology* magazine, and Dr. Lester Kirkendall, prominent in the American Humanist Association. To him, any moral absolute was unthinkable.[4] These are a sample among those who led the movement to capture American culture through government schools. To these people, "sex without guilt" includes adultery, sex perversion, and premarital sexual relations. Organizations prominent in the business world have continually assisted with funds and promotions for decades, while the top spheres of government have provided the majority of funding.

These sex leaders boldly praised Sweden for their approval of vast freedom to young people to enjoy "sexual activities without shame." *Look* magazine reported that "most high-school Swedes regard premarital sex as natural and acceptable."[5]

Many honorable people remained ignorant of the degrading content in the school programs, yet chose to believe that a sex-education program in schools might reduce sexual activity among teens. However, without a moral foundation, without a strong sense of right and wrong, how could they expect moral choices? They clearly desired to promote *im*morality.

Another name to remember is Dr. Joseph Fletcher, "religious" author of *Situation Ethics: The New Morality*. He urged amending the Commandments to the following: "Thou shalt not covet, ordinarily. Thou shalt not kill, ordinarily. Thou shalt not commit adultery, ordinarily."[6] There should be no rules. Everything depends on the situation. According to the House Committee on

---

4. Ironically, such supposed relativists don't seem to realize that excluding the Christian faith is absolute in itself, as is insisting on any particular behavior or propensity. A *new* normal is still a normal and, inherently then, absolute. —Ed.
5. "Sweden and Sex: What 10 years of sex education have taught the Swedes," *Look* (November 15, 1966).
6. *The Review of the News*, vol. 15 (Madison, WI: Correction, Please, 1979), 30.

Un-American Activities, Fletcher also associated himself with the communists. The new morality in American schools based itself in situational ethics. What is right for me might not be right for you. No absolute right or wrong exists or should exist.[7] How prevalent is this attitude in today's culture? Far more than we choose to believe.

Grassroots Opposition Begins to Form: 1968

Dr. Melvin Anchell, world-renowned Jewish psychiatrist from California, expertly published on human sexuality. Called upon by California legislators with grievances over textbook content in the classrooms, Dr. Anchell sounded the alarm over real damage to children from the sex program. He explained that the physical component of sexual activity must be inseparably fused with spiritual and mental needs. After researching the way that teachers presented sex in the classroom, Dr. Anchell wrote that legislators may just as well give the same children "guns and a cache of ammunition with the admonishment not to use them."[8] He continued to speak and publish and sound alarms.

It was my great privilege to work closely with Dr. Melvin Anchell for several years in the 1980s when we both worked for Protect America's Children. I witnessed his expertise in both writing and in active testimonies in courtrooms in America, to protect children from sexual abuse and other dangers. Later, the Hoffman Education Center published a book that he authored, titled *What's Wrong with Sex Education?*

Much of the content of school textbooks is too pornographic for me to quote, but it is easily researched.

A Long Process

"Congress shall make no law respecting an establishment of religion, or prohibiting the free exercise thereof."

Alabamians, including teachers, were among the strongest voices in the opposition to the removal of school prayer from

---

7. Again, how is this not absolute? —Ed.
8. *The Review of the News*, vol. 5 (Madison, WI: Correction, Please, 1969), 27.

schools. Parents in Baldwin County were among the most vocal in exposing a degraded bias in Alabama textbooks. Parents from other towns and counties joined in the exposure of false and demeaning content in school texts. But the removal of school prayer in 1962 generated alarm and fear for the children and their future in this "land of the free."

In reviewing textbooks used in Alabama, Dr. Paul Vitz, professor of psychology and history at New York University, exclaimed "that Alabama history and social studies textbooks convey a message that religion is irrelevant or that it more or less doesn't exist."[9]

School textbooks would be challenged in the October 6, 1986–March 1987 trial held by District Judge W. Brevard Hand in Mobile, Alabama. An earlier case involving school prayer took place in 1981 when Ishmael Jaffree challenged Alabama's school-prayer laws. Hundreds of people were involved in this case. The State Board of Education, the defendant, declined to sign a pre-trial settlement agreement. The prayer advocates contended that the teaching of humanism, a man-centered theory (or religion) rejects the teaching of Christianity and Judaism. People for the American Way and the American Civil Liberties Union entered the case as "interveners." Then attorney Tom Parker and attorneys Tom Kotouc and Bob Sherling took the lead role on behalf of the prayer advocates. The Freedom Council Foundation of Chesapeake, Virginia, assisted.

The people of Alabama have consistently stood for America's Christian founding and the rule of law articulated in the constitutions of the national and state governments. The state voiced a ringing call when 81 percent of Alabamians stood for traditional marriage in a state constitutional amendment. Our Alabama Supreme Court has remained valiant in interpreting the laws of our nation. They do not take it as their role to rewrite old or make new laws, but to uphold the standards of eternal Biblical law—to

---

9. Paul Vitz, n.d., from author's library. Probably *Censorship: Evidence of Bias in Our Children's Textbooks* (University of Michigan: Servant Publications, 1986). —Ed.

protect law, life, and liberty. The greatest jurist of the founding era, Judge William Blackstone, would applaud them. Meanwhile, the judges on the federal benches across the land having placed their hand on the Bible then deny the God of the Bible as the Source of Truth and law.

A friend in California called to say, "Thank you, Alabama, for taking a stand for us all. If you fail, we all fail." I say, thank you, Alabama Supreme Court. As a retired history teacher, I am one of many Alabamians blessed and encouraged by your opinion.

The following list of rulings against "We the People" clearly reveals the attack on faith, family, and freedom—war declared on moral absolutes by unelected federal judges:

- A verbal prayer in school is unconstitutional, even if non-denominational and voluntarily participated in. Engle v. Vitale, 1962; Abington v. Schempp, 1963.

- Freedom of speech and press is guaranteed to students UNLESS the topic is religious, at which time such speech is unconstitutional. Stein v. Oshinsky, 1965; Collins v. Chandler Unified School District, 1981.

- Kindergarten children may not recite: "God is great. God is good, let us thank Him for our food." Wallace v. Jaffree, 1984.

- It is declared unconstitutional to hang a plaque of the Ten Commandments in the classroom, because it might lead children to read and meditate and perhaps obey them. Stone v. Graham, 1980; Ring v. Grand Forks Public Schools Dist., 1980; Lanner v. Wimmer, 1981. By contrast, the Supreme Court upheld a Ten Commandments display as constitutional in Van Orden v. Perry 2005.

"If the foundations be destroyed, what can the righteous do?"
(Psalm 11:3)

"Be on the alert, stand firm in the faith, act like men, be strong."
(First Corinthians 16:13 NASB)

"And ye shall know the truth, and the truth shall make you
free." (John 8:32)

CHAPTER 39

Exposing the Dangers of International Agreements to Children, Families, and American Sovereignty

September 2015

Many years ago, we had Dr. Allen Quist speak at a regional Eagle Forum meeting. He spoke about the changes in American education and spent a great deal of the speech that evening on the *new math* then under development and the International Baccalaureate, a brainchild of UNESCO and the United Nations.

Dr. Quist, a highly respected professor of political science at Bethany Lutheran College in Mankato, Minnesota, theologian, and popular speaker throughout the United States, served three terms in the House of Representatives in the Minnesota legislature from 1983–88. An author of numerous books including bestseller *FedEd: The New Federal Curriculum and How It's Enforced*, he expertly exposes the dangers of international agreements to our children, our families, and our American sovereignty. "FedEd" is short for the new *Federal Education Curriculum*. Quist's articulate passion for self-evident truth and unalienable rights in preserving liberty for our children and grandchildren was most informative and inspirational, even while exposing serious dangers to that liberty we have long enjoyed.

Recently, I discovered a brilliant review of the *FedEd* book by Steven Yates, whom I heard speak at the von Mises Institute at

Auburn. His review of the book is right on target and much more articulate than I could write. So I am taking the liberty of using much of his review. I know you will gain more understanding of events now occurring today in your community by first thoughtfully reading this chapter, and then searching for the full review. The review is titled, "FedEd: Education for Global Government," by Steven Yates (Steven Yates Archives).[1] I am very grateful to draw from his review at this time.

Dr. Quist reviews the public education system for the last hundred years, when Horace Mann and the Harvard Unitarians studied the humanistic, utilitarian, and military "Prussian model" in Europe.[2] The concept of "the state raising children to meet the needs of the state" crept in even with the very young. "This model gave us the word *kindergarten*," reflecting the idea of "growing" children (*kinder*) in a garden (*garten*).

Evidence shows that there has been a slow decline in American education since Dewey's "progressive education" became the fad, as well documented. Dr. Quist points to much evidence that the progressives' "intent has been to dumb down the citizenry of this country and produce a 'new serfdom'—a global workforce totally subservient to the needs of omnipotent world government and its internationalist corporate partners." To name those corporate partners: Goals 2000 Educate America Act and the School-To-Work Opportunities Act. A bill known as HR6, "a funding appropriations bill for most federal education programs," was created to achieve the goal. "Bill Clinton signed all three." George W. Bush signed the No Child Left Behind Act of 2001. Together, all of these turned over the "curricular content to federal educrats, resulting in the New Federal Curriculum: FedEd," which Allen Quist brilliantly exposes in detail.

---

1. Steven Yates, "FedEd: Education for Global Government," review of *FedEd: The New Federal Curriculum and How It's Enforced*, by Allen Quist. *EdWatch*, February 22, 2003, edwatch.org/lewrockwell/yates.htm.
2. See "Prussian Education System," at *Wikipedia*, en.wikipedia.org/wiki/Prussian_education_system, for an introduction.

He identifies seven themes running through the FedEd in his book (pp. 43, 100, 131–32):

1. Undermining national sovereignty (moving us toward world government under the auspices of the United Nations).

2. Redefining natural rights (substituting for the American view a Marxist and internationalist view justifying massive redistribution of wealth).

3. Minimizing natural law (essentially by neglect).

4. Promoting environmentalism (emphasizing the global nature of environmental issues, including promoting the pagan pseudo-religion of Gaia, Mother Earth).

5. Requiring multiculturalism (including acceptance of homosexuality).

6. Restructuring government (toward the idea that we live in a "global village," defining citizenship in global terms).

7. Redefining education as job skills (preparing "human resources" for the global workforce).

What will the future look like if these numerous multi-culturalist and environmentalist groups are teamed up with Marxists educrats? Can we imagine "a world in which the majority of people are Information Age serfs ruled over by a global elite,... celebrating diversity, embracing tolerance, and worshipping Mother Earth"? If they succeed, gone will be students' "grasp of economics or constitutional principles, any significant knowledge of their historical origins or even much knowledge of basic math (they will have calculators, after all)." How do these "world-class standards" sound for your child and grandchild?

Steven Yates points to Professor Quist's explanation of *themes* in the curriculum. Traditional American education stressed academic subject content in math, science, geography, literature, history, and so on. The new concept of *themes* "emphasizes attitudes, values, and beliefs in what educrats call the affective domain (cf. p. 42)." More important than communicating information and real cognitive skills is "inculcating the right attitudes and values

. . . —indoctrinating, in other words, instead of educating" in the historical sense.

Consider this discussion of sovereignty that Quist singles out: "'The world is divided into nation-states that claim sovereignty over a defined territory and jurisdiction over everyone within it' (quoted on p. 47)." This stresses a "unified world" of internationalism "viewed not just as desirable but inevitable."

Changes in standardized tests "reflect the preoccupations and values of FedEd." Students who "have not adopted the desired attitudes will simply not do well on the test." A federal funding bill, HR1, requires that all states administer the NAEP: National Assessment of Educational Progress. In the edition of the test Quist reviewed, fourteen key terms relate to environmentalism, eighteen terms relate to multiculturalism, thirty-nine terms relate to vocationalism, and zero terms relate to geography. The number of terms involving history, "apart from the history of government-designated victim groups," was zero. The number of terms referring to national sovereignty, godly or natural law, and godly or natural rights was zero.

"Among the chief goals of FedEd is to turn out 'global villagers'." We can now interpret "*education* as *job skills*." The curriculum imposes a merely vocation-centered worldview on every child, with career choices emphasized "via 'career clusters' as early as eighth grade." Who knows in the eighth grade what career path they want to pursue? Isn't it obvious that the FedEd proponents seek to cast off God's principles of individuality and liberty to choose? The article points toward the devaluation of personhood—the free individual under God—in favor of being a "human resource," a mere drone worker.

FedEd is sold in many places as "good for business." Both Quist and Yates take this on. Some Chambers of Commerce buy the idea that FedEd will turn out "loyal, technology-savvy, and business-savvy employees." The key phrase is "private-public partnership." Quist says that too close ties with government and business leads to corporatism, not capitalism. Corporatism may sound good to some, but it leads to a "statist and collectivist" society. "The New Federal Curriculum sets out to indoctrinate and train individuals to meet the needs of the state and its corporate partners."

Parents might ask, How will they enforce this? While presented as "voluntary," the new Federal Curriculum, according to Professor Quist, is the law of the land. "HR6 stipulates that the U.S. Department of Education can simply withhold national money from any state not signing on to the new program (pp. 92–93)." All fifty states have signed on. "Every federal dollar comes with strings attached."

How Professor Quist Envisions that the FedEd Program Will Be Enforced

The three bills outlined above gave control of education to the government in 1994: Goals 2000 Educate America Act, the School-To-Work Opportunities Act, and ESEA Authorization Act (the infamous HR6). The overall package developed in progressive legislative installments. Goals 2000 uses the word *voluntary* over and over again. But HR6 says that if a state doesn't comply, it will lose its national education money. The bills and laws are deceptive.

While HR6 mentions the Constitution and Bill of Rights, the authority lies with the feds to determine what they mean—not your local school board or their teachers. Dr. Quist reminds us that you cannot have a free society if the national government determines what is true.

National law authorized the non-governmental organization Center for Civic Education (CCE) to determine curriculum in civics and government. Dr. Quist states that not one member of this unelected body ever faces the voters. They are self-appointed.

Page 2 of the National Standards states that "Civic education instead should be considered central to the purposes of American education." The Standards state that every academic subject shall include civics and government instruction, clearly a self-serving element designed to entrench centralized government. Dr. Quist believes that the FedEds can only achieve their desired change in our form of government through inculcating a new form of government.

Dr. Quist explains the use of "themes" in the curriculum. For example, he cites theme 4: environmentalism. A lesson from a textbook titled, *The People Who Hugged the Trees*, declares: "Before she left the forest, Anrita kissed her special tree. Then she whispered, 'Tree, if you are ever in trouble, I will protect you.' The tree whispered back with a rustle of its leaves." Though anthropomorphism is common in historic literature, this clearly suggests pantheism to a young child, or at least elevating a God-given, useful plant to the status of person.[3]

The text *We the People* states: "The culture we live in is becoming cosmopolitan, that is, belonging to the whole world.... National corporations have become international.... Environmental concerns transcend national boundaries.... Entertainment—music, sports, and film—command worldwide markets. The achievements of modern technology are turning the world into a global village with shared cultural, economic, and environmental concerns."[4]

Quist concludes another article with this statement: "We have come to grips with the fact that, in the core curriculum now required by federal law, there is one unifying theme, which is the disbanding of the United States of America as a sovereign, free people, and the creation of an international one-world government. This is the glue that holds it all together."[5]

Most of the public does not know what is taking place. Money is tight and most states are dependent on national dollars.

This chapter has just touched the surface, and I am so grateful both to Professor Quist and Steven Yates to provide this excellent review. Please take time go to the articles online and read them in full, for the sake of the children who are the victims.

---

3. Allen Quist, *FedEd: The New Federal Curriculum and How It's Enforced* (St. Paul, MN: Maple River Education Coalition, 2002), 69.
4. Quist, *FedEd*, 94–95.
5. Allen Quist, "The New Federal Curriculum and How It's Enforced," *EdWatch*, edwatch.org.

America: A Christian Nation from Birth— Men in Black Robes, Then and Now

August 2015

In this year of 2015, it would be very interesting to know if our good reader ever heard the name of David Josiah Brewer, an associate justice of the U.S. Supreme Court from 1889 to 1910. Has any modern law student studied Brewer's decisions on the court? His most important case was the Church of the Holy Trinity v. United States, decided February 29, 1892, on the eve of the twentieth century.[1]

If the case has been so buried for the past century, why should we study it and its opinion penned by Justice David Josiah Brewer? Believe me, it has tremendous meaning in both the political and spiritual life of our nation. It was important in 1892, and it is important today. Understanding the case's significance or ignoring it may well forebode the very future of religious liberty for your children and grandchildren.

Seven years before this case came to trial, on February 26, 1885, Congress passed a law. It intended "to prohibit the importation and migration of foreigners and aliens under contract or agreement to perform labor in the United States, its Territories, and the District of Columbia."

The Church of the Holy Trinity employed a minister from England, E. Walpole Warren, to come to the United States to

---

1. Church of the Holy Trinity v. United States, 143 U.S. 457 (1892), available online at supreme.justia.com/cases/federal/us/143/457/.

serve as its pastor. The United States government charged the church with violating the 1885 law by making a contract with the minister, "importing an immigrant to do labor."

At trial, the church did not plead the First Amendment to the U.S. Constitution, but argued that the law should not apply to the church and its foreign pastor. The lower court rejected the defense and ruled against the church. The case went to the Supreme Court.

Justice Brewer demonstrated that the lower court was in error in its decision because the court based its judgment on the letter of the law and not on the intent of the law. For the lower court to rule that the church's contract with the minister was illegal would be absurd in the eyes of the court.

It is interesting to note that the justices had no problem with the law in question—in fact they made allowance for "large capitalists in this country" to contract with "an ignorant and servile class of foreign laborers ... at a low rate of wages," thereby breaking down "the labor market...to reduce other laborers engaged in like occupations to the level of the assisted immigrant."

Justice Brewer used the opportunity in this case to show how damaging it would be for the government to inject itself and appear to be "against religion."

In the unanimous decision, Justice Brewer documented the evidence that America's earliest colonists, and continuing through our founding as a nation, "came pursuant to the Great Commission."

Secondly, he documented the organic evidence that the providential purpose of America had never changed in over three hundred years. He declared America a Christian nation based on solid evidence. The Supreme Court ruled, on evidence, that *America is a Christian nation*.

Justice Brewer rendered seven hundred decisions in his career, which spanned forty-six years in numerous judicial positions, including the Supreme Court of Kansas, the Eighth Circuit Court of Appeals, and the U.S. Supreme Court (1889–1910).

Remarkably, he also made himself available to lecture on our Christian heritage with its relationship both to religious liberty and to the political sphere. He saw the role of religion in American life as the cause of her prosperity, and much more:

"Churches and church organizations ... abound in every city, town, and hamlet; the multitude of charitable organizations [exist] everywhere under Christian auspices; the gigantic missionary associations, with general support ... [aim] to establish Christian missions in every quarter of the globe."[2]

Supporting the influence of the Christian faith, Justice Brewer observed that the American people established our civil orders based on the laws of God. That the nation's "founding purpose was to advance the Christian faith" is evident. This great truth, as the source of liberty, was his passion.

Brewer was born of missionary parents in Smyrna, Asia Minor, in 1837. His family returned to New England during his childhood. He entered Wesleyan College at age fifteen. He settled in Kansas and held numerous judicial positions with great acclaim. A noted scholar and devout Christian in both his personal and public life, he consistently lived according to his understanding of this nation's providential founding and mission.

His decisions and opinions consistently stated that no legal government action may harm the Christian religion—neither state nor national government—because this is a religious people. In reviewing the evidence, Justice Brewer cited the commission to Columbus by Ferdinand and Isabella: "By the Grace of God,... continents and islands ... will be discovered."

The First Charter of Virginia stated its purpose: "By the providence of Almighty God ... in propagating of the Christian Religion to such People, as yet live in Darkness and in miserable Ignorance of the true Knowledge and Worship of God." He quoted the colonial charters, one by one, citing Divine Providence and the establishment of the Christian religion foremost in every new territory.

---

2. Church of the Holy Trinity v. United States.

The importance of these documents has been lost to modern history and to the American classrooms. William Penn, in his charter of Pennsylvania, 1701, wrote, "Because no People can be truly happy, though under the greatest Enjoyment of Civil Liberties, if abridged of the Freedom of their Consciences,... Faith and Worship ... doth enlighten the Minds, and persuade and convince the Understandings of People...."

Brewer cites the rich Christian wording in the Declaration of Independence. In support of that Declaration, our Founders pledged to each other "our Lives, our Fortunes, and our sacred Honor."

Every state constitution recognized religious obligations upon the people. Many explicitly stated that office holders must believe in God to hold office in government. The justices affirmed that a universal language declares this is a religious nation, and that "the morality of the country is deeply engrafted upon Christianity, and not upon the doctrines or worship of those imposters."

American Vision republished the court record of Church of the Holy Trinity v. United States and a review of the case as a book entitled *The United States: A Christian Nation*.[3] A large portion of the book is a republication of the original as published by John C. Winston Co. in 1905. It also includes material on Justice Brewer's lectures, an introduction by Gary DeMar, founding president of American Vision, and a review of the case by Dr. Herb Titus, prominent attorney and university professor serving multiple institutions with great distinction.

For all the recent generations who did not study America's true history in school, this book documents that this nation's legacy of liberty comes from Biblical Christianity in faith and practice. Without the profession of faith in the one true God, there will not be liberty and the blessings of Providence.

With the heritage of the Protestant Reformation, can we say with Martin Luther, "My conscience is captive to the Word of God"?[4]

---

3. Available online at store.americanvision.org.
4. From Luther's appearance before the Pope at the Imperial Diet of Worms, 1521. See luther.de/en/worms.html.

Can we agree with George Washington, "Of all the dispositions and habits which lead to political prosperity, religion and morality are the indispensable supports. In vain would that man claim the tribute of Patriotism who should labor to subvert these great pillars of human happiness"?[5]

The clergy served in general assemblies, conceived of the first common schools, penned charters and constitutions, and preached the principles of liberty without compromise. This discipled the nation.

John Witherspoon, president of the College of New Jersey (later Princeton), trained a vice president, three Supreme Court justices, ten cabinet members, twelve governors, sixty congressmen, and many state leaders—too numerous to list. Pastors in those black robes brought us the Great Awakenings with their Reformation messages. The men in black robes on the courts of America were Biblically literate, and the majority was committed to the Christian faith. The words of their decisions displayed their commitment to upholding the law of God and our Constitution.

Today, what picture prevails in our minds when we see men in black robes? Certainly, here in Alabama, we are thankful that our Supreme Court displays faithfulness to the cause of Christian liberty. Sadly, this is not true nationwide in the courts of the land. We see the destruction of our religious and civil liberty at every turn, and we sometimes cry aloud with the psalmist, "If the foundations be destroyed, what can the righteous do?" (Psalm 11:3).

We find our mandate clearly expressed in Scripture: "Proclaim liberty throughout all the land" (Leviticus 25:10). This Scripture is inscribed on the Liberty Bell in Philadelphia, Pennsylvania.

The Lord says, "As surely as I live, your children will be like jewels that a bride wears proudly" (Isaiah 49:18 NCV).

---

5. George Washington, *Farewell Address* (New York: Houghton Mifflin Company, 1913), available online at *The Avalon Project* at Yale Law School, avalon. law.yale.edu/18th_century/washing.asp.

The Origin of Liberty in Government Established by the U.S. Constitution

March 2016

With the death of Justice Antonin Scalia, the court is now equally divided between the constitutionalists and those who oppose traditional interpretation of our law. With recent drastic changes in American culture, cases pending before the high court could further destroy the moral absolutes in our culture. As of now, the court is equally divided between "right and left." There is great speculation about Justice Scalia's replacement on the bench.[1]

Immigration and the aggressive refugee resettlement movement are moving swiftly at the present time, and the case before the court could reverse a lower court ruling to delay the Obama plan.[2]

Religious non-profits are seeking an exemption from the Affordable Care Act's mandate that employers must pay for the cost of collective bargaining, even if they object to the union demands.

Affirmative Action, long a hot topic in university admission programs that take race into consideration, will come under scrutiny by the court. Perhaps the most controversial case challenging the court will be the abortion issue. Reproductive rights have been

---

1. As we now know, under great opposition, President Trump nominated to the Supreme Court, and the United States Senate confirmed, constitutional conservatives Neil Gorsuch to replace Justice Scalia, and Brett Kavanaugh to replace Anthony Kennedy, giving the court a nominal conservative edge. Chief Justice John Roberts remains something of a wild card on this score. —Ed.
2. President Trump has now proposed eliminating the program. —Ed.

front and center since 1992. The "rights of a woman and her own body" have clouded the issue of a "right to life." Will the court place restrictions on physicians and facilities to protect that most fundamental right of all, which is life?

The real issue behind these rulings concerns the Constitution as the supreme rule of law in America. While our citizens have enjoyed freedom and liberty since 1788, it has not always been so with any other people, in any other country or continent on the globe. This is an amazing story.

Men tried to establish a government for centuries before 1788, but their experiments never produced freedom and liberty for the individual. The cycle moved from a mob, to a monarchy, sometimes to democracy, more often to tyranny, to autocracy, or feudalism. None brought the promise of "life, liberty, and the pursuit of happiness." No indeed, each one brought suffering, oppression, misery, and most often violence. Tyranny and military despotism crushed the hearts and ideals of men, and left them with no security. There was no regard for, or even recognition of, an individual's God-given rights.

The English, more than any other people, understood their own history. They knew well the oppression of their kings, and preserved the Magna Carta in their hearts, while it was ignored and denied in the daily life of England's ruling classes.

We as Americans truly claim the Magna Carta, or Great Charter, as the basis of American liberty. Behind that parchment lies the history that you and I have enjoyed. The story of this history has been denied to generations in America's government schools since the early 1900s. This glorious history belongs to every American as it relates to the long and relentless struggle by a brave and united people against the misrule of kings.

I have visited numerous times that meadow at Runnymede, on a little island in the River Thames, where King John of England was given the choice of a pen or the sword. He chose the pen—signing the Great Charter—rather than the sword, which would cost his life. It was his admission of having used arbitrary rule and his acceptance of limited powers. In that meadow in June, the year 1215, they established the law as supreme in England.

For the first time in history, the Magna Carta provided the restraint of written law to apply to all men. This marked a decisive step toward what would become constitutional government in the future.[3]

The Magna Carta did the following:

1. Clarified rights.
2. Ensured that government could dispossess no one of his property except by due process of law, or by a judgment of his peers.
3. Assured trial by jury, with the right of an appeal.
4. Assured fair taxation by consent of the people's representatives.

That last provision will of course remind us of the slogan of the American Revolution: "No taxation without representation."

The Great Charter established four fundamental principles into law that live today. They are:

1. A king or ruler must rule in accordance with the law and desires of his people.
2. Government is a contract with each party accountable and called to account.
3. Individual rights are clearly stated.
4. The king has specific restrictions.

Four hundred years later, King Charles I violated the ancient rights and principles of the Magna Carta. The people acted. On June 7, 1628, Parliament withheld money, forcing Charles to sign The Petition of Right.

Continuing to ignore those rights cost Charles his life on the headman's block in 1649, and the monarchy was not restored to rule in England until 1660.

---

3. The Magna Carta arguably restored an ancient Christian tradition in England where law is supreme, notably dating at least from the reign of King Alfred the Great. —Ed.

Those principles in the Petition of Right are a vital part of our United States Constitution:

1. The government may levy taxes only with the consent of Parliament.
2. Troops may no longer quarter in private homes.
3. The government may not declare martial law in time of peace.
4. Citizens have the right to trial by jury of their peers.

England lived another twenty-eight years of peace through the rule of law under the Petition of Rights, until King James II attempted an absolute monarchy, prompting his abdication. The revolution of 1688 finally settled the power of Parliament and English law. Parliament then elected William and Mary as rulers. Political liberty triumphed in England with the Bill of Rights in 1689.

The first eight amendments to our United States Constitution enacted into law the influence and indeed the very principles of the English Bill of Rights and the Petition of Rights.

In the 1600s, when these events took place in England, the founders of the American colonies followed their consciences to seek liberty elsewhere. It meant facing uncertainty, privation, and sufferings, but they conquered a wilderness and reached their goal of freedom and liberty in a new world.

The Founding Fathers of our nation knew their history and learned its lessons. One of the greatest tragedies of our day is that recent generations of Americans do not know their own history. If they did, we would expect a public outcry to protect liberty in every public square, and in every voting booth.

The American Founding Fathers learned history by reading the writings of the men who fought for liberty. Among them were John Locke, William Blackstone, and the French philosopher Baron de Montesquieu. Providentially, they learned from the political sermons of John Witherspoon, Charles Wesley, George Whitefield, Samuel Davies, Jonathan Mayhew, and so many others.

John Locke led the political philosophy of the Whig Party in England. He outlined his vision for civil government in his *Treatise of Government*, published in 1690. According to Locke, the "God-given rights of man are 'life, liberty, and property'." To protect his God-given rights, man must form a community by a social contract.[4] The ends of political society are to have a uniform interpretation of the law, to establish those rights of "life, liberty, and property" given to the individual. The first eight amendments to the Constitution set forth those rights, privileges, and immunities.

The French Baron de Montesquieu approved of the English system, but he added to it something dramatic and essential due man's inherent sinful greediness—the separation of powers.

We see the wisdom of his promoting the division of power into the executive, legislative, and judicial branches of government as set forth in our Constitution. Sadly, we see the tragic damage from abuse of good law in the Constitution through neglect and overreach in the various branches of government at every level in our nation.

Sir William Blackstone, in his *Commentary of the Laws of England*, analyzed and clearly set forth what would become the basis of American law. Every signer of the Declaration of Independence, and those at the Constitutional Convention, had internalized Blackstone's writings. Righteous law was a sacred trust to them, as it should be to us.

The writings and lives of James Madison, Thomas Jefferson, John Adams, and his son, John Quincy Adams, with so many others, affirm their understanding and commitment to the rule of law. Locke and all the others mentioned above vowed that no man could be deprived of these rights, because God gave them.

---

4. As Mary-Elaine Swanson notes in the Nordskog Publishing title *John Locke: Philosopher of American Liberty* (Ventura, CA: Nordskog Publishing, 2011), while Locke's thinking was essentially Biblical, he used secular arguments to avoid losing his influence amid expected sectarian bickering. His social contract—interpreted as two-way—between men alone—eventually came to replace the Biblical three-way covenant, which always includes God in the manner of an oath. We believe we ought to restore the three-way covenant. —Ed.

Could it be that any group of people has actually lived out such a faith and practice? After many decades of studying history, including personally visiting Plymouth, Massachusetts, so many times, I am still inspired by the lives and history of the Pilgrims. I have already written about them and their Mayflower Compact. No people has ever displayed more Christian courage and charity than this group of Christians seeking freedom of religion. Their faith and persistence saw them through every tragedy and every challenge. Their Compact written and signed aboard the Mayflower, represented a political covenant in harmony with their religious doctrine that guided their relationships and their worldview. Even in the wilderness and with only a tiny community of people, they understood the necessity of law.

The American Constitution has truly served the cause of human freedom. Yet today, because the hearts of many American citizens no longer hold the Constitution sacred, it is in danger. Too many judges and politicians holding elected offices do not revere this document. Its future in our land will determine our freedom and our liberties. It will determine our right to life, the expression of our thoughts and values, our freedom of religion, our rights of assembly, petition, and action, and our property rights and civil liberty.

In my library, I have a recently republished book of *Political Sermons of the American Founding Era, 1730–1805.*[5] It contains a thousand pages of these political sermons. Today, the pulpits of America are silent concerning our great God-given heritage of law, which is clearly based on God's Word.

For thirty years, Justice Antonin Scalia faithfully exercised his charge to protect our God-given rights through faithful loyalty to the Constitution. His intellect, his brilliance, and personal faith shine through his faithfulness in the following words.

---

5. Ellis Sandoz, *Political Sermons of the American Founding Era, 1730–1805,* 2 vols. (Indianapolis: Liberty Fund, 1998).

Quotes from Justice Antonin Scalia

It is of overwhelming importance ... who it is that rules me. Today's decree says that my Ruler, and the Ruler of 320 million Americans coast-to-coast, is a majority of the nine lawyers on the Supreme Court.... This practice of constitutional revision by an unelected committee of nine, always accompanied ... by extravagant praise of liberty, robs the People of the most important liberty they asserted in the Declaration of Independence and won in the Revolution of 1776: the freedom to govern themselves. (Obergefell v. Hodges)

Except as limited by a constitutional prohibition agreed to by the People, the States are free to adopt whatever laws they like, even those that offend the esteemed Justices' "reasoned judgment." A system of government that makes the People subordinate to a committee of nine unelected lawyers does not deserve to be called a democracy. (Obergefell v. Hodges)

[T]he enshrinement of constitutional rights necessarily takes certain policy choices off the table.... Undoubtedly some think that the Second Amendment is outmoded in a society where our standing army is the pride of our Nation, where well-trained police forces provide personal security, and where gun violence is a serious problem. That is perhaps debatable, but what is not debatable is that it is not the role of this Court to pronounce the Second Amendment extinct. (District of Columbia v. Heller)

THE DANBURY BAPTISTS, THOMAS JEFFERSON, AND "THE WALL OF SEPARATION"

January 2015

Amendment I. Congress shall make no law respecting an establishment of religion, or prohibiting the free exercise thereof; or abridging the freedom of speech, or of the press; or the right of the people peaceably to assemble, and to petition the Government for a redress of grievances.

On New Year's Day, 1801, Thomas Jefferson used a metaphor in a letter to the Danbury Baptists Association of Connecticut, which has profoundly affected policy in recent generations.

Jefferson's intention, clearly stated, reflected the constitutionally mandated purpose and safeguard of the First Amendment's protection of religious liberty.

Go back in history to colonial times, and recall that numerous colonies had an established church, as in Connecticut, where the state established Congregationalism. The Connecticut Baptists were a religious minority who supported Jefferson because of his unflagging commitment to religious liberty.[1] They found themselves a political minority as a small Republican community, as well as a religious minority in their faith and practice.

In their letter to the new president, they wrote to congratulate him on his election and to voice their concerns: "Our sentiments

---

1. Americans, including Jefferson, always meant by *religion* the Biblical Christian faith.

are uniformly on the side of Religious Liberty—That Religion is at all times and places a Matter between God and individuals—That no man ought to suffer in Name, person, or effects on account of his religious Opinions—That the legitimate power of civil Government extends no further than to punish the man who works ill to his neighbor. But sir, our constitution of government is not specific." They expressed concern about their religious liberty, that it was enjoyed more as "religious privilege" than "inalienable rights." If "favors" were "granted" by states, could they not be withdrawn? They expressed belief that God in His providence had raised up Jefferson, having heard the voice of the people.

Jefferson circulated the letter from the Danbury Baptists and a draft of his intended response to Attorney General Levi Lincoln, a Massachusetts Republican, and Postmaster General Gideon Granger, a Connecticut Republican. The president was eager to explain why he did not issue proclamations designating days for prayer, thanksgiving, and public fasting, as had his presidential predecessors. It is clear that Jefferson wanted to use the occasion to express his personal convictions on the matter of faith. Levi Lincoln urged caution, as the New Englanders were accustomed to "observing fasts and thanksgivings in performance of proclamations from their respective Executives. This custom ... being handed down from our ancestors." Granger also referred to the offense to the New England clergy, but believed that "it is but a declaration of *Truths* [emphasis added] which are in fact felt [held] by a great Majority of New England."[2] After deleting a small section, Jefferson responded to the Danbury letter.

> Gentlemen,
> The affectionate sentiments of esteem and approbation which you are so good as to express towards me, on behalf of the Danbury Baptists association, give me the highest satisfaction. My duties dictate a faithful & zealous pursuit of the interests of my constituents, & in proportion as they are persuaded of

---

2. Daniel L. Dreisbach, *Thomas Jefferson and the Wall of Separation between Church and State* (New York and London: New York University Press, 2002), 45, 47.

my fidelity to those duties, the discharge of them becomes more pleasing.

Believing with you that religion is a matter which lies solely between Man & his God, that he owes account to none other for his faith or his worship, that the legitimate powers of government reach actions only, & not opinions, I contemplate with sovereign reverence that act of the whole American people which declared that their legislature should "make no law respecting an establishment of religion, or prohibiting the free exercise thereof," thus building a wall of separation between Church & State. Adhering to this expression of the supreme will of the nation in behalf of the rights of conscience, I shall see with sincere satisfaction the progress of those sentiments which tend to restore to man all his natural rights, convinced he has no natural rights in opposition to his social duties.

I reciprocate your kind prayers for the protection & blessing of the common father and creator of man, and tender you for yourselves & your religious association, assurances of my high respect & esteem. —Thomas Jefferson[3]

As governor of Virginia, in 1779, Jefferson wrote "A Bill Establishing Religious Freedom." He was the chief architect of proclamations designating days of fasting and prayer through the 1770s. Jefferson saw his position as consistent with the Constitution and the establishment of Federalism. State governments were free to accommodate and prescribe religious practices. Jefferson viewed the powers of the executive branch as derived from the creative powers of the legislative branch. He should be respected for his allegiance to the Tenth Amendment principles of Federalism and strictly delegated powers.

Jefferson's reference to the "wall of separation" was simply a figurative device in reference to the First Amendment mandate that prohibited congress from making laws concerning the "establishment of religion or prohibiting the free exercise thereof." The letter went into public circulation almost immediately, but it would not end the Church-State debate in America.

---

3. Dreisbach, *Thomas Jefferson and the Wall of Separation*, 48.

Philip Schaff, church historian, noted that the phrase "wall of separation" entered the lexicon of American constitutional law in 1878, almost a hundred years later. Quoting Schaff, we note: "In Reynolds v. United States, the U.S. Supreme Court opined [claimed] that the Danbury letter 'may be accepted almost as an authoritative declaration of the scope and effect of the [First] amendment thus secured'." Nearly seven additional decades later, in the landmark case, Everson v. Board of Education (1947),[4] the Supreme Court returned to the metaphor: "In the words of Jefferson, the [First Amendment] clause against establishment of religion by law was intended to erect 'a wall of separation between church and state'." "That wall," the justices concluded in a sweeping separatist declaration, "must be kept high and impregnable. We could not approve the slightest breach." It is interesting how the court found, 170 years after the fact, an innovative legal principle no one before had recognized.

Contrary to the Supreme Court justices voicing their opinion in *Everson*, no evidence in America's early history exists that our Founders and Framers ever intended to construct a wall of separation between church and state to keep faith out of government. Few letters in American history have been so abused as to have such a deep, deceptive, and disruptive impact in the public square. Had no strong voice in favor of Biblical Christianity existed in early America, so to impact government, we would have no U.S. Constitution as we have it, and certainly no First Amendment.

The writing of James Burgh (1714–75)—an admired Scottish schoolmaster and one of Britain's most popular spokesmen for political reform—evidently inspired the "wall" metaphor Jefferson used. Burgh was a radical Whig, espousing the rights of resistance, separation of powers, freedom of thought, religious toleration, advancing public education, and extending the "rights of Englishmen" to all mankind. Burgh, and others of like mind, advocated reforms in English government, including legislative representation, rotation of offices, annual Parliaments, etc. His writings,

---

4. Dreisbach, *Thomas Jefferson and the Wall of Separation*, 4.

circulating widely in the colonies, included the three-volume *Political Disquisitions* (1774–75), a work found in Jefferson's library.

Burgh greatly influenced Jefferson and the other American Revolutionary leaders. Interestingly, Jefferson recommended this reading to his future son-in-law Thomas Mann Randolph, who would study law. He also recommended the study of Montesquieu's *Spirit of Laws* and "Locke's little book on Government." Historical documents testify to the influence of Burgh on Jefferson, Washington, Adams, Hancock, Rush, Sherman, and many others. Burgh may easily have influenced the construction of the First Amendment. No English or European writer came closer to the American thought than James Burgh. He was a man of deep orthodox Christian faith, the "wellspring of his politics and moral code." His belief in religious tolerance inspired his recommendation for building "an impenetrable wall of separation," to prevent government intrusions.

Having been a great admirer of Burgh, Jefferson most likely adopted Burgh's figure of speech. George Washington shared these concerns and wrote of establishing "effectual barriers against the horrors of spiritual tyranny, and every species of religious persecution."[5]

Jefferson's letter to the Danbury Baptists has had a negative legal impact through the courts of the land through accidental or purposeful misperceptions of the "wall of separation." American culture continues to suffer through the effects of this bad doctrine, as we further abandon a faithful teaching of American history in schools and family life.

American Federalism is unique in world history. America's founders discovered the way for Christianity to be protected by law, but not controlled or dictated by law. It took America to determine how to build American Federalism. The combined principles of local self-government in a balanced tension with the limited

---

5. "From George Washington to the United Baptist Churches of Virginia, May 1789," *National Archives*, Founders Online, founders.archives.gov/documents/Washington/05-02-02-0309.

power of union—such as the two great divisions of power between the states and the nation—gave America the ability to produce a great nation while maintaining individual liberty.

I believe that our constitutional form of government cannot exist without a Biblically educated people capable of self-government. Only the Biblically educated will see that the price of liberty will always be eternal vigilance.

Inspired by President Ronald Reagan and passed as joint resolutions of Congress, the nation declared 1983 the "Year of the Bible," Public Law 97-280, October 4, 1982. In a beautiful proclamation, Reagan urged all Americans to "reexamine and rediscover [the Bible's] priceless and timeless message." He affirmed that the Bible is the source for inalienable rights of the individual and our system of law and government.[6] As James Madison said, the uniqueness of America was "the capacity of mankind for self-government."

"My people are destroyed for lack of knowledge: because thou hast rejected knowledge, I will also reject thee, that thou shalt be no priest to me: seeing thou hast forgotten the law of thy God, I will also forget thy children" (Hosea 4:6).

---

6. Ronald Reagan, *Public Papers of the Presidents of the United States: Ronald Reagan, January 1 to July 1, 1983* (Washington, D.C.: U.S. Government Printing Office, 1984), 180.

CHAPTER 43

THE INHERITANCE OF THE COMMON LAW
IN WESTERN CIVILIZATION

Will we live under the rule of law, or the rule of man?

July 2014

The concept of man in the common law of England is one of the most civilizing forces in all of history. For centuries, history recorded and declared the English common law "the highest inheritance of the King, by which he and all his subjects shall be ruled. And if there were no law, there would be no king; and no inheritance."[1] In the last decade of Elizabeth's reign, an entry in her court cases was this affirmation, "The Common Law is the surest and best inheritance that any subject hath, and to lose this is to lose all."[2]

In the eighteenth century, our Founding Fathers brought to our shores with them the *Commentaries on the Laws of England*, by William Blackstone. Blackstone called our common-law rights "the best birthright and noblest inheritance of mankind."[3]

Men of God have long appealed to the rule of His law given by Moses and throughout Holy Scripture. In every century since

---

1. From "an anonymous scribe in the Year Book" (the law reports of medieval England), "Natural Law and the Common Law," *University of Notre Dame Natural Law Institute Proceedings*, book 3, ed. Edward F. Barrett (Notre Dame, IN: College of Law, University of Notre Dame, 1950), 38.
2. Richard O'Sullivan, *The Inheritance of the Common Law* (London: Stevens & Sons Ltd., 1950), 3.
3. O'Sullivan, *The Inheritance of the Common Law.*

God permitted Israel a human king, the line of succession had been to the king, to his subjects. Appealing to the original law of Moses, early America restored God's intended system of covenantal, republican civil representation, a ground-up system of self-government.

In the decade before the signing of the Declaration of Independence, the colonies of the North Atlantic seaboard received more than 2,500 copies of Blackstone's *Commentaries*, nearly as many as circulated in England. Every college and university in early America used them as the gospel on law. Within my lifetime, we used Blackstone with our Christian high school students for more than forty years. The common law provided the organic unity in legal institutions for all states except for Louisiana. Australia and New Zealand also belong to the living tradition of the common law.

Considered by many scholars the true origin of the common law are the laws of King Alfred, in which no sign of Roman law appeared. Rather, Alfred translated the Ten Commandments and passages from Exodus, as well as apostolic history. When William the Conqueror took control of England, he proclaimed his wishes that "one God ... be venerated throughout his whole kingdom, [and] one faith of Christ always ... be kept inviolate."[4]

The first clause of the Magna Carta confirmed a separation of the king's courts from the courts Christian, later to be called the Ecclesiastical Courts of the Church of England: "We have granted to God, and by this our present Charter have confirmed, for us and our Heirs for ever, That the Church of England shall be free, and shall have all her whole rights and liberties inviolable."[5]

The twofold jurisdiction and discipline of temporal and spiritual courts was a regular feature of England and America from the 1600s until the 1800s, when erosion slowly took place.

4. "No. 4. Norman Period, 1066–1087 A.D.: Laws of William the Conqueror, 1066–1087 A.D.," in *Documents for English Constitutional and Legal History During the Middle Ages*, ed. Norman MacLaren Trenholme (Columbia, MO: University of Missouri, 1905).
5. Edwardo Coke, *The Second Part of the Institutes of the Laws of England* (London: E. & R. Brooke, 1797), 1.

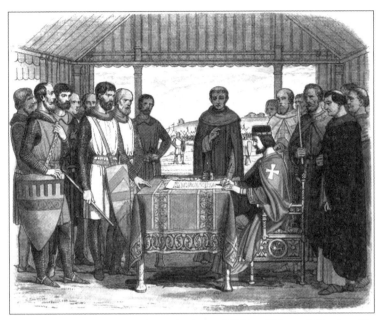

King John Signs the Magna Carta, by James William Edmund Doyle, 1864

The Conqueror concerned himself with family inheritance, the matter of private property rights. The charter he gave to the people read, "I will that every child be his father's heir after his father's day, and I will not endure that any man offer any wrong to you. God keep you."[6] He believed that a mark of tyranny is to rob man out of his rightful inheritance.

When the Conqueror arrived in England, the slave trade thrived. Men and women usually were slaves from birth, usually attached to the soil, and often sold with the land. Such practice greatly contradicted the proclamation of Augustine of Hippo, who declared, "God did not make rational man to lord it over his rational fellows, but only to be master of the irrational creatures."[7] He also wrote, "The desire to rule over our equals is an intolerable lust of soul."[8]

---

6. Theodore F. T. Plucknett, *A Concise History of the Common Law* (Union, NJ: The Lawbook Exchange, Ltd., 2001), 13.
7. A. J. Carlyle, *A History of Mediaeval Political Theory in the West*, vol. 1 (Edinburgh & London: William Blackwood & Sons, 1903), 114.
8. O'Sullivan, *The Inheritance of the Common Law*, 9.

In 1215, the year of the Magna Carta, a decree from the Fourth Lateran Council called for all men and women to confess sins, and to receive holy communion, acknowledging the sinfulness of every human being. Calls for repentance individually and corporately were frequent throughout the land. The sense of human equality was espoused in church and in literature, becoming a leading principle of English law. From the writing of Sir Thomas More ("Everyman is to Everyman an 'even Christian'") to Chaucer's *Canterbury Tales*, we see where men and women are to meet on equal terms and follow life's pilgrimage. William Langland's thought is explicit in *Piers Plowman*:

> For we are all Christ's creatures, and of his coffers rich,
> And brethren as of one blood, alike beggars and earls.[9]

The common law did not tolerate slavery. Through a slow process, the social system came to recognize the intellectual and moral autonomy of Everyman. "A free man ... is able to manage and maintain his own family and rear and educate his own children;... administer his own property ... living in the fellowship of a free community."[10]

Here are the thoughts of Erasmus: "Nature, or rather God, hath shaped this creature [that is, man] not to war but to friendship, not to destruction but to health, not to wrong but to kindness and benevolence."[11]

In stark contrast, Thomas Hobbes and others sharing his worldview look at man in need of external authorities (the State) and sees a solution for man in totalitarianism. Do we not see this all over the world today: where the moral law does not exist as supreme, tyranny fills the void?

In the classical and Christian tradition that animates the common law, the political community consists of three parts: the individual, the family, and the city or state. On the deepest level in

---

9. O'Sullivan, *The Inheritance of the Common Law*, 10.
10. O'Sullivan, *The Inheritance of the Common Law*, 21–22.
11. O'Sullivan, *The Inheritance of the Common Law*, 22.

the life of the individual, the life of the conscience and mind is where Everyman is alone with his Creator, and hopefully, his Redeemer. On the next level is the life of the individual within his family. As for the level of community, Aristotle and Aquinas both greatly influenced the philosophy of the common and moral law. They saw three levels of living in community—ethics, economics, and politics—but they saw that the basis for living on these levels is personal responsibility in and quality of family life. The good must be achieved by "the science of living," applied to a unique training for ethics, for family life, for economics, and for politics.[12] If political philosophy here sounds very different from what the schools teach today, indeed it is.

The Law of Succession protected family private property. Sanctity of the family requires protection of its property to ensure adequate foundations for development of the next generation to its highest potential. Generational community requires peaceful transition with justice and liberty. It requires godly law, once revered by the people.

English courts cite with approval the language of an Irish judge: "The authority of a father to guide and govern the education of his child is a very sacred thing bestowed by the Almighty and to be sustained to the uttermost by human law."[13] Christianity never condoned ignorance. Educating the child was imperative. The law held the family accountable. Naturally varying views on child education mean varying content, methods, and occupational goals. This reflects the historic principle of liberty under law. Christian families and greater society held reading, writing, and reasoning from the Scriptures paramount.

The Reformation transformed the worldview over England and Europe, and the Pilgrims and Puritans brought the principles of the Reformation to our shores with true piety. They lived out the Gospel in their communities, applying its understanding to everything they did. They certainly left us a great model for faith and

---

12. O'Sullivan, *The Inheritance of the Common Law*, 84–85.
13. O'Sullivan, *The Inheritance of the Common Law*, 41.

practice in general, and for education of children in particular. The Massachusetts Act of 1642 addressed the importance of teaching children to read, toward their understanding of the principles of the Christian religion. In January 1643, Dedham, Massachusetts, recorded a grant of land for schools to provide free schooling. Local citizens voted for themselves the necessary finances. The Old Deluder Satan Act, a Massachusetts Bay law of 1647, read, "It being one chief project of the old deluder, Satan, to keep men from the knowledge of the Scriptures,... that learning may not be buried in the grave of our fathers." This act provided for a community of fifty families to establish a school and a community of a hundred families to establish a grammar school. They intended to preserve Christianity and to prepare for college those capable youth seeking to enter certain professions such as the pastorate and law.

American statesmen—to the man—valued education. They were passionate about diffusing knowledge more generally through the masses of the population than ever before. Ben Franklin, among others, led a "Committee of Guardians" who, at their own expense, provided education for free blacks. The Guardians also personally superintended the instruction in the schools. Then they made efforts to procure employment for these youths among various trades.

A public-school society, meeting in Connecticut in 1809, recorded the comment that "It is as uncommon [in New England] to find a poor man who cannot read and write, as it is rare to see one in Europe who can."[14]

To understand the importance of the First Amendment to the U.S. Constitution, one must understand the life of the early republic and the inheritance of the common law, so dearly cherished and defended for centuries by our colonial antecedents. When the officers of the crown and a series of royal governors threatened their liberty, Samuel Adams and others—recognizing the threat of tyranny lurking just over the horizon—organized the Sons of

---

14. William Oland Bourne, *History of the Public School Society of the City of New York* (New York: G. P. Putnam's Sons, 1873), 16.

Liberty. They fought one battle after another: The Stamp Act, The Sugar Act, the Townsend Act, and on and on. When the colonies saw their common danger, they recognized the need to unite in their actions, for mutual protection and defense.

When the movement came to replace the Articles of Confederation, state leaders offered the idea of a federal constitution. Sam Adams was hesitant to support a national government. Elected a delegate to the national ratification convention, he revealed his conviction, "As I enter the Building I stumble at the Threshold. I meet with a National Government, instead of a Federal Union of Sovereign States."[15] Adams feared that a national government would have too much power and not long remain free. Others among those who gave us the Declaration and the Constitution overpowered his voice. With an understanding of the unique Scriptural principle of liberty *and* union, the Founders could preserve both the moral and common law. America's Federalism has its root in the two commandments of Christ—love God, and love your neighbor. Patrick Henry has been called the true "Trumpet Voice" of freedom.[16] Educated at home by his father and in a local common school, Henry certainly possessed an eloquence unmatched in his day. He too was skeptical of a national government and an enemy of government overreach. He, George Mason, John Tyler, Benjamin Harrison, James Monroe, and others are largely responsible for the assurance that the Constitution would have the Bill of Rights from the beginning. The First Amendment has remained the most crucial one, and the protection of conscience today is a vital issue for families as regards education, as in all of life matters.

While some remnants of Christian orthodoxy remained, the results of Unitarianism were devastating. By the early 1800s, the Unitarian influence on New England churches had become cemented. In 1837, Massachusetts formed the very first state board

---

15. Samuel Adams, *The Writings of Samuel Adams: 1778–1802*, vol. 4 (New York: G. P. Putnam's Sons, 1908), 324.
16. William J. Federer, *America's God and Country: Encyclopedia of Quotations* (St. Louis: Amerisearch, 2000), 758.

of public instruction. Other states followed suit. Until the Unitarian influence became prominent in New England churches and legislature, all schooling had been Christian education. Horace Mann was then president of the Massachusetts state Senate, and close to Governor Edward Everett. Both followed Germany's Hegelian philosophy, which claimed that nothing was absolute, and that man's ideas were superior to the Bible. Massachusetts formally adopted into education secular humanism as taught in the German state of Prussia. This introduced a radical change away from the principles of a Biblical perspective to create two paths of education—Biblical Christian and secular. For example, beginning in 1836, the original *McGuffey's Readers* continued the Biblical heritage throughout the states, until revised editions appeared in 1879. Other textbooks retained much explicitly or implied Christian content for many years in many states. The 1828 Webster's *Dictionary* with its Biblical references throughout also remained a force in the early era of the American republic.[17]

With John Dewey came even greater and sweeping changes in the textbooks. A philosophy professor at Columbia University and the University of Chicago, Dewey was a Hegelian, holding that truth is always in process. Morals change, society changes. His theme was *change and adjust, change and adjust*. He was the first president of the American Humanist Society and he signed the *Humanist Manifesto* in 1953. The *Manifesto* opens with this declaration: "The time has come for widespread recognition of the radical changes in religious beliefs throughout the modern world." He offered a new religion: humanism—meaning that man is the measure of all things. The time had passed for theism. Dewey's

---

17. With the republication of the 1838 Sixth Edition *McGuffey's Readers* by Mott Media in 1982, American children can now continue to enjoy the blessings of this work. Also, Webster's *Dictionary*'s new publisher, Merriam-Webster, secularized the original Christian work. The good news is that the Foundation for American Education republishes the great Christian 1828 Christian edition, available at FACE.net/noah-websters-1828-dictionary/. Webster's 1828 *Dictionary* can also be accessed online at webstersdictionary1828.com/. *McGuffey's Readers* can be purchased online at mottmedia.com/mcguffey-s-readers-2.

most ardent followers were university professors training the next generation of educators. Most of those early ones came from Europe, schooled in Hegel's philosophy. The National Education Association went along with the dramatic shift in education's content and objectives. To achieve their goals, humanists must distort history to remove the greatness of Western Civilization, and they must give children a new inheritance to replace the Hebrew-Christian foundation, which had for generations proclaimed liberty to Everyman.

It would be a new religion to which the curriculum would now conform.

Dr. Paul Vitz, a famed psychologist, and many others, have sounded alarms for the public. They condemned the educational mind-control techniques of Values Clarification, Magic Circle, Quest, and all the programs that government schools have used for many decades. Many educators, including myself, have joined in that condemnation. Keenly aware of these programs' undermining of the literate and moral training of our children over the years, we have remained steadfast in our opposition to them.

We recently observed D-Day across our land. Nothing less than our freedom was won that day on the Normandy beaches. Yet today, is not our freedom in even more danger than it was then? Five Supreme Court justices—Blackmun, Kennedy, O'Connor, Stevens, and Souter—told you that you have a fundamental right to kill a human being and even encouraged it. Can we say that we live under the rule of moral law? When a parent no longer has the right to educate his child by the dictates of his conscience, do we really have liberty? How will Christian parents deal with Deuteronomy 6:7?

> And thou shalt teach them [God's laws] diligently unto thy children, and shalt talk of them when thou sittest in thine house, and when thou walkest by the way, and when thou liest down, and when thou risest up.

Isn't the issue, for all of us in all of life, this: obedience to the

Lord? And is the First Amendment still protection for this liberty of conscience? We need the kind of education that the Pilgrim and Puritan fathers brought with them—fear of and disdain for tyranny, a love of the moral and common law, building on the cherished liberties. If only one generation submits itself as the "mere creature of the State," America will no longer exist as we have known it. Restoration begins with a courageous and faithful individual mind and heart. Then we must reproduce that courage and faith in the children of our families. Malachi 2:15 says, "He seeks godly offspring. Therefore take heed to your spirit, and let none deal treacherously with the wife of his youth" (NKJV). Also, be not afraid: "The fear of man brings a snare, but whoever trusts in the LORD shall be safe" (Proverbs 29:25 NKJV).

The Crisis We Face Today, and Its Only Solution

December 2017

On the Occasion of Christmas

We have heard the thirteenth century called the Age of Faith, the eighteenth century called the Age of Reason, and the twentieth century called the Atomic Age.

Some call our current era the Age of Irrationalism.

Today, many who are labeled *intellectuals* commonly despair of true knowledge. Their pagan philosophers have completely undermined any materialistic foundation for knowledge. Government schools and colleges have accordingly given up the possibility of moral absolutes.

For centuries, people of faith—Old Testament and New Testament believers and scholars—believed that Holy Writ alone effectively communicates to man trustworthy knowledge—that is, truth, or reality. In fact, God gave its writs for man's redemption and restoration of relationship with God and men.

Theologian Charles Hodge takes *rationalism*, in general, in its ordinary sense. He says rationalism is a cognitive faculty for perceiving, comparing, judging, and inferring. Man is capable of thought either through his natural sinful bent, the result of the Edenic fall, or through the lens of Scripture by the power of the Holy Spirit. Generations of Christians accepted rational thought, in the context of Biblical revelation and God's intellectual gifts to man, as normal. God is ultimately and transcendentally rational, and He gave the gift of rational thought to man.[1] When we discard Biblical thought and the foundations of reason, what do we lose? We lose objective truth and all the safety that goes with it. Due to man's fall into sin, humanistic rationale—apparently self-serving—always ends badly.

Dr. Sinclair Ferguson has written passionately about the spiritual power of the printed word, and especially since the birth of the printing press. Even earlier, Paul asked Timothy from prison to bring his "books, but especially the parchments" (Second Timothy 4:13). Yet today, our lack of reading and literacy is alarming. Reading Christian literature, in addition to our Bible reading, adds to the health of the Christian Church. Dr. Ferguson writes that Martin Luther was responsible for, amazingly, one-third of all the books published in the German language in the first half of the sixteenth century. We really must remember and celebrate the Reformation—again and again.[2]

Libraries are declining in possession of books, selecting technology instead. To me, this is a travesty. Imagine every church resolving to build a library filled with sound theology and good applied-faith books. We need books that take us toward "the stature of the fulness of Christ" (Ephesians 4:13).

---

1. A full treatment of the philosophy of knowledge is far beyond our scope here. In summary, we understand rationalism with due apprehension of our tendency to sinful irrational thought. Our capability for rational thought rests entirely in ability given by and through Christ alone by His special redemption or by common grace. In Athens, Paul the Apostle dialogued, reasoned, or argued (Gk. *dialégomai*) daily from Scripture (Acts 17:17). True knowledge bears good fruit. It is tested and proved, as with the Christian origin of the historic scientific method. It is an application of the Biblical understanding of learning. Trusting God and Scripture leads to knowledge. Ultimately, the Bible clearly says that we can only *know* through relationship with God. Consider First Corinthians 8:2. Faith is an essential element of knowledge. See Charles Hodge, *Systematic Theology*, vol. I, Introduction, chapter III, "Rationalism" (Woodstock, Ontario: Devoted Publishing, 2016). —Ed.
2. Sinclair B. Ferguson, *Read Any Good Books?* (Edinburgh: Banner of Truth Trust, 1992).

Would not Christian parents determine to have their children learn from the great historic Christian leaders—Augustine, Calvin, Spurgeon, Bunyan, or Baxter? Paul longs for us to connect with the saints and prays so in Ephesians 3:18–19: "May [you believers] be able to comprehend with all saints what is the breadth, and length, and depth, and height; and to know the love of Christ, which passeth knowledge, that ye might be filled with all the fulness of God."

Many in today's world repudiate the belief that man can possess true knowledge. They despair of knowledge, unable to fully accept and embrace God's Word. If we cannot affirm the virgin birth, how can we affirm the inerrancy of Scripture? We walk by faith. The alternative—if we are honest about the materialists' presuppositions and philosophical history—only produces intellectual suicide. To them, knowledge is impossible. Let's face it—irrationalism has permeated our culture. Apart from intelligent defense by the faithful, presumptuous and arrogant contemporary attacks—on truth, on revelation, on logic—do great damage.

As Christian believers, we pray for revival. Is it possible to have a truly Christian revival if irrationalism has even invaded our churches through compromises? As our first duty, we must affirm sound doctrine and the best theoretical models. Then we must apply these to our everyday practice, testing the fruit and making whatever corrections are necessary. If American Christians do not affirm and assert true knowledge, how can the Church extend the power of the Gospel?

Decades ago, a missionary of worldwide travel came into the life of our family and ministry, visiting us numerous times while in the States. He brought a new understanding of Paul's writing in Romans to us all. He took us through the eleven chapters expanding on doctrine and theory, and then the last chapters on living out that doctrine in daily practice. Paul clearly explained it to help us avoid confusion and irrationalism. This is a promise: "Sin shall not have dominion over you: for ye are not under the law, but under grace" (Romans 6:14).

However, note this: Sin is not entirely dead in us or as an operating power in the world. We must remain aware of sin's working in us, availing ourselves of the Christ's power to efface it. We must remain vigilant against sin in the world, opposing it as God gives grace in our spheres (John 16:33; Romans 12:21; First John 4:4).

In every season, we have the assurance of God's Word. We have the personal revelation of who He is. He is the

> "I am," the personal God. All the names and titles given to him; all the attributes ascribed to Him; all the works attributed to Him, are revelations of what He truly is. He is the Elohim, the Mighty One, the Holy One, the Omnipresent Spirit; He is the creator, the preserver, the governor of all things. He is our Father. He is the hearer of prayer; the giver of all good. He feeds the young ravens. He clothes the flowers of the field. He is Love.
>
> He so loved the world as to give his only begotten Son, that whosoever believeth in Him might not perish but have everlasting life [John 3:16]. He is merciful, long-suffering, abundant in goodness and truth. He is a present help in every time of need; a refuge, a high tower, an exceeding great reward.... He is our ruler, and father, with whom we can commune. His favour is our life, his loving-kindness better than life. This sublime revelation of God in his own nature and in his relation to us is not a delusion.... It makes God known to us as He really is. We therefore know God, although no creature can understand the Almighty unto perfection.

As we view the Son, we view the Father.

> God has revealed Himself in the person of His Son.... He and the Father are one [John 10:30; 14:10–11].... The revelation which He made of Himself was the manifestation of God.... The words of Christ were the words of God [Luke 21:33]. The works of Christ were the works of God [John 3:34; 14:11]. The love, mercy, tenderness, the forgiving grace, as well as the holiness, the severity and power manifested by Christ, were all manifestations of what God truly is. We see, therefore, as with

our own eyes, what God is.... Philosophy must veil her face in the presence of Jesus Christ, as God manifest in the flesh. She may not presume in that presence to say that God is not, and is not known to be, what Christ himself most clearly was. This doctrine that God is the object of certain and true knowledge lies at the foundation of all religion, and therefore must never be given up.[3]

This writer is so grateful for the opportunity to write on the tragic cultural decay in our beloved republic connected to the deep meaning of Christmas—the incarnation of the Christ, the only true solution. May every Christian embrace the Gospel more intimately, and reach out more passionately to others. May the Scriptures and the carols have more meaning than ever before in our hearts. May we, in our family life, renew our faith commitment to each other, to our local congregation, and to the embracing of the Word more diligently and more thankfully.

> Romans 8:1: "There is therefore now no condemnation to them which are in Christ Jesus, who walk not after the flesh, but after the Spirit."

> Romans 8:28: "And we know that all things work together for good to them that love God, to them who are the called according to His purpose."

---

3. Charles Hodge, *Systematic Theology*, vol. I (Woodstock, Ontario: Devoted Publishing, 2016), 164.

CHAPTER 45

INDEPENDENCE DAY, JULY 4

July 2018

An Independent People Are Wholly Dependent upon God

The creation itself also will be delivered from the bondage of corruption into the glorious liberty of the children of God. (Romans 8:21 NKJ)

I will walk at liberty: for I seek Thy precepts. (Psalm 119:45)

The Pennsylvania State House was hot, humid, and charged with emotion as representatives for the thirteen colonies came together in June and July of 1776. They worked to consider severing their allegiance to the mother country, now an oppressive regime abusing the colonies for financial gain. They pledged their lives, fortunes, and sacred honor. They risked conviction for treason in order to gain liberty for themselves and posterity. On July 4, 1776, the Continental Congress passed the Unanimous Declaration of the Thirteen United States of America. Eleven years later, a similar group of patriotic statesmen framed the Constitution on the Declaration's principles.

These dates are more important than most of us realize. On July 4, 1776, God providentially birthed a nation. Its citizens have enjoyed a greater degree of civil liberty than any other nation in history since the early days of the nation of Israel in the Old Testament.

Samuel Adams, called the Father of the Revolution, after signing the Unanimous Declaration on August 2, said that

We have this day restored the Sovereign, to whom all men ought to be obedient, and from the rising to the setting of the sun, let His kingdom come.[1]

Is it true that with the birth of our nation, mankind restored the sovereign God to His rightful place in civil, and all human, affairs? Did this providential act make way for His kingdom to come on the earth in a fuller measure than previously? Let us explore these questions more fully.

Take Thirty Minutes

Take time to read the actual Declaration document and examine how its principles are timeless, giving us wisdom for the restoration of our great nation.

In addition to the indirect references to God and Biblical principles, there are four direct references to God in the Unanimous Declaration. The first reference is the phrase, "laws of nature and of nature's God entitle them...." This is a powerful statement indicating God as the supreme Lawgiver. The "laws of nature" refer to the laws that God made that apply to all men, knowable even if one does not have God's written revelation.[2]

These include laws against murdering and stealing. This natural law condemned Cain for killing his brother, many years before God put in writing "Thou shalt not kill."

The laws "of nature's God" refer to the law of God as codified in the Bible—His written revelation. America's Founders taught that men must subject themselves to the supreme Lawgiver and to His law, His Word. They knew that only then would the Lord, the first Founding Father, bless this new nation. As George Washington stated in the *First Inaugural Address*, "The propitious smiles

---

1. David Barton, *The Myth of Separation* (Aledo, TX: WallBuilder Press, 1989), 98.
2. These laws of nature remain subjective and inexact apart from special revelation. Only in America did their application redound to their highest expression in history, due to its hundred and fifty years and more of diligently applying the Word of God to all of life. We accept the laws as of nature from Romans 1, but emphasize the need to study Scriptures to guide and correct us into "all truth," so that we do not presume upon God (John 16:13; Second Timothy 3:16). —Ed.

of Heaven, can never be expected on a nation that disregards the eternal rules of order and right, which Heaven itself has ordained."[3]

Commentators have written volumes on the Preamble to the Unanimous Declaration, particularly concerning this sentence:

> We hold these truths to be self-evident, that all men are created equal, that they are endowed by their Creator with certain unalienable Rights, that among these are Life, Liberty, and the pursuit of Happiness.

The truth that all men are created equal is derived from the Bible,[4] and for the first time in history, an attempt was made for a nation to live by it. We also observe that the authors of this document declared their belief in and reliance upon God, the Creator. This is a powerful affirmation, for He who creates must also sustain. This is why they often referred to God as their provider, calling Him *Providence*. Finally, they also highlighted God as the all-powerful Creator who alone is the Author of rights. No one can take away inherent rights. This was a deliberate and bold break from the past, for in the history of mankind, civil government always established *itself* as the grantor of rights.

> That to secure these rights, Governments are instituted among Men, deriving their just powers from the consent of the governed.

The next section of the Declaration details that right, and even duty, of the people to properly steward their civil government. A morally responsible people must steward themselves—practice self-government—steward their family with family government, their church with church government, and their voluntary associations with voluntary government of ministry. They also must steward their civil governments. God gives this responsibility. Men

---

3. John Frederick Schroeder, compiler, *Maxims of George Washington* (Mount Vernon, VA: The Mount Vernon Ladies' Association, 1942), 170.

4. For example, Acts 10:34 says that God is "no respecter of persons," and Exodus 12:49 says, "One law shall be to him that is homeborn, and unto the stranger that sojourneth among you."

must then alter or abolish their civil government as necessary to conform to ruling Biblical principles. In First Samuel 12, we see Samuel giving an account of his judgeship to the people. He asks the people to judge him, that they may have an opportunity to practice due stewardship over their civil government. Of course, we know that they chose foolishly in asking for a king. And God judged them (First Samuel 12:19).

Tyranny Exposed and Rebuked

Thomas Jefferson once spoke of "the holy author of our religion, who being lord both of body and mind, yet chose not to propagate it by coercions on either, as was in his Almighty power to do."[5] The essence of tyranny in civil government is the abuse of power. The next section of the Declaration lists the abuses of King George. The list is quite extensive and makes very interesting reading, especially in light of historic parallels. If we brought similar charges to our civil governments today, those exerting powers beyond their Biblical jurisdiction, we would have quite a long list as well. Let us enumerate a few examples, appropriate to America today:

Establishing a Secular Culture

1. Demanding an application of the "separation of church and state" that effectively denies many public expressions of Biblical Christianity, such as displaying Christian symbols and public prayer
2. Favoring non-Christian expressions over Biblical ones

Suspending Assemblies

1. Persecuting, harassing, and in some cases closing down Christian schools and homeschools
2. Forbidding Bible studies, prayer, or other expressions of Christianity in government schools

Usurping Power

1. Judicial activism effectively turning judges into lawmakers

---

5. Carl J. Richard, *The Founders and the Bible* (Lanham, MD: Rowman & Littlefield, 2016), 296.

2. Executive orders that greatly expand the power of the executive branch beyond its constitutional limits

3. Mandating school attendance through compulsory education laws, usurping the rights of parents

Harming the Citizens through Policies and Practices

1. The establishment of public schools producing millions of functionally illiterate citizens

2. Overstepping its jurisdiction and passing many laws thought to protect us (seat-belt and helmet laws, mandatory vaccinations, minimum wage laws, etc.)

Economic Tyranny

1. Interfering in the free market in myriad ways

2. A taxation rate that is way beyond what is Biblically considered tyrannical (e.g., 10 percent was considered tyrannical (see First Samuel 8)

3. False philanthropy: multitude of wealth redistribution plans that effectively steal from some to give to others

Violations of Conscience

1. Enforcing attendance in government schools where unbiblical ideas are diligently inculcated on a daily basis

2. Taxpayers forced to finance such things as government schooling, welfare, and abortion

3. Removing rights of health-care providers to refuse to perform procedures to which they are opposed

God Is the Supreme Judge

We, therefore, the Representatives of the united States of America, in General Congress, Assembled, appealing to the Supreme Judge of the world for the rectitude of our intentions, do, in the Name, and by Authority of the good People of these Colonies, solemnly publish and declare, That these United Colonies are, and of Right ought to be Free and Independent States;... And for the support of this Declaration, with a firm reliance on the protection of divine Providence, we mutually pledge to each other our Lives, our Fortunes and our sacred Honor.

Declaration of Independence, by John Trumbull, 1819

After pleading their case by listing the grievances against King George, the signers of the Unanimous Declaration submitted their case to the One Judge. They knew and recognized the fact that lesser judges existed. However, they presented their case for trial before the Supreme Judge of the world, the Lord Jesus Christ. God indeed makes men judges, but the absence of a just human authority forces an appeal to heaven, as Jephthah did when the Ammonites threatened Israel (Judges 11:12–27). "Appealing to the Supreme Judge of the world," declared that God is the ultimate and supreme Judge—judged by no man, yet standing in judgment of all, including civil rulers and governments (Psalm 2). When they made their appeal "for the rectitude of our intentions," they declared they believed their cause just and right. That is, that they acted in accordance with God's Word, while the King did not.

The Unanimous Declaration made a declaration of *dependence* as much as a declaration of *independence*. God used Dr. John Witherspoon, Presbyterian pastor and later president of the College of

New Jersey, to urge adding the phrase with "a firm reliance on the protection of divine Providence." This declared that their hope and trust in this life is not in man but in the God who cares for His creation and watches over all, orders their steps, and intervenes for good in their lives. We know that God did intervene many times during the long war to finally win their independence. They repeatedly acknowledged the evident protection of God. In so many circumstances, their enemy would have defeated them had not God miraculously intervened. Washington at one point was prompted to acknowledge this:

> The great Director of events has carried us thro' a variety of Scenes during this long and bloody contest in which we have been for Seven Campaigns, most nobly struggling.[6]

Finally, they continued to act according to Biblical covenant as they vowed to, "mutually pledge to each other our Lives, our Fortunes and our sacred Honor." Of the fifty-six signers, many of them would soon lose their lives, and many would have to forfeit their wealth. There is a cost to liberty, and they were more than willing to pay it.

We Still Must Purchase Liberty at Some Cost

Liberty never was and never will be free! John Philpot Curran, Irish statesman and orator stated:

> It is the common fate of the indolent to see their rights become a prey to the active. The condition upon which God hath given liberty to man is eternal vigilance; which condition if he break, servitude is at once the consequence of his crime and the punishment of his guilt.[7]

As Biblical Christians, God holds us responsible for the stewardship of the liberty He grants us. Accordingly, we must continuously ask ourselves questions:

---

6. Schroeder, *Maxims of George Washington*, 166–67.
7. George Stimpson, *A Book about a Thousand Things* (New York: Harper & Brothers, 1946), 5.

1. Do I understand God's view of liberty, both internal and external?

2. If so, am I willing to submit myself to Him, that I may walk in liberty?

3. Do I have the heart of God for the liberty of my posterity? Based upon my actions today, will my children, grandchildren, and succeeding generations have a greater degree or lesser degree of civil liberty?

4. What is God asking me to do so that this generation and the many to come will walk in the glorious liberty of the children of God?

CHAPTER 46

What Can We Do to Restore America's Christian Heritage?

October 2018

Freedom[1]

But they that wait upon the LORD shall renew their strength; they shall mount up with wings as eagles; they shall run, and not be weary; and they shall walk, and not faint. (Isaiah 40:31)

Nowhere in history is God's hand more evident than in the establishment of the United States of America. The signing of that great and noble document, the Declaration of Independence, not only gave birth to a new nation, it gave birth to a new hope for all nations, ushering in a new era in the history of government on earth.

John Adams, our second president, and one of the signers of the Declaration, was so awestruck by the event in which he had participated, that he wrote his wife Abigail that it "ought to be commemorated as the day of deliverance, by solemn acts of devotion to God Almighty. It ought to be solemnized with pomp and parade, with shows, games, sports, guns, bells, bonfires, and illuminations, from one end of this continent to the other, from this time forward forevermore."[2]

---

1. This chapter first appeared as an article in 1986, when Bobbie Ames served as the Alabama State Director of the Freedom Council.
2. Cited in many works, e.g., Charles Francis Adams, *Familiar Letters of John Adams and His Wife Abigail Adams, During the Revolution* (New York: Hurd & Houghton, 1876), 194.

While Americans have been faithful in following the latter part of Adams's suggestions—the pomp, parades, and illuminations—we have been less so in adhering to the first. Our celebration of the "day of deliverance," like our celebration of Thanksgiving, instituted by the Pilgrims at Plymouth, has tended more and more to the merely secular. The "solemn acts of devotion to God Almighty" advocated by Adams have not only for the most part disappeared, but they would likely be mistakenly rebuffed by many as unconstitutional intermingling of church and state.

But Adams's comment to his wife reveals a recognition found in the writings of all the Founding Fathers—that something far greater than the mere will of men surrounded the events of our nation's beginning. Indeed, all bear reverent testimony to the sense that the mighty hand of God was at work in the affairs of men. They, by responding to the crisis of their time, participated in a turning point in history almost incredible and certainly miraculous given the typical evils of the past.

Beyond their own recognition indeed of their need for firm reliance upon God and His providence, the Founding Fathers represented a people well prepared for this new development in history. The American people—though from thirteen unique colonies and loyal to sundry denominations—had yet received from the same Bible a thorough schooling in the gospel of Truth, including its justice and liberty, and so submitted to it as one people. Many men or women, or descendants of men or women, came to America to escape the religious tyranny of Europe. Here they became accustomed to principled liberty. They thus were quick to recognize tyranny in the following acts of the mother country: The Navigation Acts, the Revenue Acts, the Stamp Act, the Quartering Act, the Townshend Act, and the Boston Port Act.

However, neither the colonists nor their leaders were predisposed to rebellion or desired it. In response to the Stamp Act, Congress entreated England for fair play. Efforts to reason with the oppressors, and reliance on God at the same time, characterized each political effort.

When clear that the king and his Parliament had hardened their hearts, the colonists acted in unison. In town meetings, one after another, they sounded the alarm! Thomas Jefferson spoke of the conviction of the multitude, when he wrote, "The God who gave us life, gave us liberty at the same time; the hand of force may destroy, but cannot disjoin us."[3]

To see the Declaration of Independence as merely a human document is to miss the underlying philosophy and faith that initiated it. To the Founders, the Declaration was a divinely inspired sacred charter to which they pledged their lives, their fortunes, and their sacred honor. It was an expression of the unmerited favor of God. To the Founders, proposition of the Declaration was essential for the good of their sons, their daughters, and all their posterity.

Let us prepare annually for Independence Day as America's "day of deliverance." Can we throughout the year treasure a spiritual deliverance and celebrate our unique form of government—Christian self-government with liberty under law? Let us consecrate ourselves—as individuals, as families, as churches—to the task of rebuilding our nation's Biblical foundation. Let us be both diligent to study and practical to do. Let each of us start where we are. Most of all, let us remember with "solemn acts of devotion," the God Whose mighty hand brought our nation into being.

In the Family

In order to restore the Biblical principles of government that established our nation, we must first restore these principles in our homes. We gain skill as we practice. As God's first institution of society, the home is the first sphere of local self-government. The family makes its greatest contribution to our nation's well-being as it trains and inculcates young men and women with Christian character.

The home trains the heart of the child to righteousness or unrighteousness. The heart is the seat of character. Out of it comes

---

3. Thomas Jefferson, "A Summary View of the Rights of British America," Yale Law School, Lillian Goldman Law Library, *The Avalon Project* at Yale Law School, avalon.law.yale.edu/18th_century/jeffsumm.asp.

either a "good treasure" or an "evil treasure," as Christ makes clear in Luke 6:45. The home ultimately affects every corner of society, by what it builds or does not build in character.

A valuable but often-neglected practice in the home is the use of literature to aid in building character through example. To take advantage of using literature for the training of hearts, modern parents need to research and use the great literature that helped form the character of our early American generations. You will not find this literature used today in government schools. However, this once-treasured literature is a wonderful contribution toward restoring our national character if we will learn from it and apply its lessons.

In the Church

No institution should be better qualified than the Christian churches to impress on believers the Christian responsibility to apply Christian principles of government to every area of life, including the civil sphere. The Reformation introduced the Biblical form of government to the Protestant churches of England. This representative and covenantal model became the pattern for civil government in the American colonies. Later it became the national form of American government created by the U.S. Constitution.

Pastors of all denominations should dare to take the lead in reaffirming the vital link between the individual spiritual freedom granted in the Gospel, and the political freedom that established our nation.

One good starting point, and an inspiring adventure, would be to review the early sermons of the pastors who lived prior to and during the American Revolution. This resource blessing to the pastors would hopefully lead to a life-changing experience for their congregations, the result being the restoration of our nation.

A great resource for this can be found in the books and other resources of FACE.net, the Foundation for American Christian Education, in Chesapeake, Virginia.

We the People

Following are ways the individual can help restore our nation to its Biblical principles of government.

1. Research the hand of God in our United States history. Study, meditate, and pray daily for our spiritual restoration.

2. Make your voice heard. Upon at least an initial preparation in the Biblical principles of justice and liberty, write to candidates, elected officials, newspapers, radio, and TV anchors to express your views. Share with your neighbors. Be ready with specific Gospel answers for the hope that lies within us regarding Christian self-government, republican representation, covenantal civil association, Federalism, justice, and liberty. (First Peter 3:15).

3. Become a public relations officer for America's Christian destiny. Set a goal of contacting numbers of people every week to win support for the cause of restoring America's Biblical foundation. Consider hosting an American Christian history study group.

4. With an election coming in November, support those candidates who stand for a godly cause.

5. Consider seriously the power of campaigning for truth. The greatest friend of liberty is truth. Truth is contained in Biblical Christianity and will ultimately triumph. We are on the winning team.

We the People of the United States, in Order to form a more perfect Union, establish Justice, insure domestic Tranquility, provide for the common defence, promote the general Welfare, and secure the Blessings of Liberty to ourselves and our Posterity, do ordain and establish this Constitution for the United States of America.

The first three words of the preamble, "We the People," may be the three most important words in the history of the American Republic![4]

4. "The Constitution of the United States," America's Founding Documents, National Archives, archives.gov/founding-docs/constitution.

EDUCATION TODAY:
RESTORING A CHRISTIAN REPUBLIC

August 1, 2014

Primary sources of American history document beyond contradiction that our Founders established these United States as a Christian republic. These sources include colonial state constitutions and our United States Constitution.

By removing these primary sources of our true history from America's classrooms, recent generations have been educated—or better, *indoctrinated*—to question our historic, orthodox, evangelical Christian roots. This brought about the continued frenzy over separation of church and state.

The United States Constitutional Convention discussed the roles of church and state. Many states had their own established churches and feared a national government might overreach with ever-increasing power. The First Amendment settled that issue. The states may freely continue to support their established churches. And they did so for some time.

The separation of church and state issue first came forward through the influence of the French Revolution, and it was not a widespread influence. All colonies were Christian republics—God ruling through the representation of free citizens in civil government. The colonists landed on our shores as Englishmen. Eventually, the colonists would no longer consider themselves English citizens. They loved their mother country, yet they began to chafe under an abusive feudal monarch. They did not need heavy-handed government. They were *self-governed*, each colony with its own separate, representative colonial government.

After the French and Indian War, the English Parliament tried to usurp power from the American legislatures. Protecting their now-long-established heritage of self-government, Americans then made their Declaration of Independence, and fought a war to settle the matter.

The people restricted officeholders in all colonies to people of faith in Trinitarian Christianity and the infallible nature of the Bible. Court records across the colonies testify that courts of law barred atheists from giving testimony in courts because they professed no ground for personal morality, had no moral ground for truth.

Alexis De Tocqueville, in his American travels, reported that a New York judge in 1831 disqualified an atheist witness, declaring "that he had not before been aware that there was a man living who did not believe in the existence of God; that this belief constituted the sanction of all testimony in a court of justice; and that he knew of no cause in a Christian country where a witness had been permitted to testify without such belief."[1]

The Constitution reflects Christian moral laws. The framers provided checks and balances because of the sinful nature of man and the distrust of power. They refrained from imposing any regulation or control of religion. America has never been without problems, because her citizens are sinners. However, Biblical Christianity dwelled in the hearts of the vast majority of her citizens for a long, long time. The laws of communities, states, and national government clearly reflect this heritage. The Northwest Ordinance provided free land for Christian schools. For many decades Christian schooling was the norm in colonial America. Unitarians were the first to reject locally governed schools and instead to establish controlling state boards of education and state-controlled schools.

---

1. De Tocqueville, *Democracy in America*, vol. I, 391.

Christians and others committed to the moral absolutes of the Bible face the challenge today to restore America's constitutional republic, along with a culture reflecting a Biblical worldview. From the earliest, most ancient times, cultures suffered destruction and, for some, rebuilding. Isaiah 58:12 reminds us that there will always be a remnant, in godly places, to rebuild: "Those from among you will rebuild the ancient ruins; you will raise up the age-old foundations; and you will be called the repairer of the breach, the restorer of the streets in which to dwell" (NASB).

As painful as it is to face today's reality, we must face it for the sake of our children and their future:

- Nineteen out of thirty young adults believe that homosexuality is an acceptable lifestyle[2]
- Out of the average thirty high school students, roughly half have been or are sexually active[3]
- Fourteen don't see a great risk in heavy daily drinking[4]
- Fifteen of them have used marijuana[5]
- Nine admitted stealing from a store[6]
- Twenty admitted lying to their parents about alcohol and/ or drugs[7]
- Nineteen admitted cheating on a test[8]

---

2. Darren K. Carlson, "Acceptance of Homosexuality: A Youth Movement," *Gallup*, February 19, 2002, news.gallup.com/poll/5341/Acceptance-Homosexuality-Youth-Movement.aspx.

3. "Key Graphics on Trends Among High School Students from CDC's National Youth Risk Behavior Survey (YRBS), 1991–2011," Center for Disease Control and Prevention, cdc.gov/nchhstp/newsroom/2012/yrbs-graphics2012.html.

4. "2010 Partnership Attitude Tracking Study: Teens and Parents," MetLife Foundation (April 6, 2011): 12.

5. "2010 Partnership Attitude Tracking Study," 9.

6. "Josephson Institute of Ethics Releases Study on High School Character and Adult Conduct," Josephson Institute (October 29, 2009), josephsoninstitute. org/surveys/.

7. Lene Arnett Jensen, Jeffrey Jensen Arnett, S. Shirley Feldman, and Elizabeth Cauffman, "The Right to Do Wrong: Lying to Parents Among Adolescents and Emerging Adults," *Journal of Youth and Adolescence* 33:2 (April 2004): 101–112.

8. "Josephson Institute of Ethics Releases Study on High School Character and

- Twenty-seven are satisfied with their own ethics and character[9]

Between 70 percent and 80 percent walk away from church by the end of their freshman year in college.[10] That means that seven out of ten of our children will not be reared in the discipline and instruction of the Christian faith. Another research group has found that 86 percent had begun to question the Bible by high school.[11] Keep in mind that 80–90 percent of Christian parents have their children in public schools.[12]

Through the centuries, when false teachings have corrupted a culture, church leaders have joined together calling God's covenant people back to Scriptural Truth. Church leaders of numerous denominations and many from across the world have united their efforts, forming an organization for such a time as this: The International Church Council Project. Their recent title, *Rebuilding Civilization on the Bible*, is a weapon targeting twenty-four areas of false doctrine that to a large degree have infiltrated the modern church, and certainly the culture. The authors advise the readers that the book does not represent *all* that the church should believe, but rather the "twenty-four battle lines on which the enemy is currently attacking the church." It will be obvious to the reader that the same false teachings have long been primary in the secular education institutions of elementary, secondary, and higher education. Poison has permeated today's culture, and the family structure and the church have been the targets.

Adult Conduct," Josephson Institute (October 29, 2009), josephsoninstitute.org/surveys/.

9. "Josephson Institute of Ethics Releases Study."

10. Jon Walker, "Family Life Council Says It's Time to Bring Family Back to Life," June 12, 2002, sbcannualmeeting.net/sbc02/newsroom/newspage.asp?ID=261; "Reasons 18- to 22-Year-Olds Drop Out of Church," *LifeWay Research*, August 7, 2007, lifewayresearch.com.

11. Britt Beemer's America's Research Group, in Sheila Richardson, "Today's Youth—Walking Away from Truth," *Answers Magazine*, July 12, 2007, answersingenesis.org.

12. Beemer in Richardson, "Today's Youth."

Just as the principles of the Bible have provided the foundation for civil government in the Constitution, these same principles are the foundation for history, law, arts, economics, science, and all of life's faith and practice.

Rebuilding Civilization on the Bible is the work of many theologians across denominational lines, compiled and edited by Dr. Jay Grimstead and the late Dr. Eugene Calvin Clingman. Meant to be a very personal call to action, it provides the tool we need to be equipped for spiritual warfare. The goal is to join forces, to identify those of like mind, to enlist others, and to be bold in proclaiming the truth.

The twenty-four documents are available separately for download free from the International Church Council Project website.[13] The documents clarify the clear teaching of Scripture on the issues bringing confusion and deconstruction of our Christian culture. The reader can order the three hundred-plus-page book, published in 2014 by Nordskog Publishing Company in Ventura, California. To review the book, contact the publisher.[14]

Jude's admonition has never been more relevant than today: "Contend earnestly for the faith which was once for all delivered to the saints. For certain men have crept in unnoticed, ... who turn the grace of our God into lewdness and deny the only Lord God and our Lord Jesus Christ" (Jude 3–4 NKJV).

---

13. ChurchCouncil.org.
14. Grimstead and Clingman, *Rebuilding Civilization on the Bible*.

CHAPTER 48

THE WORLD JESUS CHRIST ENTERED AND THE IMPACT HE MADE

January 2013

Hundreds of millions of people have again recently celebrated Jesus's birthday. The tri-county area of Alabama was then filled with lights, carols, rituals, and special services. Ironically, many celebrate the season without even knowing or caring about Jesus's birth, life, death, or resurrection. And most importantly, those who celebrate in ignorance have no clue that His birth brought our very invitation, by faith, to His salvation.

The birth of Jesus is the most important event in all of history—for indeed, history is, after all, *His Story*. We date all of history—B.C. and A.D.—as before or after that great event, His birth. What was so life- and world-changing about His birth? He was born and lived in small towns in Judea and Galilee, insignificant parts of the Roman Empire by world standards, and He only lived thirty-three years. One of His own followers betrayed him. Imperial Rome proudly but unjustly executed Him. What a world to come into! Yet His earthy ministry was only the beginning of His impact. Three days after His murder, He came out of His borrowed grave. He was and is the Second Person of the Holy Trinity—the Son, the Logos, the Word, the Wisdom of God.

For centuries the Hebrew people had expected His coming. God's Word foretold His coming and His kingdom that would know no end. Indeed, His coming did bring a new kingdom, a totally new civilization to mankind. The world into which Christ came was one of violence in Greece and Rome. The government school where I grew up taught the revisionist view of history, which portrayed Greece and Rome as civilized societies, of enlightenment and democracy. They taught that we derived ideas of justice and law from these empires. My grandfather was part Jewish, and he loved Israel and spent time there. He determined to know true history. My mother's father taught her not to credit Greece and Rome as having inspired Western Civilization, but to credit men living out of God's Word by His Spirit through history. Rome and Greece did not build Western Civilization. The entry of Jesus Christ into the world accounts for all of mankind's progress. Roman cruelty and greed built an empire of violence, of conquest and slavery. She built her empire with military legions whose generals proudly used blood to maintain the peace.

The Christian faith first challenged the religions of Greece and Rome. The pagan culture produced gods and goddesses larger and supposedly more powerful than humans, but with sinful qualities like humans. They invented false gods to intervene in their lives from birth to death, for harvest, for love, for wars, for fertility, etc.[1] Astrology, witchcraft, animism, and ghosts, animal and human sacrifices, and polytheism prevailed. The arena's gladiatorial gore illustrates the sinful love of violence and infliction of pain. At times, one third of Italy's population consisted of slaves. They lived and died merely to serve and entertain their masters.

Neither Rome nor Greece educated the individual with knowledge or wisdom to establish individual calling and purpose. In fact, the Greek culture, which Rome emulated, never processed the idea of individualism. The Greek culture especially stressed community and the sense of belonging to the community. Leaders ruled over the community. Even in the great Athens direct democracy, only a small minority of the population participated.[2] Ignorance

---

1. We would argue that, on one hand, the classic pagans, in conceiving their gods, merely deified themselves, and on the other hand, gave themselves an excuse when their lives went wrong. They could blame the gods' intervention. —Ed.
2. See, for example, "Athenian Democracy," *Wikipedia*, en.wikipedia.org/

and illiteracy reigned in both Greece and Rome. Only a few elite knew or understood their philosophy. Both Rome and Greece, as virtually every other ancient nation, were called church-states. Rome eventually called the emperor divine.

The earliest teaching of Christianity emphasized as essential for the early Church that individual members *know truth*. "Ye shall know the truth, and the truth shall make you free" (John 8:32). After some time, the church of Rome gained power. To control the people, it used images, statues, frescoes, and other mixed pagan elements of worship with Christian teachings. Even after the spread of Christianity, Roman law remained relatively uninfluenced by Christianity. It never embraced what we know as justice, but remained filled with corruption. Against the historic totalitarianism of nearly the whole pagan world, Christ and his followers taught the Scriptures, introducing the God of the Bible to the world as a rational, loving, teaching, personal God who reveals Himself to His people through his Word. Believers learned the Ten Commandments. This law authoritatively and comprehensively treats against the use of idols in worship, the rightful place of parents, purpose of the Lord's Day, and condemnation of lying, murder, and covetousness. Jesus elaborated on the Ten Commandments in Matthew 5–7, in the Sermon on the Mount. He gave the invitation to saving justification, by faith, trusting in His righteousness alone. He made the believer acceptable to God for all eternity through His own death and resurrection. This is the Gospel of Christianity and the theological basis for a new civilization that Jesus Christ brought into the world. Imagine the suffering of the early church persecutions as pagan rulers lost their power over men.

No longer would Aristotle's view prevail: "The State is the highest of all.... Citizens belong to the State." Now men knew the truth. Man is a creation of God, made in His image. God created the earth for man. How liberating to know that there is neither

---

wiki/Athenian_democracy, and "Democracy Is Born," *Ancient Civilizations*, ushistory.org/civ/index.asp. —Ed.

Jew nor Greek, slave nor free, but all are of one body in Christ Jesus. (Galatians 3:28)

In the Middle Ages, many attacks came on the truths of God's Word. For one, many tried to urge combining pagan and Christian elements of worship on churches across Europe and the Middle East. The Roman Empire, largely upon the example of Constantine, focused on building Christendom—a religious-political order. Constantine assisted the Bishops to become a ruling class of the church, and local self-governing churches became nearly extinct. Freedom of religion was outlawed. Despite Constantine's claiming he saw a vision of the cross before the Battle of Milvian Bridge, no evidence exists that Constantine truly understood the Gospel. His edict against the Jews made it a crime for them to proselytize. As the Middle Ages moved on, superstition and magic still prevailed in everyday living. How could an individual know the truth? Only priests, monks, and scribes were allowed to read the Bible. Bibles themselves were very large and heavy, chained to the pulpits of the cathedrals of the Roman world. The common man could not truly know for himself what God "hath said."

The Protestant Reformation of the Sixteenth Century

It was not until the sixteenth century that God providentially, through the influence of the Gospel of Jesus Christ, removed the chains from His Word. In the small village of Wittenburg, a thirty-four-year-old Augustinian priest walked to the Castle Church and nailed a paper to the church door. It contained a list of theological propositions for debate. Martin Luther's debate assertions turned the world upside down indeed. These acts unleashed the Protestant Reformation. With it came world-transforming reforms in religious and civil liberty. Constitutional government resulted. Biblical principles birthed those ideas of liberty, civil rights, free markets, free exchanges of ideas, and the sanctity of private property—internal intellectual property, as well as tangible property. These revolutionary ideas resulted from Luther's bold stand for the Bible in the hands of the common man. Little did he realize, through his primary stand on salvation and justification by faith, what would follow. All resulted from breaking the intellectual and spiritual chains that had held man in ignorance of the Gospel, and placing the Word of God in his hands. Luther saw himself as protesting the sale of indulgences, as he knew that man is saved through faith in Christ alone, through Christ's righteousness and not our own. Luther believed that the Scriptures properly guide all of life. The issue of salvation was personal for Luther. When he could stand so before His Christ, he realized the liberation of God. No man could stand between himself and God. This was his faith.

The central idea of the Reformation is *sola scriptura*—the Bible alone. Luther translated the Bible from the Hebrew and Greek into German, so that his people could read it in their own language. The Bible formed the Constitution for the Protestant Church. This limited the authority of any church leader over the individual conscience of the believer. The Founding Fathers of America insisted on a written constitution for the very same reason. We live and prosper as we live in relation to God's moral law.

The Reformation not changed only the church, but transformed law and economics with the concept that all work accomplished for God's glory is honorable labor and acceptable to Him. Christianity birthed a free market, a free society, and capitalism. Active Christian leaders gleaned these and other new insights from the Protestant Reformation largely through the writing of leading Reformers, primarily John Calvin. Calvin organized the theology of Luther and others, systematizing them into writing more thoroughly than anyone else. Certainly we cannot overstate his influence with regard to England's liberties and America's founding principles. One cannot find a single virtue in early America not rooted in Biblical principle. What in early America could so uniquely produce the greatest liberty and prosperity the world has ever seen? Could it have been this secret? "But seek ye first the kingdom of God, and His righteousness; and all these things shall be added unto you" (Matthew 6:33). America's New England ministers read Calvin. They preached from his writings. The sermons, still in print, focused on their devotion for godly education, piety, liberty, and representative government. Their patriotism demonstrated that they were giants in the land. D. James Kennedy called these ministers "watchmen on the wall." They preached liberty under fire. They preached liberty through the entire formation of our Constitution and the building of America. Their election sermons were filled with passion and wisdom, with warnings against tyranny in all forms. They understood the cultural mandate of Genesis 1:26–28. They confronted the culture to subdue it to Christ's liberty. Christ's Great Commission goes out to every generation of believers. All power and authority in heaven and earth belong to Him. They spoke out on law, education, politics, government, entertainment, foreign influences, and anything else that influenced the culture.

What Happened to the Modern Church?

The late Dr. D. James Kennedy observed, "By the middle of the 20th century, America's pulpits fell silent. Most Christians today, and probably ministers, are under the mistaken assumption that they should not take an active role in the moral and political climate of our nation."[3] How many laypeople in our churches take the time to become well informed about what really goes on in the world? You cannot get the whole story from television or daily news headlines.

Dr. Francis Schaeffer wrote, "Truth demands confrontation.... Here is the great evangelical disaster—the failure of the evangelical world to stand for truth as truth. There is only one word for this—namely *accommodation*."[4]

What happened and what do we do now? Our nation is over twenty-three trillion dollars in debt.[5] China finances national debt. The government tramples on individual liberties. Many in

---

3. D. James Kennedy, *Today's Conflict, Tomorrow's Crisis* (Fort Lauderdale, FL: Coral Ridge Ministries, 2002), 10–11.

4. Francis A. Schaeffer, *The Great Evangelical Disaster* (Wheaton, IL: Crossway Books, 1984), 37.

5. See US Debt Clock, usdebtclock.org.

American leadership acclaim the failed economic socialism of Germany, and President Obama declared that we are no longer a "Christian nation."[6] Well, we have murdered over sixty-one million babies in the womb,[7] and now declare that every woman of any age has a *right* to kill a baby in the womb or even after delivery.[8] Families in America present a tragic picture of brokenness, divorce, children out of wedlock, single parents in poverty, and crime at staggering levels.

A completely different worldview has taken over our nation from that of the Protestant Reformation and America's founding. In Jeremiah's day, an exchange took place. The prophet demanded, "Hath a nation changed their gods, which are yet no gods? but My people have changed their glory for that which doth not profit" (Jeremiah 2:11). What will be the legacy for our children and grand-children? Will they ask us, "What did you do?" And what will our answer be?

---

6. "Call to Renewal," address given June 28, 2006, at Washington D.C.

7. "Number of Abortions - Abortion Counters," United States since Roe v. Wade, numberofabortions.com.

8. Caleb Parke, Gregg Re, "Dems Block 'Born Alive' Bill to Provide Medical Care to Infants who Survive Failed Abortions," *Fox News*, February 25, 2019, foxnews.com.

CHAPTER 49

GOD'S ASTOUNDING GRACE IN A MANGER

December 2012

"For unto you is born this day in the city of David a Saviour, which is Christ the Lord.... Ye shall find the babe wrapped in swaddling clothes, lying in a manger." (Luke 2:11–12)

Every year at this time, the season beckons us to relive the search of the humble shepherds for the long-awaited anointed One, the One Who will rule. The voice of the angel rings out with the Good News of the Babe of Bethlehem. Wouldn't it be sad not to recognize the magnitude of His birth, the magnitude of God's love, His grace? Grace! Free grace! John Newton wrote the wonderful words that we sing: "Amazing grace, how sweet the sound that saved a wretch like me!" The Gospel may be summed up in that word *grace*.

We have discovered close to two hundred different names for our Lord in the Scriptures, beginning with Genesis 3:15, where the text calls Him the seed of the woman. "And I will put enmity between thee and the woman, and between thy seed and her seed."

Yes, the baby in the manger came from the bosom of the Father to become the Seed of the woman. In Genesis 49:10, our Lord is called the Peacemaker, Shiloh. "The sceptre shall not depart from Judah, nor a lawgiver from between his feet, until Shiloh come; and unto Him shall the gathering of the people be." Later, that same chapter refers to our Lord as "the Stone of Israel," the chief cornerstone (Genesis 49:24; see also Psalm 118:22). Leviticus 2:1 and 3:1 call for special offerings, meat offerings, and peace offerings, calling for special times for intimate communion with the Lord. This is not legalism. The freewill offerings brought the previously slavish Israel to know and love the gracious God on His terms, for their own good. Today, these provisions of God's law assure you, with faith as a believer, no obstacle can come between you and your Lord.

Numbers 24:17 pictures our Lord as "a Star out of Jacob." "I shall see Him.... I shall behold Him." Throughout, the Old Testament invites us to see our Lord through the Word of prophecy. He is the "Captain of the host of the LORD" (Joshua 5:14), "the Rock of my salvation" (Second Samuel 22:47), "the Light of the morning," and He shall be "as the tender grass ... shining after rain." (Second Samuel 23:4) What a beautiful picture! God's shepherds lead their flock to the pastures with the tender grass.

Psalm 18:2 inspired the hymn we all love: "The LORD is my rock, and my fortress, and my deliverer; my God, my strength, in whom I will trust." The hymn goes, "A mighty fortress is our God, a bulwark never failing; our Helper He, amid the flood of mortal ills prevailing." Every failure in our lives comes about when we turn to a different fortress than the One prepared and kept for us by our Deliverer. That beloved hymn ends with, "And He must win the battle."

The book of Proverbs calls Jesus Wisdom (3:19), and Understanding (4:4–7), and "a Friend that sticketh closer than a brother" (18:24). In figure, Solomon calls Christ "the Rose of Sharon, and the Lily of the valleys" (Song of Solomon 2:1), and Him "whom my soul loveth" (1:7), "the Chiefest among ten thousand" (5:10), and "altogether lovely" (5:16).

For Isaiah, our Lord will be "a Sanctuary" (8:14) and "a great Light" (9:2), and the most familiar of Isaiah's names for our Lord: "Wonderful, Counsellor, The mighty God, The everlasting Father, The Prince of Peace" (9:6).

In the New Testament, Matthew 1:1 first names our Lord in his "book of the generation of Jesus Christ." In using that name, we see important meanings: Jesus, or Yeshua in Hebrew, means

"Savior." Christ means "the Anointed One," the One commissioned to rule. One day, every knee shall bow to Him in heaven and on earth. The name of Jesus (or Yeshua in Hebrew, from the name Joshua) appears over seven hundred times in the New Testament. Indeed, Joshua was a type of our Lord Jesus, as he led Israel to the Promised Land in Old Testament times. Matthew 1:23 calls forth Isaiah 7:14, where the prophet announces our Lord as Immanuel, which means, "God with us." In Matthew 28:19–20, we have His own Word, "I am with you alway, even unto the end of the world."

Every name in the New Testament tells a story. Matthew 11:19 shines the light on Jesus as a "Friend of publicans and sinners." In 13:37, He is the Sower who sowed "the good seed," which is the Word of God. He sows the living seed of grace. He is called the Prophet, the Bridegroom, the Holy One of God, the Son of the Most High God, the Son of Man, the Son of the Highest, the Salvation of God, the Word, the True Light, the Only Begotten of the Father, the Lamb of God, Man of Sorrows, Messiah, and over one hundred fifty more names in some versions.

Whatever else one may conclude, our Lord's birth is the dynamic focal point of Biblical Christianity, *and* of all history. The Gospel of Christ is "the grace of God" (Acts 20:24). We find the message of grace throughout the Bible, from cover to cover. We sing, "Marvelous grace of our loving Lord, grace that exceeds our sin and our guilt."[1]

For the first time since the landing at Jamestown in 1607, a majority of our citizens do not profess to be Bible-believing Christians. The electorate has rejected the moral law of God at the polls in all fifty states, on one issue after another. Rebellion against the moral law is nothing new. It began in the Garden. Not only do we practice sin, we are *born* sinners, rebellious against God. Only by the grace of our Lord, freely given, can we escape bondage to that sin. Romans 3:10 tells man's story: "There is none righteous, no, not one."

---

1. Julia H. Johnston (1849–1919), "Grace Greater than Our Sin," (1911).

When Christmas time once more comes around, as we unpack the Christmas decorations, light the tree, and place the manger in a prominent place, let us all ask God to heal us from spiritual blindness, that we might see Him as He has been shown to be across the entire Bible. He is the giver of grace for life eternal. Grace is God's unmerited favor. Nothing we do or can do merits this grace (Deuteronomy 9:6–8). God gives grace freely to us, though it is costly to Him. As we look at the manger scene and all the decorations for Christmas, it is fitting to keep the cross in sight to remind us of the actual cost of our salvation. Christ became a man to bring us the Gospel. He died a sacrificial death and He rose from the dead for our justification. By grace, He convicted us of our individual sin, and He will continue to enrich our salvation with sanctification. He will fellowship with us for all eternity in heaven. Don't miss it.

CHAPTER 50

THE COMING OF CHRIST:
THE FULFILLMENT OF COVENANT PROMISE

December 2015

Our Creator God has always, by grace, extended covenants to His children. To Adam, He clearly stated that he might eat of "every tree of the garden," except "the tree of the knowledge of good and evil" (Genesis 2:16–17). God obligated Adam to mere faithful obedience.

To Noah, who found grace in the eyes of the Lord, God spoke thusly: "With thee will I establish My covenant; and thou shalt come into the ark, thou, and thy sons, and thy wife, and thy sons' wives with thee" (Genesis 6:18). Noah's reward came through obedience and trust.

After the Tower of Babel and the dispersion of the people, God still offered grace through covenant with Abraham:

> I will make of thee a great nation, and I will bless thee, and make thy name great; and thou shalt be a blessing: And I will bless them that bless thee, and curse him that curseth thee: and in thee shall all families of the earth be blessed. (Genesis 12:2–3)

Over the centuries, theologians have placed emphasis on the covenants of God. For reformers John Calvin and John Knox, the very substance of the covenants of the Old and New Testaments was the same: Jesus Christ and the Gospel of salvation from the beginning of Creation to the fulfillment of the Second Coming.

Other theologians also saw a covenant of works, along with Calvin and Knox's covenant of grace. The covenant of works is sometimes called a legal or *natural* covenant, founded in nature, but also founded in the law of God, written (engraven) in man's heart from the beginning. For obedience, God promised Adam eternal life, yet Adam could not obey. Though Adam could not obey in his own strength, God's grace transcends. Truly, man always and from the beginning needed God's sovereign and unilateral grace in a relationship of faith with Him.

Reformation thought heavily influenced our early American churches. Especially cherished among the writings of the Reformers was that of one Samuel Rutherford (1600–1661). Rutherford wrote what he embraced as "the covenant for life," owing all that we are and have to Him, who gave Himself for us.

Writing in his *Covenant of Life*, Rutherford declared, "The Lord punished Christ for us to declare the glory of His justice in punishing sin in His own Son, who was the sinner by imputation."[1]

His book *Christ Dying and Drawing Sinners To Himself* provides another example of Rutherford's depth of understanding. He alerts us to the fact that the atoning sacrifice for sin was much more profound than the satisfaction of justice. The sacrifice took place in the inner heart, the inner person of Jesus Christ.[2]

As Christmas approaches and we contemplate celebrating the birth of Jesus Christ and his fulfillment of the covenant of grace, how do we experience that covenant in a very personal way? As we think of the baby Jesus in a manger, can we even fathom the Father's only begotten Son, before the world began already appointed the sacrificial Redeemer of the Father's creation?

How difficult even to imagine the love leading to the Son taking on human flesh, submitting himself to the law, suffering the death of the cross, and redeeming all who believe from sin and death. Before the world began, Christ agreed to pay the price for

---

1. Samuel Rutherford, *The Covenant of Life Opened: Or a Treatise of the Covenant of Grace*, ed. Matthew McMahon (Edinburgh: Andro Anderson, 1654; repr., New Lenox, IL: Puritan Publications, 2005), 71.
2. Samuel Rutherford, *Christ Dying and Drawing Sinners to Himself* (Glasgow: Niven, Napier & Khull, 1803), 687.

our redemption and purchased for us all the benefits of *free* grace and reconciliation.

The sacraments of circumcision, baptism, and the Lord's Supper foretell or remember the covenant of grace. The sacrifice of the Paschal Lamb beautifully portrays what should constantly enrich our everyday life and bow us to constant worship.

Respected contemporary theologian Dr. Morton H. Smith taught in several seminaries, including Reformed Seminary in Mississippi and Greenville Presbyterian Seminary in South Carolina, where he served as dean of the faculty. He also served as stated clerk in the general assembly of the Presbyterian Church in America from its founding in 1973 to 1988.

Dr. Smith's writing on covenant theology would likely bring a new revival to many churches if taken to heart by pastors. We highly recommend it.[3] Writing on the covenants, he reminds us, "The covenant idea stressed the legal, binding relation between God and His people.... Since the covenant binds men to God, covenants can only be effected on the basis of reconciliation between the holy God and sinful men. It is this that is the essence of the covenant designated the covenant of grace."[4]

When a person accepts Christ by faith as their personal savior, a spiritual union binds us to God. The covenant of grace provides the judicial ground of that union. Sin separated us from God as the just legal consequence of it. In response, Christ sealed the covenant with His own blood, the only possible legal payment for our sin. This glorious Truth, writes Dr. Smith, enables us "to become partakers of the redemption purchased by Christ through the federal, spiritual, and vital mystical union with Him. Scripture sets forth this union as embracing every phase of the saving

---

3. For more information about Dr. Morton H. Smith's writing on covenant theology, a good source is the bookstore of Greenville Presbyterian Theological Seminary, P.O. Box 690, Taylors, SC 29687, or online at gpts.edu/?s=morton+h.+smith.

4. Morton H. Smith, "Covenant Theology," *Journal of the Evangelical Theological Society* (March 1978): 68–86.

relation, both in the purpose of God and in its realization."[5] In other words, Christ represents both the spiritual cause for our reuniting with God, and the cause of the resulting full and good life in His people, now and for eternity.

First Corinthians 15:19–49 and Romans 5:12–21 establish that, just as Adam was head of the fallen human race, Christ constitutes the Head of the new redeemed humanity. Christ represents life to His elect. We die because of our relation to the first Adam, but we live by faith in Christ. Yes, He gives us both present and eternal life.

Romans 16:25 addresses the "mystery" kept "secret since the world began." Paul also speaks of the "mystery" in Ephesians chapter 1 (vv. 4–9), and again in Colossians chapter 1, which is "Christ in you, the hope of glory" (vv. 26–27). The very thought of the God of the universe loving us enough individually to indwell us is beyond human understanding. Scriptures promise and declare fulfillment of our unity with other believers. Read John 17 over and over, and then rejoice in the glory found there.

Glorious union with Christ gives us daily, even moment-by-moment, communion with the Father, the Son, and the Holy Spirit. We can experience the continual love of Christ the Bridegroom, since, through His Covenant, He reconciles us to Him.

God's covenant of grace represents *the* central unifying theme of the entire Bible. Once we are united in Christ, no power can remove us from His grace (John 6:39 and John 10:28–30).

As we next gather together to sing our Christmas carols and to reach out to others at this glorious time of the year, may the covenant remain our focus. "For God so loved the world, that He gave His only begotten Son, that whosoever believeth in Him should not perish, but have everlasting life" (John 3:16).

---

5. Morton H. Smith, *Systematic Theology*, vol. 2 (Eugene, OR: Wipf & Stock, 1994), 491.

Postscript: The Road Ahead for America

January 2017

If the foundations be destroyed, what can the righteous do?
—Psalm 11:3

Divine Providence is God Himself, directing history, through individuals, nations, and even in using nature for Gospel purpose. America is a unique nation, in that we were founded through reliance on providential history, and we rejoiced in the liberty that resulted, both religious and civil liberty.

Today, all of this is in danger, and American citizens are perplexed, confused, and mostly ineffective in the public square. There is an explanation for it all. The explanation centers in family life and in American education. Also, the church of today heavily reckons in the mix. The church is too often silent. Dr. Al Mohler addressed our current cultural dilemma in his wonderful book *We Cannot Be Silent.*[1] We recommend it highly.

In the past, I have written on the FACE conference in Virginia, in which our school ministry was honored. This is the Christian education program of the Foundation for American Christian Education. Theirs is the strongest Christian education program in America that is consistent with Biblical providential history. Early generations of Americans were so confident and knowledgeable

---

1. R. Albert Mohler Jr., *We Cannot Be Silent: Speaking Truth to a Culture Redefining Sex, Marriage, & the Very Meaning of Right & Wrong* (Nashville: Thomas Nelson, 2015).

about God's merciful providence that the spiritual life and the cultural life merged without conflict and confusion. Americans based schooling on God's Word as infallible. No source in America has more of America's true Christian history and education curricula for every age. We urge readers to check out the website.[2]

Dr. Max Lyons is their teaching consultant. Dr. Lyons graciously makes himself available to answer questions. Also available from FACE is Noah Webster's 1828 *American Dictionary of the English Language*, well representing the English Biblical language of liberty. I consider this extremely valuable for understanding liberty and Christian history.

Today's culture commands Christians to keep their spiritual life in the closet. We must not invade the current culture of secularism. How have we come so far from the individual liberty that no other nation on earth has enjoyed?

Our Founding Fathers learned Biblical law, and through that, they established a constitutional government with limited powers. The Founders insured individual rights of private property, freedom of conscience, and a free-market-free-enterprise system through constitutional law.

Families assumed responsibility for the education of their own children. Many parents schooled their children at home. Communities formed locally governed schools, reflecting the Christian worldview the vast majority of families embraced.

James Madison declared, "It is the duty of every man to render to the Creator such homage.... This Duty is precedent both in order of time and degree of obligation, to the claims of Civil Society. Before any man can be considered as a member of Civil Society, he must be considered as a subject of the Governor of the Universe."[3]

---

2. The Foundation for American Christian Education, FACE.net.
3. Ralph Ketcham, ed., *Selected Writings of James Madison* (Indianapolis: Hackett Publishing, 2006), 22.

John Adams declared, "Our Constitution was made only for a moral and religious people. It is wholly inadequate to the government of any other."[4]

What about public education today? The totally secular school has expelled God and His Word from the classroom and the textbooks. With moral absolutes omitted from the teaching, how can we attain moral character? It is no wonder that modern secular education is a threat to the American Christian church and the Christian home.

This writer graduated from high school in 1948, and in our classrooms we were already then introduced to a conflict between science and religion. *Strange* theories—at least they were strange to Southern children at that time—included the writings of Hegel, Dewey, and others. John Dewey's *experimentalism* rejected *supernaturalism*, as did Rousseau. He followed Darwin in evolutionary science.

The influence of John Dewey is tremendous, with his embracing humanism, rationalism, and naturalism. With his current following in public education, we are not surprised that moral absolutes are missing from today's classrooms. The all-out *war* on true education continues. I read recently that we rejected the Bible's "Gospel of John," but instead turned to the "Gospel of John … Dewey" in education. What a tragedy is robbing American children of their rightful heritage of individual religious and civil liberty.

More than 90 percent of American children know nothing of their rightful heritage as heirs of a Christian constitutional republic. Little do they know of the Pilgrims' landing at Plimouth in search of religious and civil liberty. They have never read the historical account written by William Bradford, governor of Plimouth Colony from 1620–49. According to Bradford, these devout Christians thought of themselves as "stepping-stones" of liberty to others. With their passion for true liberty came Christian self-government, the value of conscience, as well as the formation of a political union for government.

---

4. Adams, *The Works of John Adams*, vol. 9, 229.

Scholars Misses Verna Hall and Rosalie Slater spent many decades writing from primary sources the true Christian history of America. Their curriculum forms the basis for many Christian and home schools, known as Principle Approach® schools. Our school is one of the many indebted to those ladies and to their continuing foundation. Our Emerald Mountain Christian School campus was blessed with an over-fifty-year school history. We began in 1965, in Marion, Alabama. It has been liberating throughout the years to use the Foundation for American Christian Education curriculum,

How the Hand of God Moved

Go, Make Disciples of All Nations

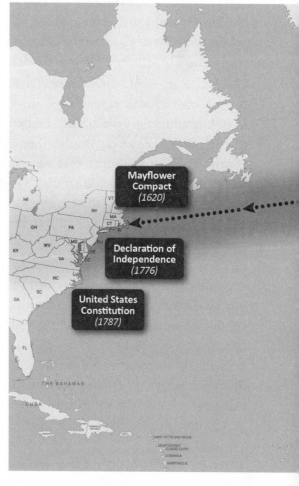

taught by faculty and staff who were serious students themselves. We love and appreciate them all greatly.

Parents face a dilemma today regarding their children's education. Proverbs 22:6 commands Christians to "Train up a child in the way he should go: and when he is old, he will not depart from it."

And Romans 12:2 has this solemn warning, "Be not conformed to this world...." Rather, as admonished in Leviticus 25:10, "Proclaim liberty throughout all the land."

Christian Civilization Westward

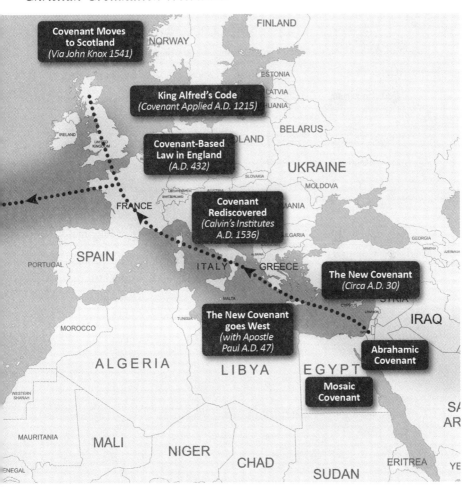

Timeline: Liberty in the English Heritage

Eternity Past

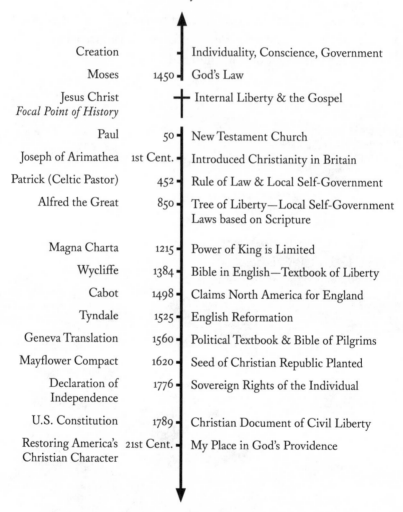

Creation		Individuality, Conscience, Government
Moses	1450	God's Law
Jesus Christ *Focal Point of History*		Internal Liberty & the Gospel
Paul	50	New Testament Church
Joseph of Arimathea	1st Cent.	Introduced Christianity in Britain
Patrick (Celtic Pastor)	452	Rule of Law & Local Self-Government
Alfred the Great	850	Tree of Liberty—Local Self-Government Laws based on Scripture
Magna Charta	1215	Power of King is Limited
Wycliffe	1384	Bible in English—Textbook of Liberty
Cabot	1498	Claims North America for England
Tyndale	1525	English Reformation
Geneva Translation	1560	Political Textbook & Bible of Pilgrims
Mayflower Compact	1620	Seed of Christian Republic Planted
Declaration of Independence	1776	Sovereign Rights of the Individual
U.S. Constitution	1789	Christian Document of Civil Liberty
Restoring America's Christian Character	21st Cent.	My Place in God's Providence

Eternity Future

Recommended Reading

Listed by Chapter

Chapter 1

Feder, Don. *A Jewish Conservative Looks at Pagan America*. Lafayette, LA: Huntington House, 1993.

Kurtz, Paul. *Humanist Manifestos I and II*. Amherst, NY: Prometheus Books, 1973. Also available online at americanhumanist.org.

Morris, Henry, III. *Your Origins Matter*. Dallas, TX: Institute for Creation Research, 2013.

Noebel, David, J. F. Baldwin, and Kevin Bywater. *Clergy in the Classroom: The Religion of Secular Humanism*. Manitou Springs, CO: Summit Press, 1995. Third ed., 2007.

Reese, Curtis W. *Humanist Sermons*. Chicago: Open Court Publishing, 1927.

Chapter 3

Grant, George. *The American Patriot's Handbook: The Writings, Spirit, and History of a Free Nation*. Nashville: Cumberland House, 2009.

Jay, John, Alexander Hamilton, and James Madison. *The Federalist Papers* (1788). Available in many publications and online at congress.gov/resources/display/content/The+Federalist+Papers.

Jefferson, Thomas. *Notes on the State of Virginia*. London: Stockdale, 1787, available online at static.lib.virginia.edu/rmds/tj/notes/index.html.

Long, Hamilton Albert. *Your American Yardstick*. Philadelphia: Your Heritage Books, 1963.

Washington, George, *Farewell Address* (1796). Available in many publications and online at *The Avalon Project* at Yale Law School, avalon.law.yale.edu/18th_century/washing.asp.

Information on Biblical Principle Approach® Education is available from at least a dozen wonderful foundations, including the Foundation for American Christian Education, Chesapeake, Virginia, as well as individual Principle Approach® Schools. Go to FACE.net to take advantage of their publications and conferences. They offer teacher training for home and Christian schools, and have curriculum available for all grades.

Chapter 4

Beliles, Mark A., and Stephen K. McDowell. *America's Providential History: Including Biblical Principles of Education, Government, Politics, Economics, and Family Life*. Charlottesville, VA: The Providence Foundation, 1989. Available from providencefoundation.com.

Hall, Verna M. *Christian History of the American Revolution: Consider and Ponder*. San Francisco: Foundation for American Christian Education, 1975.

———. *The Christian History of the Constitution of the United States of America: Christian Self-Government*. American Revolution Bicentennial edition. San Francisco: Foundation for American Christian Education, 1976.

———. *The Christian History of the Constitution of the United States of America: Christian Self-Government with Union*. San Francisco: Foundation for American Christian Education, 1979.

Hall, Verna M., and Rosalie Slater. *The Bible and the Constitution of the United States of America*. San Francisco: Foundation for American Christian Education, 1983.

Slater, Rosalie J. *Teaching and Learning America's Christian History*. San Francisco: Foundation for American Christian Education, 1975.

Slater, Rosalie J., and Verna M. Hall. *Rudiments of America's Christian History*. San Francisco: Foundation for American Christian Education, 1968.

Webster, Noah. *American Dictionary of the English Language: Noah*

Webster 1828. Facsimile edition. Anaheim, CA: Foundation for American Christian Education, 2006. Available for purchase from FACE.net. Webster's 1828 *Dictionary* is also available online at webstersdictionary1828.com/.

———. *Value of the Bible and the Excellence of the Christian Religion.* Original, 1834. Reprint by Foundation for American Christian Education, 1988.

Chapter 5

Webster, Noah. *American Dictionary of the English Language: Noah Webster 1828.* Facsimile edition. Anaheim, CA: Foundation for American Christian Education, 2006. Available for purchase from FACE.net. Webster's 1828 *Dictionary* is also available online at webstersdictionary1828.com/.

Chapter 6

Hutton, Ann Hawkes. *Portrait of Patriotism: Washington Crossing the Delaware.* Radnor, PA: Chilton Book Company, 1959. Available online at archive.org/details/portraitofpatrio006992mbp.

Chapter 7

Frothingham, Richard. *The Rise of the Republic of the United States.* Boston: Little, Brown, and Company, 1872.

Hall, Verna M. *The Christian History of the Constitution of the United States of America: Christian Self-Government.* American Revolution Bicentennial edition. San Francisco: Foundation for American Christian Education, 1976.

Washington, George. *Rules of Civility.* Washington's transcription, 1744. Available online at *President George Washington,* georgewashington.us/p/the-rules-of-civility-were-composed.html.

Chapter 9

Farrand, Max, ed. *The Records of the Federal Convention of 1787.* New Haven: Yale University Press, 1966.

Hall, Verna M. *George Washington: The Character and Influence of One Man.* San Francisco: Foundation for American Christian Education, 1999.

Wilbur, William H. *The Making of George Washington.* DeLand, FL: Patriotic Education, 1973. Available for borrowing at archive.org/details/makingofgeorgewa00wilb.

Chapter 10

Calvin, John. *Biblical Commentaries of Calvin*. Grand Rapids, MI: Baker Publishing Group, 2009. Available in many publications and online at *Christian Classics Ethereal Library*, at ccel.org.

——. *Institutes of the Christian Religion*. Peabody, MA: Hendrickson Publishers, 2009, and other publications. Available in many publications and online at *Christian Classics Ethereal Library*, at ccel.org.

Kelly, Douglas. *The Emergence of Liberty in the Modern World: The Influence of Calvin on Five Governments from the 16th through 18th Centuries*. Phillipsburg, NJ: Presbyterian and Reformed Publishing, 1992.

Locke, John. *Two Treatises of Government* (1691). Cambridge: Cambridge University Press, 1988. Available in many publications.

Montesquieu, Baron. *The Spirit of Laws* (1742). London, New York: The Colonial Press, 1900. Available in many publications.

Rutherford, Samuel. *Lex Rex: The Law and the Prince*. London: John Field, 1644. Available in many publications.

Swanson, Mary-Elaine. *John Locke: Philosopher of American Liberty*. Ventura, CA: Nordskog Publishing, 2012.

Westminster Divines. *Westminster Confession of Faith* (1646). Available in many publications and online at reformed.org/historic-confessions/.

Chapter 11

Irving, Edward. *Confessions of Faith and Book of Discipline; Of Date Anterior to the Westminster Confession*. London: Baldwin and Cradock, 1831.

Kelly, Douglas. *The Emergence of Liberty in the Modern World: The Influence of Calvin on Five Governments from the 16th through 18th Centuries*. Phillipsburg, NJ: Presbyterian and Reformed Publishing, 1992.

The London Baptist Confession of Faith (1689). Available in many publications and online at the1689confession.com/.

The Magdeburg Confession (Lutheran), 1550. In Matthew Colvin, trans. *The Magdeburg Confession: 13th of April 1550 AD*. North Charleston, SC: CreateSpace, 2012.

Olson, Roger E. *The Westminster Handbook to Evangelical Theology*. Louisville, KY: Westminster John Knox Press, 2004.

Chapter 12

Cole, Franklin P. *They Preached Liberty: An Anthology of Timely Quotations from New England Ministers of the American Revolution on the Subject of Liberty, Its Source, Nature, Obligations, Types, and Blessings*. Indianapolis: Liberty Press, 1976.

Salter, Richard. *A Sermon, Preached Before the General Assembly of the Colony of Connecticut, at Hartford, on the Day of Their Anniversary Election, May 12th, 1768*. Farmington Hills, MI: Gale Ecco, 2018.

Chapter 13

Bennett, Mabel R. *Old Glory: The Story of Our Flag*. Largo, FL: Snibbe Books, 1984.

Our Flag House Document 100-247. Washington, D.C.: U.S. Printing Office.

Chapter 15

Adams, John. *The Works of John Adams, Second President of the United States*, 10 vols. Edited by Charles Francis Adams. Boston: Little and Brown and Company, 1856.

Adams, John Quincy. *Writings of John Quincy Adams*, 7 vols. Edited by Worthington Chauncey Ford. New York: The MacMillan Company, 1913.

Jefferson, Thomas. *The Works of Thomas Jefferson in Twelve Volumes*. Edited by Paul Leicester Ford. New York: G. P. Putnam's Sons, 1905.

Madison, James. *The Writings of James Madison: Comprising His Public Papers and His Private Correspondence, Including Numerous Letters and Documents Now for the First Time Printed*. Edited by Gaillard Hunt. New York: G. P. Putnam's Sons, 1903. Reprinted Sacramento: Creative Media Partners, 2018.

Wootton, David, ed., *The Essential Federalist and Anti-Federalist Papers*. Indianapolis: Hackett Publishing, 2003.

Chapter 16

Slater, Rosalie J. "Noah Webster, Founding Father of American Scholarship and Education," in *American Dictionary of the English Language*. San Francisco: Foundation for American Christian Education, 1967.

Webster, Noah. *Sketches of American Policy*, (1785). Clark, NJ: The Lawbook Exchange, Ltd., 2008. Available in many publications.

Chapter 17

Hall, Verna M., and Rosalie Slater. *The Bible and the Constitution of the United States of America*. San Francisco: Foundation for American Christian Education, 1983.

Chapter 18

Chambers, Whittaker. *Witness*. Washington, DC: Regnery, 1969.

Root, Edward Merrill. *Collectivism on the Campus: The Battle for the Mind in American Colleges*. New York: Devin Adair Company, 1956.

Chapter 20

Adorno, Theodor, Else Frenkel-Brunswik, et al. *The Authoritarian Personality*. Frankfort School, 1951.

Anchell, Melvin. *What's Wrong with Sex Education?* Montgomery, AL: Hoffman Center for the Family, 1991.

Bloom, Allan. *The Closing of the American Mind: How Higher Education Has Failed Democracy and Impoverished the Souls of Today's Students*. New York: Simon and Schuster, 1987.

Buchanan, Patrick J. *The Death of the West: How Dying Populations and Immigrant Invasions Imperil Our Country and Civilization*. New York: Thomas Dunne Books, St. Martin Press, 2002.

Chapter 21

The Declaration of Independence, 1776. Available in many publications and online at *National Archives*, archives.gov/founding-docs/declaration-transcript.

O'Gara, Cuthert. *The Surrender to Secularism*. St. Louis: Cardinal Mindszenty Foundation, 1967.

Chapter 22

Kirk, Ronald. *Thy Will Be Done: When All Nations Call God Blessed*. Ventura, CA: Nordskog Publishing, 2013.

Chapter 23

Most of the following classics are available in many publications.

Alighieri, Dante. *The Divine Comedy of Dante Alighieri*. Edited by Charles Eliot Norton. Boston: Houghton Mifflin, 1920.

Andersen, Hans Christian. *Hans Christian Andersen's Complete Fairy Tales*. San Diego, CA: Canterbury Classics, 2014.

Augustine, *Confessions*. New York: The Modern Library, 2018.

Bach, Richard. *Jonathan Livingstone Seagull*. New York: Scribner, 1970, 2014.

Baring-Gould, William S., and Ceil Baring-Gould. *The Annotated Mother Goose: Nursery Rhymes Old and New, Arranged and Explained*. New York: Clarkson N. Potter, 1962.

Bennett, William J. *The Book of Virtues*. New York: Simon & Schuster, 1993.

Burton, Sir Richard, trans. *The Arabian Nights: Tales from a Thousand and One Nights*. New York: The Modern Library, 2004.

Chaucer, Geoffrey. *The Canterbury Tales*. New York: Simon & Schuster, 1948.

Dickens, Charles. *David Copperfield*. Oxford: Oxford University Press, 1981. Many other fine works of Charles Dickens are worthwhile.

Grahame, Kenneth. *The Wind in the Willows*. New York, Charles Scribner's Sons, 1908.

Greenaway, Kate, illustrator. *Mother Goose, or the Old Nursery Rhymes*, Secaucus, NJ: Castle Books, 1979.

Grimm, Jakob, and Wilhem Grimm. *Grimm's Fairy Tales*. New York: Sterling, 2009.

Homer. *The Iliad and Odyssey of Homer*. Boston: Joseph T. Buckingham, 1814.

Kipling, Rudyard. *Just So Stories*. New York: Macmillan Publishers, 1902.

Longfellow, Henry Wadsworth. *Poems and Other Writings*. New York: Literary Classics of the United States, 2000.

McDonald, George. *At the Back of the North Wind*. Philadelphia: J. B. Lippincott Company, 1914. Also, many other stories in various books.

Malory, Sir Thomas. *Le Morte d' Arthur*. London: J. M. Dent & Sons Ltd., 1906.

O'Hagan, John, trans. *The Song of Roland*. London: C. Kegan Paul & Co., 1880.

Palsson, Hermann, trans. *Hrafnkel's Saga and Other Icelandic Stories*. London: Penguin Classics, 1971.

Shakespeare, William. *Mr. William Shakespeare's Comedies Histories Tragedies and Poems*. Boston and New York: Houghton Mifflin Company, 1911.

Stevens, Burton Egbert, ed. *Home Book of Verse for Young Folks*. New York: Holt, Rhinehart and Winston, 1976.

Chapter 24

Barton, David. *America: To Pray Or Not To Pray*. Aledo, TX: Wall-Builders, 1989.

Bloom, Allan. *The Closing of the American Mind*. New York: Simon & Schuster, 1987.

Farrand, Max, ed. *The Records of the Federal Convention of 1787*. New Haven: Yale University Press, 1966.

McGowin, N. Floyd (President of W. T. Smith Lumber Company). "Can the Humanities Be Dispensed with in an Age of Crisis?" Presented at Southern Humanities Conference, University of Alabama. Chapman, AL, 13 April 1963.

Tocqueville, Alexis de. *Democracy in America*. Cambridge: Sever & Francis, 1863. Available in many publications.

Chapter 25

Guinness, Os. *The American Hour: A Time of Reckoning and the Once and Future of Faith*. New York: Free Press, 1993.

Johnson, Samuel. *The Works of Samuel Johnson, LL.D.: With Murphy's Essay*. Edited by Rev. Robert Lynam. London: George Cowie and Co, 1825.

Chapter 26

Buckley, William F. *God and Man at Yale*. Washington, D.C.: Regnery, 1951.

Imprimis. Hillsdale, MI: Periodical of Hillsdale College.

Kurtz, Paul. *Humanist Manifestos I and II*. Amherst, NY: Prometheus Books, 1973. Also available online at americanhumanist.org.

Chapter 28

Darwin, Charles. *On the Origin of Species*. New York: D. Appleton and Company, 1869. Available in many publications.

Chapter 29

Morris, Barbara. *Change Agents in the Schools*. Ellicott City, MD: Barbara M. Morris Report, 1979.

Morris, Henry. *The Twilight of Evolution*. Grand Rapids, MI: Baker Publishing Group, 1963.

Morris, Henry, and John Whitcomb. *The Genesis Flood*. Phillipsburg, NJ: P&R, 1961.

Schaeffer, Francis. *Back to Freedom and Dignity*. Downers Grove, IL: Inter-Varsity Press, 1972.

Chapter 30

Schlafly, Phyllis, and George Neumayer. *No Higher Power: Obama's War on Religious Freedom*. Washington, D.C.: Regnery Publishing, 2012.

Chapter 31

Hall, Verna M. *The Christian History of the Constitution of the United States of America: Christian Self-Government*. American Revolution Bicentennial edition. San Francisco: Foundation for American Christian Education, 1976.

Hall, Verna M., and Rosalie Slater. *The Bible and the Constitution of the United States of America*. San Francisco: Foundation for American Christian Education, 1983.

Chapter 32

Eidsmoe, John A. *Historical and Theological Foundations of Law*. Ventura, CA: Nordskog Publishing, 2016.

Engels, Friedrich, and Karl Marx. *Manifesto of the Communist Party* (1848). New York: Rand School of Social Science, 1919. Available in many publications.

The New American. A periodical of American Opinion Publishing, Inc.

Tocqueville, Alexis de. *Democracy in America*. Cambridge: Sever & Francis, 1863. Available in many publications.

Chapter 33

Articles of Confederation. Library of Congress (1781). Available online at guides.loc.gov/articles-of-confederation?loclr=bloglaw.

Eidsmoe, John. *Christianity and the Constitution: The Faith of Our Founding Fathers*. Grand Rapids: Baker, 1995.

Jay, John, Alexander Hamilton, and James Madison. *The Federalist Papers* (1788). Available in many publications and online at congress.gov/resources/display/content/The+Federalist+Papers.

Plymouth Rock Foundation has a wealth of resources on "Pilgrim principles and characteristics" and those generations that followed, who forged our nation's Christian heritage. Go to plymrock.org.

Simpson, James. *The Red-Green Axis: Refugees, Immigration and the Agenda to Erase America*. Washington, D.C.: The Center for Security Policy, 2015. Also, visit The Center for Security Policy, at centerforsecuritypolicy.org/2019/06/19/the-red-green-axis-2-0-an-existential-threat-to-america-and-the-world/.

Starnes, Todd. *God Less America*. Lake Mary, FL: Charisma Frontline, 2014.

Chapter 34

Engels, Friedrich, and Karl Marx. *Manifesto of the Communist Party* (1848). New York: Rand School of Social Science, 1919. Available in many publications.

Magna Carta (1215). Available in many publications and online at *Constitution Society*, constitution.org/eng/magnacar.htm.

Rush, Benjamin. *Letters of Benjamin Rush*. Edited by Lyman Henry Butterfield. Princeton, NJ: Princeton University Press, 1951.

Warren, Mercy Otis. *History of the Rise, Progress, and Termination of the American Revolution*. Boston: Manning and Loring, 1805.

Webster, Noah. "Letters to a Young Gentleman," *Rudiments of America's Christian History and Government: Student Handbook*. San Francisco: Foundation for American Christian Education, 1968.

Chapter 35

Common Core Standards, corestandards.org/read-the-standards/.

The Constitution of the United States. Available in many publications and online at *National Archives*, archives.gov/founding-docs/constitution-transcript.

Jonathan Elliot, ed. *Journal and Debates of the Federal Convention, Held at Philadelphia, from May 14, to September 17, 1787*. Washington, D.C.: Jonathan Elliot, 1830.

Chapter 36

Grimstead, Jay, and Eugene Calvin Clingman. *Rebuilding Civilization on the Bible: Proclaiming the Truth on 24 Controversial Issues*. Ventura, CA: Nordskog Publishing, 2014.

Henry, Carl F. H. *God, Revelation and Authority*. Wheaton, IL: Crossway Books, 1999.

Hulse, Erroll. "Postmodernism: Attack on the Heart of Biblical Christianity." *Reformation Today Series*. Pensacola, FL: Chapel Library, 2007. Available online at chapellibrary.org.

Chapter 38

Anchell, Melvin. *What's Wrong with Sex Education?* Montgomery, AL: Hoffman Center for the Family, 1991.

Chapter 40

Brewer, David Josiah. *The United States a Christian Nation*. Philadelphia: John C. Winston, 1905.

Washington, George, *Farewell Address* (1796). Available in many publications and online at *The Avalon Project* at Yale Law School, avalon.law.yale.edu/18th_century/washing.asp.

Chapter 41

Blackstone, William. *Commentaries on the Laws of England*. Oxford, UK: Clarendon Press, 1765.

English Bill of Rights (1689). Available online at *The Avalon Project* at Yale Law School, avalon.law.yale.edu/17th_century/england.asp.

Locke, John. *Two Treatises of Government* (1691). Cambridge: Cambridge University Press, 1988. Available in many publications.

Magna Carta (1215). Available in many publications and online at *Constitution Society*, constitution.org/eng/magnacar.htm.

Montesquieu, Baron. *The Spirit of Laws* (1742). London, New York: The Colonial Press, 1900. Available in many publications.

Obergefell v. Hodges, No.14-556, U.S. United States Supreme Court decision, 2015.

Sandoz, Ellis. *Political Sermons of the American Founding Era, 1730–1805*. 2 vols. Indianapolis: Liberty Fund, 1998.

Swanson, Mary-Elaine. *John Locke: Philosopher of American Liberty*. Ventura, CA: Nordskog Publishing, 2012.

Chapter 42

The Bill of Rights (1791). Available in many publications and online at *National Archives*, archives.gov/founding-docs/bill-of-rights-transcript.

Burgh, James. *Political Disquisitions: Or an Enquiry into Public Errors, Defects, and Abuses.* 2 vols. 1774.

Dreisbach, Daniel L. "'Sowing Useful Truths and Principles': The Danbury Baptists, Thomas Jefferson, and the 'Wall of Separation.'" *Journal of Church and State* 39:3 (Summer 1997): 455–501. Available online with subscription at academic.oup.com/jcs.

———. *Thomas Jefferson and the Wall of Separation between Church and State.* New York and London: New York University Press, 2002.

"From George Washington to the United Baptist Churches of Virginia, May 1789." Available online at *National Archives*, Founders Online, founders.archives.gov/documents/Washington/05-02-02-0309.

Jefferson, Thomas. "Letter to the Danbury Baptists" (1802). Available online at Library of Congress, loc.gov/loc/lcib/9806/danpre.html.

Journal of Church & State. Waco, TX: Baylor University. Available online at academic.oup.com/jcs.

Locke, John. *Two Treatises of Government* (1691). Cambridge: Cambridge University Press, 1988. Available in many publications.

Montesquieu, Baron. *The Spirit of Laws* (1742). London, New York: The Colonial Press, 1900. Available in many publications.

Reagan, Ronald. *Public Papers of the Presidents of the United States: Ronald Regan, January 1 to July 1, 1983.* Washington, D.C.: U.S. Government Printing Office, 1984.

Schaff, Philip. *History of the Christian Church.* Third rev., 8 vols. New York: Charles Scribner's Sons, 1891.

Chapter 43

Adams, Samuel. *The Writings of Samuel Adams: 1778–1802.* New York: G. P. Putnam's Sons, 1908.

Blackstone, William. *Commentaries on the Laws of England.* Oxford, UK: Clarendon Press, 1765. Available in many publications.

Erasmus, Desiderius. *Against War* (1515). Boston: The Merrymount Press, 1907. Available in many publications.

Federer, William J. *America's God and Country: Encyclopedia of Quotations.* St. Louis, MO: Amerisearch, 2000.

Magna Carta (1215). Available in many publications and online at *Constitution Society*, constitution.org/eng/magnacar.htm.

McGuffey, William. *McGuffey's Readers*. Sixth ed., 1838. Fenton, MI: Mott Media, 1982. Available for sale online at mottmedia.com/mcguffey-s-readers-2.

O'Sullivan, Richard. *The Inheritance of the Common Law*. London: Stevens & Sons Ltd., 1950.

Chapter 44

Ferguson, Sinclair B. *Read Any Good Books?* Edinburgh: Banner of Truth Trust, 1992.

Hodge, Charles. *Systematic Theology*. New York: Charles Scribner and Company, 1871. Available in many publications.

Chapter 45

Barton, David. *The Myth of Separation*. Aledo, TX: WallBuilder Press, 1989.

The Declaration of Independence, 1776. Available in many publications and online at *National Archives*, archives.gov/founding-docs/declaration-transcript.

Schroeder, John Frederick, compiler. *Maxims of George Washington*. Mount Vernon, VA: The Mount Vernon Ladies' Association, 1942.

Washington, George. *First Inaugural Address* (1789). Available in many publications and online at *National Archives*, archives.gov/legislative/features/gw-inauguration.

Chapter 46

Adams, Charles Francis. *Familiar Letters of John Adams and His Wife Abigail Adams during the Revolution*. New York: Hurd and Houghton, 1876.

Chapter 47

Fournier, Ray. *Education Reformation: A Teacher's Call for Christian Parents to Abandon the Public Schools and Return to the Word of God*. In 6 Days Evangelism, 2014.

Grimstead, Jay, and Eugene C. Clingman. *Rebuilding Civilization on the Bible: Proclaiming the Truth on 24 Controversial Issues*. Ventura: CA: Nordskog Publishing, 2014.

Rushdoony, Rousas J. *This Independent Republic: Studies in the Nature and Meaning of American History*. Vallecito, CA: Ross House Books, 1964.

Tocqueville, Alexis de. *Democracy in America*. Cambridge: Sever & Francis, 1863. Available in many publications.

Chapter 48

Kennedy, D. James. *Today's Conflict, Tomorrow's Crisis*. Ft. Lauderdale: Coral Ridge Ministries, 2002.

Schaeffer, Francis A. *The Great Evangelical Disaster*. Wheaton, IL: Crossway Books, 1984.

Chapter 50

Calvin, John. *Institutes of the Christian Religion*. Peabody, MA: Hendrickson Publishers, 2009, and other publications. Available in many publications and online at *Christian Classics Ethereal Library*, at ccel.org.

Rutherford, Samuel. *Christ Dying, and Drawing Sinners to Himself*. Glasgow: Niven, Napier & Krull, 1803.

———. *The Covenant of Life Opened: Or a Treatise of the Covenant of Grace* (1654). Edited by Matthew McMahon. Coconut Creek, FL: Puritan Publications, 2005.

———. *Lex Rex: The Law and the Prince*. London: John Field, 1644. Available in many publications.

About Bobbie Ames

Bobbie Ames is a woman whose life has been marked by accomplishment. Her legacy is one of tireless commitment to Biblical truth, reflected in the establishment of Christian schools, service to her community, and a wealth of published writings. She has spent her life advancing the cause of the restoration of America's Christian heritage. Bobbie has received numerous awards in her lifetime, but the one she cherishes most is the Verna Hall Research Award, which she received in 2016. The following is the press release[1] from that special celebration:

VERNA HALL RESEARCH AWARD
2016 RECIPIENT MRS. BOBBIE AMES

Chesapeake, Virginia, November 11, 2016

Acknowledging outstanding lifetime achievement in education and America's Christian history has been the purpose of the

---

1. Based on and updated from the press release from the Foundation for American Christian Education (FACE) in *The Alabama Gazette* (December 2016).

Foundation for American Christian Education for over fifty years. Periodically, the Foundation awards an individual of distinguished service with the Verna Hall Research Award. This year the recipient of this prestigious award is Alabama native and leader in Christian education Bobbie Mae Hackney Ames of Montgomery, Alabama.

Delegates at the "Reason for Hope" Conference held November 11–12 in Virginia Beach, Virginia, gave Mrs. Bobbie Ames a resounding ovation as they heard the story of Mrs. Ames's accomplishments in founding and establishing Christian schools, in political and community service, and in her scholarly writing for publication in Christian history and government. Conference participant, Carey Dudkovsky, Executive Vice-President of the Foundation for American Christian Education, said, "Mrs. Ames's life and work are an inspiration to parents, grandparents, teachers, administrators, and scholars." The Foundation for American Christian Education commends the life and contribution of Mrs. Ames to the field of Biblical Classical education and America's Christian history and heritage.

Bobbie Ames was born in Washington, North Carolina, attended Greensboro College, then East Carolina Teacher's College, now East Carolina University, majoring in Elementary Education. She married John Brewer Ames in 1950 and lived in Selma, Alabama, and later in Marion, Alabama, while raising their five children. Today, there are twelve grandchildren and nine great grandchildren.

Mr. and Mrs. Ames founded Perry Christian School in 1965, where Mrs. Ames taught and was the school administrator. She pursued graduate work in Library Science and a Masters Degree in School Administration.

Over the years, Bobbie was active in Republican political circles, having served as President of the Federation of Republican Women at the county and state levels, and as Republican National Committeewoman from Alabama, from 1968–1972.

Along with teaching for many years, Mrs. Ames oversaw the library built at Emerald Mountain Christian School. This vast and valuable collection was used as her main research source that enabled her to write for an area newspaper, *The Alabama Gazette*, for many years, writing on issues of education and history from the Biblical worldview. Mrs. Ames's articles ran in *The Alabama Gazette* from 2009–2019. A selection from that collection of articles has been transformed into this amazing book that we hope will inspire Americans to return to our spiritual foundations that are moored to God, Family, and Country.

More from Nordskog Publishing...

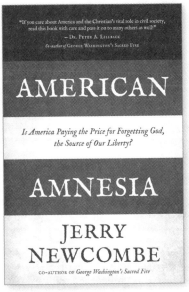

American Amnesia: Is America
Paying the Price for Forgetting
God, the Source of Our Liberty?

BY DR. JERRY NEWCOMBE

With his latest book, Dr. Newcombe continues to press the cause of Christ through his powerful commentary on current affairs from a Biblical worldview. He wields the mighty weapons of God's grace, love, and wisdom in this compilation of his essays syndicated on outlets such as *WorldNetDaily*, djameskennedy.org, *Town Hall*, *Newsmax*, & *Christian Post*, among others.

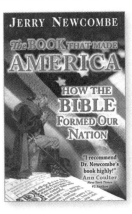

ALSO BY DR. JERRY NEWCOMBE

*The Book that Made America:
How the Bible Formed Our Nation*

Our first civil compacts, the *New England Primer*, every state constitution, and the United States Supreme Court's Trinity decision of 1892 all cry out that America's traditions have resulted from an abiding faith in the God of the Holy Bible.

Now available in Mandarin

*The Battle of Lexington:
A Sermon & Eyewitness Narrative*

BY JONAS CLARK, LEXINGTON PASTOR, 1776

Includes Clark's sermon, eyewitness narrative, biographical information on Clark, facsimile title page from original 1776 publication, four classic poems, and illustrations.

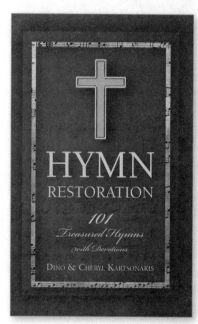